Let the
Word of God
fill your heart
with peace

God Bless~

Penny Zen

Within the pages of this book you will find the most creative, compelling, easy to understand version of the Holy Bible ever written. The author has brilliantly and successfully taken the amazing Word of God to new heights. Without question, this is an inspired work of anointed genius.

—WINK MARTINDALE
RADIO/TV PERSONALITY

I am lost for words. Listening to you read brought tears to my eyes. I felt like I was there at the Cross, among the throngs of onlookers, as our Lord went home to His Father. May God richly bless you for this book. His words jump out at me.

—REV. ROSS A. LICATA
MINISTER TO VETERANS AND BIKERS

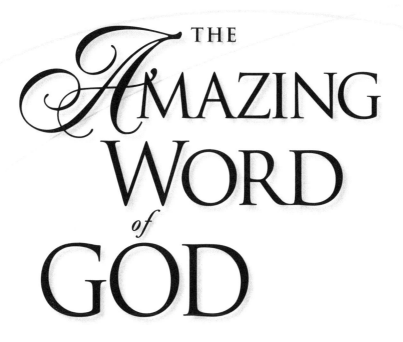

THE AMAZING WORD *of* GOD

PENNY ZEE

CREATION HOUSE
A STRANG COMPANY

THE AMAZING WORD OF GOD by Penny Zee
Published by Creation House
A Strang Company
600 Rinehart Road
Lake Mary, Florida 32746
www.strangbookgroup.com

Design Director: Bill Johnson
Cover design by Nathan Morgan

Library of Congress Control Number: 2010922534
International Standard Book Number: 978-1-61638-161-5

First Edition

10 11 12 13 14 — 9 8 7 6 5 4 3 2 1
Printed in the United States of America

$\mathcal{C}$ontents

Part 1—The Old Testament

Part 2—The New Testament

* A detailed list of the poems in this section follows this table of contents.

Detailed Table of Contents of the Life of Jesus

Acknowledgments

$\mathcal{A}$LL OF THE glory for this book goes to the Author of Life, who is the true Author of this book. This has been an extremely humbling experience, and I am very thankful that He chose to involve me in this project.

I would like to thank (in alphabetical order) Mitchell Berger, Sylvia and Ron Cayouette, Sue Ellen Cypkin, Sandy Dinse, Tom Kane, Donna Kearney, Rev. Ross Licatta, Wink Martindale, Bonnie McNair, Thelma Reid, Sue Repsher, Jessa and Brian Valentine, Linda Weise, Terri Zito and Charlie Zollo for their prayer support, special input, and enthusiastic encouragement.

Special thanks to the following pastors, who welcomed me into their churches to read to their congregations before the book was even published:

- Pastor Buddy Tipton, Central Assembly of God, Vero Beach, Florida
- Pastor Mike Lyle, Crossroads Christian Fellowship, Sebastian, Florida
- Rev. Jace Wills, First Christian Church, Fort Lauderdale, Florida

Special thanks also to Pastor Angel and Annette Bracero of Lighthouse International Ministries for inviting me to be their guest on Trinity Broadcasting Network's *Praise The Lord* program, also before the book was published.

Last, but certainly not least, a big thank you to my publishing team at Creation House—Allen Quain, Amanda Quain, Ginny Maxwell, Atalie Anderson, Candace Ziegler, and Jihan Ruano—for their faith in this project, their patience, their wisdom, and their creativity.

Introduction

EAR READER:

Welcome to *The Amazing Word of God: A Refreshing, Uncomplicated Reading of the Most Popular Books of the Bible, Including Prophecy.*

This book is not another translation of the Bible, nor is it meant to replace your Bible. In fact, I believe that when you read these stories, you will be inspired to go back to your Bible to read them in their entirety and that you will do so with a clearer understanding. Since it takes more than one page of rhyme to cover one page of the Bible, it is written in an abbreviated fashion.

However, I truly believe in my heart that this entire work was inspired and directed by the Lord from its very beginning, and I give *Him* all the glory. This project has taken seven years to complete, and many, many times I would sit at my computer and be totally "dry." I would then bow my head and pray, "Lord, please give me the words, because if You don't, this won't get written. I cannot do this on my own." Then, miraculously, within minutes, the words would begin to flow. And now, when I read these stories myself, I am amazed by them.

Also, the Lord has ways of letting us know when He is "in the middle" of something. For example, on several occasions I awoke in the night with a stanza or two on my lips, which I immediately wrote down. I always knew it came from Him because it was never a scripture I was currently working on or had been thinking about, but rather something I would be tackling at a later date.

Most people love and remember a story told in rhyme. For example, everyone knows, "'Twas the Night Before Christmas." Therefore, it seems to me that the Scriptures, told in rhyme, should be easy to read, understand, and remember. Obviously, since the Bible is not written in rhyme, I had to take the liberty of rearranging the sequence of words to retell the various Scriptures. However, even though I *did* paraphrase, I worked very hard to do so without changing the meaning.

On several occasions I have listened as other people have read these stories. A couple of times, I found that people attempted to read an entire verse as though they were reading a sentence. In doing so, the cadence and the rhyme were lost, which defeats the purpose.

Therefore, in order to fully enjoy these stories:

- Read each line individually and then pause briefly.
- When you see a comma (,) it is there to indicate another brief pause.
- When you see three periods (…) they are there to indicate a dramatic pause, which is a bit longer.
- Words that are *italicized* should be emphasized by saying them in a little stronger tone.

If you keep this in mind, I believe you will get the most out of each story and will "hear" them in the way they were meant to be heard.

I pray and I believe that you will enjoy this book to the fullest and be abundantly blessed by it.

I would love to hear from you. Please visit my Web site, www.TheAmazing-WordofGod.com, where you can send me an e-mail, watch videos, and find out where the Lord is taking the book and me.

Sincerely yours, in His service.

—PENNY ZEE

Part 1

The Old Testament

The Beginning

In the beginning God created the heavens
And then He created the world
And as His Spirit hovered over the waters
His magnificent plan unfurled

Now the earth was formless and empty
Darkness was over the deep
But as God continued to work His creation
Not long…would it sleep

He did not want it to always be dark
So He said, "Let there be light"
And He liked the light and He called it "day"
And He called the darkness "night"

Then He made the sky and He made dry land
And He separated the seas
He said, "Let the land bring forth vegetation
And fruits that grow on trees"

Then God said, "Let there be lights in the sky"
And He made the moon and the sun
He placed billions of stars across the heavens
One…by one…by one

The lights were to separate the light from the darkness
To govern the day and night, they would
And God looked at the sun, the moon and the stars
And He saw that it was good

The Lord God wanted to fill the earth with life
So He made fish of every size
He made all kinds of animals to roam the land
And birds to fill the skies

Then God created man in His own image
And He created woman too
He blessed them and He spoke to them
And told them what to do

"Be fruitful and increase in number," He said
"Fill the earth and subdue it
Rule over the fish of the sea and birds of the air
And every creature that moves through it"

"I give you every seed-bearing plant," said the Lord
"All the fruit bearing trees that grow
They will be yours for food," He continued
.   He spoke it and it was so

God saw His creation and it was very good
It had taken Him just six days
On the seventh day He rested from His work
And blessed it for always

Adam and Eve

God formed a man out of dust from the ground
He used His own image as a plan
Then He blew into his nostrils...the breath of life
And created...a living man

Then the Lord took the man and put him in a garden
In a land called Eden, in the east
And He told the man to care for the garden
Which had food enough for a feast

For God had filled the garden with fruit trees
In the middle was the Tree of Life
And the Tree of Knowledge of Good and Evil
Which would later be an object of strife

For the man was not allowed to eat from *this* tree
God spoke...and told the man why
"Do not eat of the Tree of Knowledge of Good and Evil
For when you do...you will surely die"

Now a river watered the garden and flowed from Eden
Then it separated into four
The first of the four rivers was the Pishon
Which flowed through Havilah and more

The second river wound through the land of Cush
The Gihon was its name
The third was the Tigris and the fourth the Euphrates
Which all from Eden came

The Lord told the man to name all of the creatures
Which He brought to him one by one
So the man worked on naming the animals and birds
Until the task was done

Then the Lord looked and said, "It is not good
That the man should be alone"
So He put him to sleep...and He made a woman
Out of one of the man's rib bones

"This is bone of my bone and flesh of my flesh,"
The man looked at her and said
"She is called woman, for she was taken from man"
And so they were...as wed

For this reason a man will leave his parents
And be united to his wife
And they will henceforth become one flesh
And they will share one life

THE FALL OF MAN

Now the man and the woman were naked
And yet they felt no shame
Then one day the devil approached the woman
Disguised as a serpent he came

God had said they could eat from all the other trees
Including the Tree of Life
But when the devil came up disguised as a snake
He was able to deceive the wife

"Did God really say you must not eat from any tree?"
The devil began his lie
"We must not eat of the Tree of Knowledge," said the woman,
"Or we will surely die"

"You will *not* surely die" the serpent shot back
"You will be like God if you do!"
So the woman ate the fruit...and gave some to the man
And he took it...and ate it too

Then the eyes of the man and the woman were opened
And their nakedness...they saw
They put fig leaves together to cover themselves
Which they had never done before

Then they heard the sound of God walking
In the garden in the cool of the day
They hid themselves...but the Lord called the man
"Where are you?" they heard Him say

"I heard you in the garden and I was afraid," he answered
"For I was naked…so I hid"
"Who told you you were naked? Did you eat from the tree?"
Though of course, He knew they did

"The woman you put here gave me fruit from the tree
And I ate it," the man replied
Then God asked the woman, "What have you done?"
And she told Him the serpent lied

"The serpent deceived me and I ate," said the woman
The Lord turned to the snake and said,
"You are now cursed above all of the animals"
And the serpent lowered his head

"You will crawl on your belly and you will eat dust
All of the days of your life
Between you and the woman and your offspring and hers
I will put enmity and strife

"And man will crush your head," He continued
"And you will strike his heel"
Then He told the woman, "I will greatly increase
The childbearing pain you will feel

"Your desire will be for your husband," He said
"And he will rule over you"
Then the Lord turned and looked at Adam, the man
And gave him…his punishment too

"Because you listened to your wife and ate from the tree
Cursed is now the ground
All of your days you will eat of it through painful toil
And thorns and thistles will be found

"By the sweat of your brow you will eat your food
Until you return to the dust
From dust you were taken…to dust you will return"
The man and woman had betrayed His trust

CAST OUT OF THE GARDEN

Adam named his wife Eve, for she would become
The mother of all mankind
But since Adam and Eve had disobeyed God
They had to leave the garden behind

"He must not be allowed to eat from the Tree of Life
And live forever," God said
And He drove them out of the Garden of Eden
To work the land instead

From then on, there were angels at the entrance
Along with a flaming sword
Which flashed back and forth to guard the Tree of Life
Placed there by the Lord

Cain and Abel

Now Adam and Eve had two young sons
The firstborn they named Cain
And when Cain grew up, he worked the land
Growing vegetables and grain

Adam and Eve named their second son Abel
Who became a keeper of sheep
And both sons knew...that what they raised
Was not all theirs to keep

One day Cain brought a portion of his harvest
As an offering to the Lord
While Abel brought the fattest and choicest of his lambs
His best...he did not hoard

The Lord was pleased with Abel's offering
But with Cain, He was not content
Then Cain became angry, his face downcast
And his anger...he would rent

Then God said to Cain, "Why are you angry?
And why is your face downcast?
If you do what is right...will you not be accepted?"
God's counsel...unsurpassed

"But if you do *not* do what is right," He continued,
"Sin...is crouching at the door
It is eager to control you, but you must subdue it"
Would Cain listen...or ignore?

Then Cain went and spoke to his brother Abel
"Let us go out to the field," said Cain
But when they got to the field...Cain attacked him
And his brother Abel...was slain

Then the Lord asked Cain, "Where is your brother?"
"I do not know...am I his keeper?" he replied
And *now*...not only had Cain killed his brother
Now also to God...he had lied

"What have you done?" demanded God
"His blood cries from the ground!
Now you shall be cursed...your land will not yield
You'll be a vagabond and wander around!"

"My punishment is more than I can bear!"
In anguish, cried out Cain
"You've driven me out...I'll be hidden from your face
When someone finds me...I'll be slain!"

"On whoever kills Cain, revenge shall be taken
Seven times over," said God
Then He put a mark on Cain, so all would know
And Cain left...for the land of Nod

Cain took a wife...and they had a son
And his son had a son too
And so it went on...through generations
And the population grew

The Flood

When Adam was one hundred and thirty years old
He had yet another son
They named him Seth...and through the generations
There were many more to come

Seth's son was Enosh...whose son was Kenan
Whose son was Mahalalel, by name
Then Mahalalel fathered a son he named Jared
And from Jared...Enoch came

Enoch grew up and had a son named Methuselah
And to Methusaleh...Lemech was born
And all of these men, starting with Adam
Had lives many hundred years long

When Lemech was a hundred eighty-two years old
Lemech also had a son
His name was Noah and he walked with God
For Noah was a righteous one

After Noah had lived for five hundred years
Three sons were born to him
And Noah and his wife named their sons
Japeth, Ham and Shem

As the three sons of Noah all became men
Each one took a wife
Noah taught them all how to love the Lord
And lead a godly life

But the rest of mankind had turned from God
From the plan He had from the start
They followed every manner of wickedness
With evil desires in their heart

The violence and corruption of man was great
Worse and worse they became
Until God regretted creating them
And His heart...was filled with pain

Since the people had become so corrupted
And violence was everywhere
God decided to put an end to the earth
And wipe away all that was there

But Noah found favor in the eyes of God
And God told Noah His plans
He said that He was going to send a flood
To cover all of the lands

He said the flood would destroy all life on earth
But He made a promise too
"Every creature with the breath of life will die
But I will establish my covenant with you"

Then God told Noah to build an ark
To make it with cypress wood
And to coat it with pitch, inside and out
Noah listened and understood

God said to make it four hundred fifty feet long
And seventy-five feet wide
He said to make the ark, forty-five feet high
With a big door in the side

Finish it to eighteen inches from the top
And inside…make many a room
Make upper and middle and lower decks
To prepare it for the coming doom

God told Noah that he and his wife would enter
And his sons and their wives too
"Bring two of all creatures, male and female," He said,
"To keep them alive with you"

"Take every kind of food there is to be eaten
And store it for you and for them"
And Noah followed all of the instructions
That God had given him

When Noah and his family finished building the ark
The animals began to arrive
Seven pair of every clean and two of every unclean
God sent...so they would survive

There were lions and elephants and rhinoceros
And hippopotamus too
Wolves and turtles and cats and dogs
Giraffe and kangaroo

Bears and leopards and sheep and hamsters
Cattle and butterflies too
Chickens and goats and horses and oxen
Gazelles and two marabou

Chipmunks and donkeys and roadrunners ran
Up the ramp they came
Spiders and snakes and pigs and lambs
Creatures of every name

Then seven pair of every kind of bird
God also sent to him
And when everyone and everything was safely inside
The Lord God shut them in

And in the six hundredth year of Noah's life
For forty days and nights
The heavens opened up and the rains came down
'Til there was no land in sight

The mountains were covered by twenty feet
And every living thing died
But Noah, his family and the creatures on the ark
All were safe inside

THE WATERS RECEDE

The ark finally came to rest on Mount Ararat
After many months of floating around
Noah sent a raven and then sent a dove
Searching for dry ground

Seven days later, he again sent a dove
Who returned with a leaf in his beak
He sent it again and it didn't come back
After waiting another week

The big door was opened and God said, "Come out"
After almost a whole year afloat
And they saw a great rainbow arched in the sky
When they came out of the boat

God promised He would never again flood the world
And He made the rainbow a sign
So whenever He would see a rainbow in the sky
His promise would come to mind

The Tower of Babel

After God had made His covenant with Noah
Noah's descendants greatly increased
And the whole world spoke one language
And had one common speech

As men moved eastward they found a plain
In Shinar and settled there
They said to each other, "Let us make bricks"
Which they could use everywhere

So then they used bricks, instead of stones
For mortar they used tar
Then the people said, "Let us make a city
With a tower that stretches far

"Up to the heavens and because of the tower
For ourselves we will make a name"
But as they were building the tower so high
Down...God came

For God wanted to see the city and the tower
Which toward Heaven did reach
He said, "If they do this, they can do anything"
And so...He confused their speech

And when the people tried to speak to each other
They could no longer understand
They were confused and stopped building the tower
And were scattered across the land

And that is why...it is called Babel
Because of what happened there
The Lord confused the language of the people
And scattered them everywhere

Abraham

THE CALL OF ABRAM

In the land of Haran, lived a man named Abram
Abram was a descendant of Shem
And he lived in Haran until one day
When God said this to him

"Leave your country, your people and your father's house
And go to the land I show you"
Then the Lord went on to tell Abram
What He was going to do

"I will make of you a great nation," He said
"I will bless you and make your name great
I will bless those who bless you and curse those who curse you"
A new nation . . . God would create

"Through you all the families of the earth will be blessed,"
Was the last thing Abram was told
So Abram left Haran as the Lord had directed
He was seventy-five years old

When Abram left Haran, he took Sarai, his wife
And Lot, his brother's son
He took all of the people they had acquired in Haran
All their goods and cattle, every one

Then they traveled to the land of Canaan
To Shechem . . . in the Moreh plain
But the land was occupied by the Canaanites
Then God appeared . . . and spoke again

"I will give this land to your offspring,"
Abram heard Him say
But there was a famine so they went to Egypt
Building altars along the way

They lived in Egypt until the famine was over
And then they returned to the land
Given to them by the Lord Himself
Arranged...by His own hand

Abram and Lot Separate

Now Abram was very blessed by God
In livestock, silver and gold
And his nephew Lot was also blessed
With many possessions to behold

But the land could no longer support them all
For the clan had grown much too large
It was time for Abram to make a decision
For he was the one in charge

So Abram told Lot to choose his portion
The land to the east or the west
Lot chose for himself the plain of Jordan
For that land...was the best

Then Lot set out with his family and possessions
Every man, woman, child and beast
They departed from Abram and the rest of the clan
And headed for Sodom, in the east

After Lot had departed, God spoke to Abram
And told him to look all around
And to walk the length and the breadth of the land
For he was giving Abram that ground

Abram Rescues Lot

Soon after that time...there was a war
And four kings rose against five
Sodom was defeated and Lot and his people
All were captured alive

One man escaped and went back to Abram
He told him what happened...and then
Abram went out to rescue Lot and his people
With three hundred and eighteen men

During the night, he divided his men
To prepare for the attack
They ran off the captors and rescued the people
And to Sodom he brought them all back

GOD'S COVENANT WITH ABRAM

After this happened, Abram had a vision
And he heard the voice of the Lord
"Fear not Abram...for I am your shield
And your great reward"

"Lord, what can you give me...for I am childless?"
Abram bowed and replied
"So a servant will have to be my heir
I have no child," he sighed

But then the Word of the Lord came to Abram,
"Not a servant but a child of your own"
Then God took Abram outside in the night
Where the moon and the stars all shone

"Look at the heavens and count the stars
If indeed you can," said He
"As numerous as the stars...shall your children
And your children's children be"

"I am the Lord who brought you out of Ur
To give to you this land"
Then the Lord told Abram to make a sacrifice
Upon an altar in the sand

As the sun went down, Abram fell asleep
And God told him what was to be
His descendants would be slaves for four hundred years
Before they would again be free

God promised him the land from the river of Egypt
To the river Euphrates too
"And all the people who dwell within it," He said,
"I have delivered to you"

Hagar and Ishmael

Ten years passed by…and Abram's wife Sarai
Still had not given him a son
So she had her servant Hagar sleep with Abram
So Hagar could give him one

But when Hagar learned that she was with child
Her mistress…she began to detest
Sarai said, "She hates me!" and Abram replied,
"Do what you think is best"

Then Sarai began to mistreat Hagar
So Hagar ran away
But when an angel found her in the desert
He sent her back that day

The angel told Hagar to submit to Sarai
And also what her baby would be
She would have a boy and would name him Ishmael
For the Lord *heard* her misery

Abraham Is Named

God appeared again to Abram when he was ninety-nine
And He changed Abram's name
He would be Abraham and his wife would be Sarah
And their lives would never be the same

For again God said that Sarah would be blessed
And she would have a son
Abraham fell facedown and laughed
How *could* this blessing come?

Abraham thought, "Will a son be born
To a man a hundred years old?
Will Sarah bear a child at the age of ninety?"
Yet once again...he was told

God said again that Sarah would have a son
And Isaac would be his name
He said Sarah would be the mother of nations
From her descendants... *kings* would reign

THE THREE VISITORS

One day as Abraham was sitting by his tent
During the heat of the day
Three men appeared...and stood nearby
Then Abraham looked their way

Abraham ran out to greet his visitors
Bowing down to the ground
"My Lords," he cried, "please do not pass by
If favor in your eyes I have found!"

"Let water be brought to wash your feet," he said
"And rest yourselves under the tree
I will go and get food to refresh all of you
Now that you have come to me"

Then Abraham hastened into his tent
Where to Sarah, his wife, he said,
"Quickly...take three measures of flour
And bake it into bread!"

Then he ran to the herd and fetched a calf
Which he gave to a servant to prepare
He took butter and milk, the calf and the bread
And served his visitors there

"Where is Sarah, your wife?" one of them asked
"There in the tent" he replied
"This time next year she will have a son," said the Lord
But Sarah listened from inside

And when Sarah heard that, she laughed to herself
For she and Abraham were old
Then the Lord said…"Why did Sarah laugh?"
It was not good…that she had been bold

"Is there anything that the Lord cannot do?" He asked
"Next year she *shall* have a son"
Sarah was afraid and denied she had laughed
"Yes…you *did* laugh," said the One

Abraham Pleads for Sodom

After the Lord and the angels visited Abraham
And they were preparing to leave
They looked toward Sodom and as they did
The Lord's words made Abraham grieve

"The outcry against Sodom and Gomorrah is great
And their sin is grievous indeed"
Then the Lord said that He would destroy the cities
And Abraham started to plead

"Will you sweep away the righteous with the wicked?
What if there are fifty righteous there?
Will you really sweep away the cities?" he cried
"For the sake of fifty…can they be spared?"

"Far be it from you to do such a thing," he said,
"To kill the righteous with the wicked alike
Far be it from you!…Will not the Judge
Of all of the earth do right?"

Then the Lord said, "If I find fifty righteous people
Then the city of Sodom, I will spare
I will spare the whole place for their sake," He said
Speaking of the people there

Then Abraham spoke up again and said,
"Now that I have been so bold
As to speak to the Lord…though I am nothing
But dust and ashes," he told

"What if the number of the righteous in the city
Is five *less* than fifty?" he cried
"Will you destroy the whole city because of *five* people?"
"I will not destroy it...if I find forty-five"

"What if only *forty* are found there?" said Abraham
"For the sake of forty...I will not do it then"
Then Abraham said, "May the Lord not be angry
But let me speak once again?"

"What if only *thirty* can be found there?" he asked
For Abraham wanted to know
"I will not do it if I find thirty," said the Lord
How far was He willing to go?

"Now that I have been so bold as to speak to the Lord,"
Abraham said again,
"What if only *twenty* can be found there?" he asked
"For the sake of twenty...I will not destroy it then"

"May the Lord not be angry...but let me speak once more,"
And once more...Abraham dared
"What if only *ten* righteous can be found?" he asked
"For the sake of ten...it will be spared"

Now Abraham knew he could ask no more
For the Lord was through speaking then
And as Abraham watched, the Lord left him there
And Abraham went home again

SODOM AND GOMORRAH ARE DESTROYED

The two angels arrived at Sodom in the evening
Where Lot was sitting by the gate
He bowed and invited them to his home
For the hour was getting late

The angels turned down Lot's invitation
"We will spend the night in the square"
But Lot insisted strongly...for he already knew
It was evil and dangerous there

So they went with Lot into his house
Where Lot prepared a meal
But after dinner...something happened
With which he would have to deal

Men from all over the city surrounded the house
And then they called out to Lot,
"Where are the men who came here tonight?"
But send them out...he would not

Instead Lot himself came out of the house
He would try to reason with them
For Lot knew that these men were all evil
But they wouldn't listen to him

"Get out of our way!" they shouted
Pressuring Lot even more
Then the angels inside reached out and grabbed him
Pulled him in...and slammed the door

The men outside began beating on the door
They were spoiling for a fight
But the angels struck them where they stood
And took away their sight!

Then the angels gave Lot a warning
Something he needed to know
They said they were going to destroy the city
And he must take his family and go

Then Lot told two men, "Get out of this place!"
They were pledged to marry his daughters
"The Lord is going to destroy the city!" he cried
But they didn't heed his orders

They thought he was joking and paid no attention
To all that he had to say
The angels said, "Take your wife and your daughters
Or you will be swept away!"

Lot hesitated but the angels grabbed his hand
And the hands of his daughters and wife
Then the angels led them safely from the city
For the Lord was sparing their life

And as soon as the angels had brought them out
"Flee for your lives!" they said
"Do not look back...do not stop in the plain!"
If they did...they would all be dead

"Flee to the mountains or you'll be swept away!"
But Lot knew that that was too far
He knew of a small town that they could run to
So he asked if they could go to Zoar

By the time they reached the town of Zoar
The sun has risen over the land
Then burning sulfur fell on Sodom and Gomorrah
Destroying them by God's hand

But as Lot and his family fled the city
His wife died...through her own fault
For she disobeyed the angel and she looked back
And turned into a pillar of salt

Early the next morning, Abraham went to the place
Where the Lord and he had spoke
And as he looked toward Sodom and Gomorrah
He saw dense billows of smoke

Isaac Is Born

The next year the promise of the Lord came to pass
And Sarah gave birth to a son
They named him Isaac, which means "he will laugh"
And a *new* life...had begun

HAGAR AND ISHMAEL ARE SENT AWAY

Abraham held a feast when Isaac was weaned
In honor of his son
But Hagar's son Ishmael…had stood by mocking
And Sarah saw what he had done

"Get rid of that slave woman," she said to Abraham,
"And Ishmael…her son"
For she didn't want Isaac to share his inheritance
With Ishmael…or anyone

Now Abraham was greatly distressed by this
For it involved his other *son*
But God assured him that he should not worry
For *God* would care for *that* one

Then God told Abraham, that through Ishmael
He would also build a nation
And that Abraham should do as Sarah desired
Which eased Abraham's frustration

So Abraham took food and a skin of water
On the very next day
And set them on the shoulders of Hagar
And sent them on their way

They wandered in the desert of Beersheba
But when the water in the skin was gone
Hagar and Ishmael…grew thirsty and weak
Until they could no longer go on

Hagar took the boy and put him under a bush
Then she went and sat nearby
She lowered her head and began to sob
For she knew…her son would die

But God sent an angel for He had heard
Their cries of desperation
The angel said that God would take Ishmael
And make from *him*…a great nation

Then God opened Hagar's eyes and she saw a well
She drank and the boy did too
They lived in the desert...and the boy became an archer
And God was with him...as he grew

ABRAHAM IS TESTED

Sometime later, God again called Abraham
To put him...to a test
A test involving his beloved son Isaac
With whom he had been blessed

God told Abraham to go to a mountain
In the region of Moriah
And sacrifice his son...as a burnt offering
An offering of fire

So early the next morning, with a heavy heart
Abraham's journey began
He took Isaac and two servants and headed to Moriah
To sacrifice...to the Great I AM

On the third day, Abraham saw the mountain
Where Isaac's life would end
He told his servants to stay with the donkey
For just he and Isaac would ascend

Abraham placed the wood on Isaac to carry
While *he* carried the knife and the fire
And along the way...his son spoke up
As they climbed higher and higher

"Father," young Isaac said to Abraham
"Yes, my son?" he replied
"The fire and the wood are here," said Isaac
"But where is the lamb?" he cried

"God will provide the lamb for the offering,"
Abraham told his son
Abraham had lied, rather than frighten
This precious, innocent one

When they reached the place where God has said
Abraham built an altar
Then he arranged the wood and bound his son
Praying he would not falter

Then Abraham gently lifted his son
And laid him down on the wood
His heart was breaking as he tried to gather
Whatever courage he could

And as Abraham reached out and took the knife
He covered Isaac's eyes with his hand
His pain was unbearable for in just a moment
His son's blood...would run in the sand

As he raised his hand...and prepared to slay
The son that he so loved
He heard the voice of an angel of the Lord
Calling...from above

"Abraham...Abraham!"...the angel called
"Here I am"...was his reply
"Do not lay a hand on the boy!" said the angel
For Isaac did *not* have to die

Abraham had passed the test of the Lord
And now the angel knew
That Abraham feared God...and there was *nothing*
That he was not willing to do

"You have not withheld from me," said the angel,
"Your son, your only son"
Then Abraham saw a ram caught in a thicket
For God has sent him one

Abraham gratefully made the sacrifice then
But now it was the ram that died
And after that, Abraham named that place
"The Lord...Will Provide"

And because of Abraham's obedience
In going through this test
The Lord swore to bless him and through his descendants
All the nations on earth would be blessed

Isaac and Rebekah

Abraham was blessed throughout his life
Blessed in every way
And when he was old, he called his best servant
With a special request one day

Abraham made his servant...swear by the Lord
That he would *not* find a wife
For Abraham's son Isaac...from the local women
The daughters of the Canaanites

"Go to *my* country and from my *own* people," he said
"Find a wife for my son"
"If she won't come," said the servant, "should I bring Isaac
To the land where you came from?"

"Make sure that you do *not* take my son back there!"
Abraham firmly said
"The Lord who promised this land to me
Will send an angel ahead"

So the servant loaded up ten camels
And traveled to the town of Nahor
Then he sat near the well where the women came
In the evening...for water to draw

"O Lord, God of my master," said the servant
As he began to pray,
"Show kindness to my master Abraham
And give me success today"

"When I ask a girl for a drink she will say,
'I'll water your camels too.'
By this I'll *know*...you show kindness to Abraham
And that *she* was chosen by you"

And before the servant had finished praying
Rebekah came out with her jar
She was a granddaughter of Abraham's brother
And the most beautiful...by far

Then the servant asked her to give him a drink
Which she was quick to do
And when he finished drinking...Rebekah said,
"I'll draw water for your camels too"

Rebekah fetched the water for all his camels
He watched without saying a thing
Then he gave to Rebekah, two gold bracelets
And a beautiful gold nose ring

Then the servant asked her who she was
And if by chance they might
Have enough room in her father's house
For them to spend the night

She told him who she was and then she said
There was room for them to stay
The servant bowed down to worship the Lord
To thank Him...and to pray

Rebekah was excited and ran on ahead
She ran to the house of her mother
When she told the household what had happened
Out ran Laban...her brother

He brought them all home and set out a meal
And gave the camels hay
But the servant said, "I will not eat a thing
Until I've said what I have to say"

Then he told them all about Abraham
Sarah and Isaac too
And he told them why he had come there
What he was sent to do

He told them about his prayer by the well
And how Rebekah had come around
How she gave him a drink and watered the camels
How he worshiped the Lord and bowed down

"Now if you will show kindness to my master,"
The servant said, "please let me know"
They said, "We can say nothing...for this is from God
Take Rebekah and go"

When Abraham's servant heard their response
He again bowed to the ground
And thanked the Lord...for Rebekah
The bride that he had found

Then he gave expensive gifts to Rebekah
And her mother and brother that day
Then they ate and drank and spent the night
The next morning...they went on their way

Now Isaac was in the field one evening
And he looked and saw the caravan
Rebekah looked up and she saw him too
And asked "Who is that man?"

And as Rebekah covered her face with a veil
"He's my master," the servant replied
And though Isaac was unable to see her face
Of course...he certainly tried

Then the servant went and told Isaac
All that he had done
Isaac married Rebekah...and he loved her
Rebekah...God's *chosen* one

Esau and Jacob

Now when Isaac was sixty years of age
His wife Rebekah had twin sons
Since the first twin was born with hair all over
They named him *Esau*...meaning "hairy one"

Isaac and Rebekah named the other twin Jacob
And during their growing span
Esau became a skilled hunter
And Jacob a *quiet* man

Isaac *loved* Esau and the wild game he hunted
While Jacob was *Rebekah's* favorite one
But Jacob was jealous of his brother Esau
For *Esau*...was the *firstborn son*

And one day when Esau came in from the field
Jacob was cooking a stew
"Quick, let me have some," Esau exclaimed
"I'm famished!...I *beg* of you!"

"First sell me your birthright," bargained Jacob
And here is the reason why
The firstborn son...would inherit *twice* as much
On the day that the father would die

"Look Jacob...I am about to *die*." cried Esau
"What good is a birthright to *me?*"
But Jacob said, "Swear an oath to me first!"
Esau had to *say* it, you see

So Esau went ahead and *swore* an oath to Jacob
And sold his birthright that day
Then Jacob gave Esau the stew and some bread
Which he ate...and went on his way

JACOB GETS ISAAC'S BLESSING

When Isaac grew old his eyes were *so* weak
That he could no longer see
One day he called for Esau and said to him,
"Go hunt some venison for me"

"For I have become an old man," said Isaac
"And I don't know the day of my death
So make me the savory meal that I love
And after that...*you* I will bless"

But Rebekah was listening and heard what he said
Then *she* told Jacob too
"Now my son...listen carefully," said Rebekah,
"And *do* what I tell you to *do*"

"Go to the flock...and bring me two goats
And I'll prepare your father a meal
Then *you* bring it to him...and *you* get the blessing"
So the blessing...Jacob would steal

"But my brother Esau is a *hairy* man," said Jacob,
"And *I'm* a man with smooth skin
What if my father *touches* me?" he asked
"He'll *know* I was tricking him"

"Then I'd bring a *curse* upon myself," he said,
"Rather than getting *blessed*!"
Then Rebekah responded..."Just do as I say,"
For *she* would take care of the rest

So Jacob went to the flock and got the goats
And brought them to his mother
He went right along with Rebekah's scheme
To steal the blessing...from his brother

Then Rebekah prepared some delicious food
And continuing on with her plans
She put some of Esau's clothes on Jacob
And goatskin on his neck and hands

Then Rebekah gave her son, the tasty meat
And the bread that she had prepared
"Father," said Jacob... "Who are you?" asked Isaac
"I am Esau, your firstborn," he dared

"I have done as you told me...please sit up and eat
Then you can give your *blessing* to me"
But Isaac asked... "How did you find it so fast?"
Jacob lied, "The *Lord* did it, you see"

"Come *near* so I can *touch* you," said Isaac,
"To see if you're Esau or not"
Jacob moved closer and his father reached out
And touched him from his cot

"The voice is Jacob's...but the hands are Esau's
Are you *really* Esau?" he said
"I am," lied Jacob...and Isaac believed him
Then he ate the meat and the bread

Then Isaac said, "Come here my son and kiss me,"
And as Jacob lowered his head
Isaac caught the smell of Esau's clothing
Then he blessed his son and said

"The smell of my son is like the smell of a field
That the Lord has certainly blessed
May God give to you of Heaven's dew
And all the earth's richness

"May nations serve you and people bow down
Lord over your brothers too
May those who curse you...themselves be cursed
And *blessed* be those who *bless* you"

Now right after Isaac had finished the blessing
And Jacob had barely left
In walked Esau...bringing food for Isaac
And wanting to be blessed

"My father…please rise up and eat," said Esau,
"So that your soul may bless your son"
But Isaac exclaimed, "Who are you?!"
"I am Esau…your *first*born one"

Isaac trembled all over as he asked his son,
"Then who brought the food to me?
I ate it and I blessed *him* before you came!
And blessed…he will be!"

When Esau heard the words of his father
He cried out in great pain
"Bless me too, my father!" he begged
But his pleading was in vain

"Your brother came to me deceitfully," said Isaac,
"And took your blessing, my son"
Then Esau said…"Isn't he *rightly* named Jacob?"
For Jacob means "deceitful one"

"He has deceived me two times!" cried Esau
"He took my birthright and my blessing *too*!
Haven't you reserved *any* blessing for me?"
But there was nothing Isaac could do

"I have made him *lord* over you," said Isaac
"And made your *relatives* his servants too
I've sustained him with grain and with new wine
What can I *possibly* do for you?"

"Is there only *one* blessing… *Bless me tooooo*!"
Esau cried as he wept aloud
But as Isaac answered…his words were as dark
As a heavy and ominous cloud

"Your dwelling will be away from earth's riches," he said
"Away from Heaven's dew
You'll live by the sword and serve your brother"
His words hurt his son…he knew

"But as time goes by...you shall grow restless
And you'll break his yoke from your neck"
As Esau heard the words...he *hated* his brother
But for *now*...he'd hold himself in check

JACOB FLEES TO LABAN

"The days of mourning for my father are near," said Esau,
"After *that*...I will *slay* my brother"
But someone told Rebekah what Esau had said
Then Jacob was warned by their mother

"Your brother Esau wants to kill you," she said,
"So obey my voice and rise!
Flee at once to my brother Laban in Haran
Until Esau's fury dies"

"When he forgets what you have done," she continued,
"I will send for you to return here
Why should I lose you both in one day?"
Rebekah exclaimed in fear

Then Rebekah went to Isaac and spoke to him
"I'm disgusted with the women of these lands
And my life will not be worth living," she cried,
"If Jacob takes one of their hands"

So Isaac told Jacob, "Don't marry a Canaanite
Go at *once* to Padan Aram
To the house of your mother's father," he said,
"And choose a *wife* from the daughters of Laban"

"May God Almighty bless you," he continued,
"And make you fruitful by His hand
May He give you the blessings He gave to Abraham
So you can possess the land"

Jacob's Ladder

Now when Jacob left the land of Beersheba
And set out on his flight
On his way to Haran he came to a place
Where he decided to spend the night

So he found a stone to use as a pillow
And he put it under his head
Then he closed his eyes and he fell asleep
Upon his makeshift bed

Jacob had a dream in which he saw a stairway
Stretching from the ground
It reached to Heaven and on it were angels
Going up and down

And there at the top...stood the Lord
Who looked down at Jacob and said,
"I am the Lord...the God of your father"
Jacob saw Him clearly from his bed

"I am the God of Abraham and the God of Isaac,"
Jacob heard Him say
"I will give to you and to your descendants
The land on which you lay

"Your descendants will be like the dust of the earth
You will spread to the east and the west
To the north and south...and through your descendants
All people on Earth will be blessed"

"I am with you and will watch over you wherever you go
And I will bring you back to this land
I will not leave you until I have done what I promised"
Then Jacob awoke on the sand

"Surely the Lord is in this place and I did not know it,"
Jacob reasoned in his head
"This is the house of God and the gate of Heaven"
And in the morning he rose from his bed

Then Jacob took the stone he had used for a pillow
Poured oil on its top and bowed
Then he called the name of that place Bethel
And to the Lord he vowed

"If God will be with me and watches over me
On this journey that I take
And gives me food to eat and clothes to wear
This vow...I shall now make

"If I return safely to my father's house," he said,
"The Lord will be my God," he vowed
"And this stone I have set up...will be God's house,"
Jacob continued out loud

"And of all that you give to me, O God
I will give a tenth to you"
And now...more than *ever before* in his life
Jacob *knew* what he had to do

Jacob and Rachel

Jacob Arrives in Padan Aran

Jacob continued his journey and finally arrived
In the land of the people of the East
As he looked around he saw a well in a field
Used by shepherds for their sheep

Now covering the well, there was a great stone
And when the flocks were gathered around
The shepherds would roll the stone off the well
Revealing the water in the ground

Jacob asked some shepherds, "Where are you from?"
"We are from Haran," they replied
When Jacob heard *this*...he was very excited
"Do you know Laban?" he cried

"We know him," answered the shepherds
"Is all well with him?" Jacob said
"All is well...and here comes Rachel, his daughter"
And Jacob turned his head

He looked and saw Rachel approaching
Bringing her father's sheep
Jacob immediately rolled away the stone
Kissed her...and began to weep

Then Jacob told Rachel that they were related
And that *he* was *Rebekah's* son
Rachel ran home and she told her father
Who hurried to meet this one

Then Laban brought Jacob back to his house
For a month he worked and stayed
Then Laban said, "You shouldn't work for nothing
Tell me, what shall you be paid?"

Now Laban also had *another* daughter
And Leah was her name
But the younger daughter was Rachel
And in Jacob...she kindled a flame

"I will work for you for seven years," said Jacob,
"If at the end of that time
You give me Rachel...your youngest daughter"
Laban agreed...that would be fine

Jacob worked for Laban for seven years
So he could earn Rachel's hand
"I've fulfilled our agreement, now give me my wife"
Laban agreed...but had *another* plan

Laban prepared for a grand wedding feast
But in the dark, with veils on her head
Laban gave *Leah*...in *place* of Rachel
And Jacob married Leah instead!

When Jacob discovered that he'd been deceived
He cried, "What have you done?"
"In *this* land," said Laban, "the *firstborn* marries
Before the younger one"

"But if you promise to serve me for seven *more* years
I'll give you Rachel...for your wife"
So Jacob worked for Laban for *another* seven years
For Rachel...was the love of his life

JACOB'S CHILDREN

Jacob married and loved Rachel more than any other
Yet Rachel was very sad
For Jacob had many sons by his *other* wives
But no children...had *Rachel* had

Then one day God smiled down upon Rachel
And gave *her*...her very own son
She named him Joseph and *he* truly became
Jacob's *favorite* one

Sometime after Rachel gave birth to Joseph
Jacob told Laban one day,
"I want to take my wives and children to my homeland
So send me on my way"

But Laban said to Jacob... "Please stay here
The Lord blessed me because of you
Name your wages and I will pay you," he said
But now Jacob *knew* what to do

"Your livestock has fared well under my care," he said
"Wherever I've been... you've been blessed
Let me sort out the spotted sheep and goats
And remove them from the rest"

"Agreed," said Laban, "Let it be as you have said"
So Jacob did what he wanted to do
His wages were the sheep, the lambs and the goats
And quickly, his herds all grew

But some years later, Laban's attitude changed
And the Lord told Jacob to go
So he packed up his wives, his children and his goods
To return to the land he loved so

And one day while Laban was sheering his sheep
Jacob left... with all he had
He hadn't told Laban that they were leaving
The day they fled to Gilead

But before they had left, Rachel went in
And stole the gods of her father
She didn't know that Laban would pursue them
She didn't think that he would bother

But as soon as Laban heard they had left
He went after them with his brothers
They were three days behind so they traveled fast
To catch up to the others

Seven days later, they caught up with Jacob
But a very strange dream Laban had
God told him, "Be careful to say *nothing* to Jacob
Either good or bad"

Now Jacob was camped on Mount Gilead
And he didn't *know* that Laban was near
Had Jacob known, he would have fled again
For he would have been filled with fear

When Laban came to Jacob he asked him,
"What did you do this for?
Why did you leave without my knowledge
Taking my daughters like captives of war?

"You didn't even let me kiss my grandchildren
And kiss my daughters good-bye
You acted foolishly...but I will not harm you"
And then he told him why

"The God of your father spoke to me last night"
And he told of the dream he had
Jacob was relieved to know that he was safe
But what Laban said next...was bad

"Now if you left because you are longing to return
To your father's house," he accused,
"Then why have you stolen my family gods?"
Now Jacob was *confused*

"I was afraid you would take your daughters from me,"
Jacob innocently said
"But if you should find anyone who has your gods
That person...shall be dead"

So Laban began to search through all of the tents
But found nothing...anywhere
When he entered *Rachel's* tent...she didn't get up
And as he searched...she sat there

"Forgive me lord for not standing...I am ill," she said
As he searched through this and that
And Laban never found the gods that were hidden
In the saddle upon which she sat

Then Jacob said, "You've searched my belongings
But what of yours did you find?
Put it all here...in front of our relatives
Let *them* be our judges...yours and mine"

"For twenty years I worked and your flocks did well,"
Jacob stated...and he was right
"The heat consumed me during the days," he said
"And I was chilled to the bone at night

"I served you fourteen years for your two daughters
And six more years for your herds
You have changed my wages ten times over"
Everyone listened to his words

"And had you not feared the God of my father
The God of Isaac and Abraham
You would have sent me away with *nothing*
But *God* saw the labor of my *hand*

"He rebuked you last night," Jacob concluded
Then Laban looked at Jacob and said,
"The women are my daughters, the children...my children
The animals are *mine*...every head

"All you see is mine...yet what can I do about my daughters
Or the children they have borne?
So come and let us make a covenant...you and I"
And so an oath...was sworn

They vowed they would do each other no harm
Jacob and Laban made a pact
Then they all ate together and spent the night
And the next day Laban went back

JACOB PREPARES TO MEET ESAU

Now Jacob was met by the angels of God
When he too, went on his way
"This is the camp of God!" he exclaimed
When he saw the angels that day

Then Jacob sent messengers ahead to his brother
But before they went on their way
He said, "This is what you shall tell my lord Esau
'Your servant Jacob wishes to say

"'That he has been staying with Laban until now
He has servants and herds of many kind
And he is sending us ahead with this message, my lord
That favor in your eyes he may find.'"

After some time, the messengers returned
And they said to Jacob then,
"We went to your brother and he's coming to meet you
And with him are four hundred men"

Jacob became greatly distressed and afraid
And divided his people in two
So if one camp was attacked...the other could flee
Which is what he told them to do

"Deliver me, I pray you, O God of my father
From the hands of my brother," he prayed
"I fear he'll attack me...and my wives and children"
Jacob was truly afraid

"Yet you *told* me...you would deal *well* with me
And make my race as the sand of the seas
Which cannot be numbered because of its multitude,"
Jacob said...as he prayed on his knees

Then Jacob selected from his possessions
A gift...for Esau his brother
Hundreds of bulls and cows and rams and ewes
Camels and goats and others

He put all of the animals in the care of his servants
Keeping each herd separate from the other
Then he told the servants, as they prepared to leave
What to say when they saw his brother

"When he asks you, 'To whom do you belong?'
And he asks you, 'Where are you going?
And to whom belong these beasts before you?'"
A seed, Jacob was sowing

"Tell him, 'They belong to your servant Jacob
They're a present for my lord Esau.'"
Jacob figured this would pacify his brother
Which was what . . . the gift was for

After his servants left, Jacob sent his wives
His sons and all he owned
Across the ford of Jabbok
Then Jacob was alone

All night long he wrestled with an angel
And at daybreak the angel said,
"Your name shall no longer be Jacob
It shall be Israel . . . instead"

Then Jacob looked up . . . and saw his brother
Coming with his four hundred men
Jacob separated the children of his wives and servants
And put the servants in *front* of them

Behind the servants were Leah and *her* children
Then Joseph with Rachel, his *mother*
Then Jacob went ahead and bowed seven times
As he approached his brother

But Esau *ran* to Jacob and he embraced him
He kissed him . . . and then they wept
Then Esau looked up . . . saw the wives and children
Who bowed down and then they all met

Now Esau went back to Seir to wait for Jacob
But Jacob went to Bethel
Where God appeared to him and blessed him
And named him Israel

"I am God Almighty," said the Lord
"I am giving you this land
A nation and kings will come from you"
This was the move of God's hand

Joseph

Now Joseph was one of Jacob's youngest sons
And Jacob loved him the best
But Joseph had eleven other brothers
And he was hated by the rest

One day, Jacob gave Joseph a beautiful coat
With colors and beads galore
His brothers were jealous because of the coat
And hated him even more

One day while tending the flocks of his father
When he was just seventeen
Joseph described to his older brothers
A very unusual dream

He dreamed their grain bowed down to his
But this made the brothers mad
"Do you think we would bow down to you?" they said
Hating him *more* for the dream he had

Then Joseph had *another* dream and told them,
"In this dream I did see
The sun, the moon and eleven stars," he said,
"*All* bowing down to me"

But this time Joseph also told his father
Now even Jacob got mad
"Will your mother, your brothers and I bow down?
What is this dream you had?"

JOSEPH IS SOLD BY HIS BROTHERS

By now Joseph's brothers had had enough
And they threw him in a well
"We'll kill him," they said, but changed their minds
And Joseph...they did sell

They dipped his colored coat in blood
And then they brought it home
And told their father that animals had killed
His favorite son...alone

Jacob mourned for a very long time
And for his son, he cried
His children were unable to comfort him
No matter how they tried

Meanwhile, the people who had purchased Joseph
Brought him to a foreign land
And as happens when people buy and sell people
He was passed from hand to hand

In Egypt, Joseph was bought by Potiphar
The captain of Pharaoh's guard
But the Lord was always with Joseph
So his life wasn't really too hard

The Lord blessed him and made him successful
In whatever he would touch
And Potipher saw that the Lord was with him
And put him in charge of much

So God blessed the house of Potiphar
And also blessed his field
With Joseph in charge, the crops grew tall
And abundant was their yield

Joseph and Potiphar's Wife

All went well for Joseph until one day
When a lie would change his life
He was arrested and thrown into prison
Because of Potipher's wife

For Joseph was well-built and handsome
As anyone could see
And after a while his master's wife
Said, "Come to bed with me"

She wanted Joseph to be her lover
To betray her husband and sin
But Joseph refused her...so Potipher's wife
Told her husband a lie about him

She said Joseph wanted to sleep with her
And she said that she refused
She said she screamed and he ran away
Now Joseph stood accused

Potiphar was furious and put Joseph in prison
But the Lord was still with him there
He gave Joseph favor in the eyes of the warden
Who put the prisoners in Joseph's care

One night, two men in prison, each had a dream
In the morning they became very sad
When Joseph asked why...they told him that *no one*
Could interpret the dreams they had

"Do not interpretations belong to God?"
Joseph looked at them and said
"Tell *me* your dreams"...and so they did
Then Joseph...the dreams...he read

To the cupbearer he said, "You will see the king
In three days...and all will be fine
Your former position will be restored to you
Handing the king his wine"

For the baker the news was not so good
But Joseph would not lie
He told him he would stand before the king
But that *he*...was going to die

Three days later...it all came to pass
Just as Joseph had said
The cupbearer was working for Pharaoh again
And the baker...indeed...was dead

Now Joseph had asked the cupbearer to remember him
And mention him to the king
Perhaps the king would release him from prison
But the man forgot *everything*

PHARAOH'S DREAMS

Two years later, Pharaoh had two disturbing dreams
Which no one could interpret for him
Then the cupbearer remembered Joseph in jail
And Pharaoh had *him* brought in

"No one can interpret my dreams," said Pharaoh,
"But I have heard you can"
"I cannot," said Joseph, "but *God* will give the answer"
So the narration, Pharaoh began

Joseph listened as Pharaoh described his dreams
Then he put the meaning in God's hands
And God told Joseph what was going to happen
All across the lands

Joseph told Pharaoh of seven years of abundance
Then seven years of famine too
He told Pharaoh that God had *sent* these dreams
Then he told him what he should do

The plan seemed good to Pharaoh and his court
Then Pharaoh asked his men,
"Can we find anyone *else* with the spirit of God?"
And he turned to Joseph again

"Since God made this known to you," said Pharaoh,
"There is no one as wise as you
You shall be in charge of my palace," he said,
"And all of my people too"

So during the seven years of abundance
Joseph had the people store
A fifth of the crops of grain throughout Egypt
Which filled the storehouses and more

In the following famine, people came to buy food
From Pharaoh's country and others
One day Joseph *recognized* some men who had come
For they...were Joseph's brothers

But the brothers did not recognize *Joseph*
For he was no longer a boy
But he certainly knew who they were
And decided with them, he would toy

He kept one brother and sent the others home with grain
And said, "Bring me the youngest son"
The brothers didn't understand what he was doing
And they were frightened...every one

Once home, they told their father what Joseph had said
That the youngest son, they must bring
Jacob *had* to let him go, but he was frightened
Not knowing what was *happening*!

And when the brothers brought the boy, Joseph said,
"I am Joseph...but do not fear"
As the brothers held each other and cried he told them,
"Now bring my *father* here"

So they went back and got Jacob and the family
Their households, goats and lambs
They all went to Egypt, where they settled down
And lived with Joseph in the land

Pharaoh gave much property to Joseph's family
Land which was the best
And for eighteen years the family thrived
Until Jacob's final rest

Then the brothers feared Joseph would seek revenge
For what they had done years before
They came before him and said, "We are your slaves,"
And bowed down...to the floor

But Joseph told them, "Do not be afraid
Though what you did was grave
The Lord intended it for good and put me here
For many lives to save"

Moses

Now when Jacob and his family went to Egypt
There were around seventy in their band
And they prospered and multiplied greatly
And soon Israelites filled the land

But after Joseph and his generation had died
There was a *new* Pharaoh on the throne
And the Pharaoh said, "There are too many Israelites
Who consider Egypt…their home"

So he told his people, "We'll make slaves of them
And put masters over each head"
But the more oppressed the Israelites were
The more they multiplied and spread

The Egyptians worked them harder and harder
But still they did multiply
Until one day a decree was issued by Pharaoh
That baby boys of Hebrews…must die

THE BIRTH OF MOSES

Now as it happened, a baby boy was born
To a woman of the house of Levi
But she hid the baby for several months
So he wouldn't have to die

Then she put him in a basket and sent him down a river
So her baby she might save
And Pharaoh's daughter found the baby in the reeds
When she went to the river to bathe

She kept the baby and she named him Moses
And raised him as her own
One day he went out to watch the slaves working
When he was fully grown

He saw an Egyptian who was beating an Israelite
Which Moses couldn't stand
And he struck the Egyptian and killed him
And buried him in the sand

The next day he stopped two *Hebrews* from fighting
One looked at him and said,
"Will you kill me as you killed the Egyptian?"
And Moses was filled with dread

For he knew that Pharaoh would kill him
And so he ran away
He kept traveling until he came to Midian
Where he decided he would stay

Now Moses was sitting by a well in Midian
Where seven sisters came one day
They were fetching water for their father's flock
But shepherds scared them away

Moses rescued the sisters from the shepherds
And helped them water their own
Then their father, Jethro, invited Moses
To come and stay in their home

Moses stayed in Midian and worked for Jethro
Jethro's daughter became his wife
They had a baby and they named him Gershom
And they enjoyed a happy life

THE BURNING BUSH

One day as Moses was tending Jethro's flock
Near Horeb, the mountain of God
He saw a bush burning…but not burning up!
Which was certainly very odd

Then God called to Moses from the burning bush
"Moses…Moses," He said
"Here I am," said Moses, but he was frightened
He hid his face…and bowed his head

Then God told Moses to remove his sandals
For the ground was holy where he stood
Then He told him to go lead the Hebrews from Egypt
To a land that would be good

A land which flowed with milk and honey
Where each man would be free, not a slave
For God had heard the prayers of His people
And saw their situation was grave

But Moses objected for his speech was faltered
He said, "Pharaoh will not listen to me"
"Your brother Aaron will be your prophet," said God
"Go...and you will see"

"I will make you a god in Pharaoh's eyes," He said,
"And you will tell him whatever I say"
He said for Aaron to tell Pharaoh to let the people go
So Moses could lead them away

"But I will harden Pharaoh's heart," God continued,
"And though my miracles he will see
He will not listen to you and let the people go"
Then He said what would finally be

He said He would bring a final judgment on Egypt
And then Pharaoh would let them go
When it happens the Egyptians would see He is God
They would surely know

Then God told Moses that He would be with him
And He blessed the staff in his hand
Then Moses and Aaron traveled to Egypt
To lead the people to the promised land

When they went before Pharaoh, Aaron announced,
"The Lord says, 'Let my people go
So they can come and worship Me in the desert.'"
But Pharaoh told them, "No"

"Who is this *god* that I should obey *him*?"
Pharaoh said with pride
"I do not know him…and I will *not* let them go!
Go back to work!" he cried

Then Pharaoh made the Hebrews' lives even worse
He made them work even more
Now they had to make the same amount of bricks
But they also had to gather the straw

The people became angry at Moses and Aaron
So Moses went before God again
But the Lord God sent him back to Pharaoh
He would show him miracles then

Aaron threw his staff to the ground before Pharaoh
The power of God they would show
The staff became a snake…and Moses said,
"*Now* let my people go!"

But the staffs of Pharaoh's wizards *also* became snakes
When *they* threw *them* to the floor
Then Aaron's snake *swallowed*…all of the others
And the wizards' snakes…were no more!

THE TEN PLAGUES

After that, Pharaoh's heart was still hardened
Just like God had said
Then Moses turned all of the waters to *blood*
And all of the fish were dead

Yet Pharaoh's heart was hardened *again*
When he saw *his* wizards do it too
And *still* he wouldn't listen to Moses and Aaron
He didn't *know*…what God would do

Seven days later Moses again went to Pharaoh
With a warning of God's plan
If Pharaoh didn't let the people go *this* time
Frogs would cover the land!

But Pharaoh paid no attention to Moses
And so the frogs...they came
Millions of frogs came out of the Nile
Covering the city and plain

Then Pharaoh summoned Moses and Aaron
And told them they should pray
He told them that he would let the people go
If God took the frogs away

So Moses prayed and the frogs all died
Not one live frog did they find
But again Pharaoh's heart was hardened
And *again*...he changed his mind

Then God told Moses to have Aaron strike the ground
He hit it with his staff...and then
The dust from the ground turned to gnats
Which covered the animals and men

But even then Pharaoh's heart was hardened
And he still told Moses, "*No!*"
Then Moses told him what would happen next
If he wouldn't let the people go

He said that the next day, to the Egyptian houses
God would send a plague of flies
Pharaoh still said, "No!" and the very next day
They came and filled the skies

Dense swarms of flies filled the palace
The Egyptian houses and ground
But in all of the houses of the Hebrews
Indeed...no flies were found!

Again Pharaoh summoned Moses and Aaron
And told them that they should pray
And *again* he said he would let the people go
If God took the flies away

So Moses prayed and God removed the flies
From the houses and the land
But Pharaoh hardened his heart yet again
He *still* didn't fear God's hand

So God sent Moses to warn Pharaoh yet *again*
There would be another plague, he said
If Pharaoh wouldn't let the Hebrews leave *now*
The livestock...would be dead

But Moses and Aaron could not convince Pharaoh
No matter how hard they tried
And though all of the Hebrews' animals lived
All the Egyptians' animals died

Then the Lord told Moses to go to a furnace
And take out a handful of soot
And throw it in the air...And boils would cover
The Egyptians...from head to foot

So Moses followed God's instructions
But Pharaoh would not yield
Then God sent a warning that there would be *hail*
On every house and field

He warned it would start the following day
When Moses stretched his staff to the sky
He said that everyone would need to take shelter
For anyone outside would die

The next day it happened, just as God said
For God's word does not fail
It was the worst storm Egypt had ever had
Thunder...lightning...and hail

Everything in the fields was beaten down
The hail stripped every tree bare
But in Goshen...where the Hebrews lived
No storm at all was there

Finally Pharaoh told Moses, "I have sinned
Make it stop...Take the people and go"
Moses raised his staff...and the hail storm ceased
But Pharaoh again...said, "No!"

Then God sent two more plagues to Egypt
Locusts and darkness like night
"Come before me again and you'll die!" said Pharaoh
And told Moses to get out of his sight!

THE PASSOVER

Moses warned Pharaoh of one final plague
Which would spread across the land
The firstborn in every household would DIE
If Pharaoh *still* challenged God's hand

But Pharaoh still refused to listen to Moses
Just as God had predicted before
Then God told Moses to tell all the Hebrews
To put lamb's blood...on each door

Then the Almighty Lord told Moses
Exactly *what* the blood was for
He said that the destroyer would pass over
Any house with blood on the door

He said the Hebrews should have a Passover dinner
He told Moses what they should eat
But He said that they should eat in a hurry
With their sandals on their feet

At midnight God came and struck the Egyptians
And all of Egypt cried
Each and every house in Egypt was affected
For all of their firstborn died

From Pharaoh's own son to every firstborn
Of every prisoner in every cell
In every house in Egypt...*someone* died
And the firstborn of the livestock as well

Pharaoh summoned Moses and Aaron and told them,
"Take the people and leave...this very night"
The Lord made the Egyptians give them gold and silver
And then the Hebrews...took flight

They left Rameses and traveled to Succoth
Around six hundred thousand men
Plus the women and children and many non-Hebrews
Who also went with them

They brought with them much livestock
Many flocks and herds
Cattle and oxen and sheep and goats
Chickens and other birds

For four hundred thirty years they lived in Egypt
'Til the Lord brought them out that night
They didn't have time to add yeast to their dough
Before they had to take flight

And with a pillar of fire and a pillar of cloud
God led them night and day
But soon Pharaoh decided to pursue them
As the Hebrews hurried away

CROSSING THE RED SEA

When the Egyptians caught up to the Hebrews
They were camped out by the Red Sea
The Hebrews were frightened when they saw them
There was *nowhere* for them to *flee*

"What have you done?!" they cried out to Moses
"Safe in Egypt...we should have stayed!"
Moses said, "Do not fear...but stand firm and *see*
The deliverance of the Lord today!"

Than God blocked Pharaoh with the pillar of cloud
The Egyptians could not get around
Then Moses raised his staff...and the sea opened up
And the Hebrews went through...on dry ground

With a great wall of water on their left side
And a wall of water on their right
The Hebrews walked through…with their flocks and herds
All throughout the night

Then God moved the cloud…The Egyptians followed
Crossing the sea on dry ground
But when Moses raised his staff…the waters flowed back
And the Egyptian army…was drowned

Mount Sinai

Now three months later, God lead the Hebrews
To a place where Mount Sinai was near
The mountain was trembling and covered in smoke
And the people were filled with fear

A great trumpet sounded and lightning flashed
As Moses climbed up alone
Then God gave Moses His Ten Commandments
And made His Covenant known

The Ten Commandments

God spoke and said, "I am the Lord your God
Who brought you out of slavery"
Then He gave to Moses the First Commandment
You Shall Have No Other Gods Before Me

The Second Commandment He gave to Moses
You Shall Not Make Idols of Anything
In Heaven Above or on Earth or in the Water
Or Punishment I Will Bring

God warned the people in the Third Commandment
You Shall Not Use God's Name in Vain
For the Lord Will Not Hold Anyone Innocent
If They Misuse His Name

Then God gave Moses the Fourth Commandment
Remember the Sabbath Day
Six Days You Will Work but God Blessed the Sabbath
To worship the Lord and pray

The Fifth Commandment holds a promise for the people
Honor Your Father and Mother Too
So That You May Live Long and Have a Full Life
In the Land God is Giving to You

In the Sixth Commandment the Lord God says
You Shall Not Murder each other
For you will receive the wrath of God
If you go and murder another

In the Seventh Commandment the Lord God warns
You Shall Not Commit Adultery
For those involved in sexual affairs
Punishment there will be

The Eighth Commandment God gave to Moses
Says *You Shall Not Steal*
There are many ways to steal…and God sees them all
Nothing can be concealed

In the Ninth Commandment the Lord says this
You Shall Not Falsely Testify
For God hears every word that is spoken
Whether truth or lie

God's Tenth Commandment says *You Shall Not*
Covet Your Neighbor's House
Nor Their Servants or Their Livestock
Their Possessions or Their Spouse

Then God gave Moses laws and instructions
On how they were to live
Laws of the Sabbath and of treating each other
When to punish, when to forgive

God promised if the people obeyed His laws
And followed everything He said
That He would be an enemy to their enemies
And send His terror ahead

He would cover their enemies with confusion
And make them turn and run
He would drive their enemies out with hornets
Before fighting had even begun

He said He would set the Israelite borders
From the Mediterranean to the Red Sea
And from the desert to the Euphrates River
Is how vast their land would be

And though He promised to give them victory
Over the people *living* there
He told them to not make *treaties* with them
He warned them to beware

For if the Israelites allowed these people to stay
In the land that God was giving
They would cause the Israelites to sin against *Him*
By bowing to false gods in their living

The People Agree to the Covenant

When Moses came down and stood before the people
And read what God had to say
In agreement the people all shouted together,
"All God has said…we will obey!"

Moses built an altar and made offerings to the Lord
Then took Aaron, Nadab and Abihu
And seventy of the elders up to see God
For God had told him to

They saw the God of Israel…and beneath His feet
Was pavement of sapphire so clear
And He harmed them not…and they ate and drank
Then He beckoned Moses draw near

So Moses and Joshua climbed up the mountain
And stopped where Joshua would stay
Only Moses was allowed to go any farther
Only he could go the whole way

The top of the mountain was covered in a cloud
A cloud of the glory of the Lord
From below it appeared to be consumed by fire
As seen by the Israelite horde

Moses and Joshua waited six days
And on the seventh day
The Lord called Moses to come into the cloud
So he went up...the rest of the way

Offerings for the Tabernacle

God told Moses to have the people bring offerings
Of gold and silver and bronze
Fine linen and goat hair and sea cow and ram skins
Purple and blue and red yarns

They should also bring acacia wood and olive oil
Spices for anointing and perfumes
They should bring onyx and other precious gems
To be set in their priestly costumes

He said to build a Tabernacle in which He would dwell
He said *exactly* how to build it
He also gave instructions as to what He wanted
In the furnishings that filled it

The Ark of the Covenant

Then God told Moses to make a chest of acacia wood
Two and a quarter feet high and wide
He said to make it three and three-quarters feet long
Covered with gold on every side

Trim it all around with a molding of gold
With four gold rings at its feet
Put two gold-covered acacia poles through the rings
And on top...a mercy seat

Face two gold cherubim to each other, looking down
One at each end of the seat
With wings spread up and covering the top
To make the Ark complete

Then God told Moses, "The Ark is for the Tablets,"
Which He would *give* to him
And He would *meet* with Moses and *speak* to him
From between the cherubim

THE TABERNACLE

Then God told Moses to build the Tabernacle
With ten curtains of linen so fine
Each six feet wide and forty-two feet long
With purple and blue and red twine

Take five of the curtains and join them together
Then join the other five the same way
Trim the end-curtain edges with fifty blue loops
He described the magnificent display

He told Moses to make fifty clasps of gold
To fasten the curtains together
Then cover the Tabernacle with a tent of goat hair
To protect it from the weather

Make eleven goat hair curtains for the tent
Make each one six feet wide
Forty-five feet long...connected with gold clasps
And covered on the topside

With skins of rams and skins of sea cows
And use the acacia wood
To make forty upright frames for the Tabernacle
Moses wrote and understood

The frames should each be fifteen feet high
And two and a half feet wide
All covered in gold, with silver bases beneath
And five crossbars on each side

Make a curtain of fine linen with gold cherubim
With scarlet and purple and blue
Then hang it with gold hooks on four gold posts
Standing on silver bases too

Put the Ark of the Covenant behind the curtain
For the curtain will divide
The Holy Place from the Most Holy Place
Where the Lord God…will reside

God said they should then make a *courtyard*
Of fine linen curtains outside
Make the courtyard a hundred and fifty feet long
And seventy-five feet wide

Then He gave detailed directions for an altar
A table and a lampstand
And all of the utensils to go on them
Each item perfectly planned

He described the priestly garments
And the manner of sacrifice
He said that those who do not observe the Sabbath
Will pay the ultimate price

For forty days and nights…God and Moses
Were on the mountain alone
Then God gave to Moses the Testament
Carved on two tablets of stone

THE GOLDEN CALF

While Moses was gone, the people grew restless
As they were waiting below
They came and told Aaron, "Make a god for us
What happened to Moses, we don't know!"

So Aaron told them to bring him their jewelry
And he would do it on their behalf
Then he heated the gold and melted it down
And fashioned...a golden calf

The people exclaimed, "Israel, *this* is your god!"
As they pointed to the beast
Then Aaron built an altar and the very next day
They had offerings...and a feast

Meanwhile, God told Moses about the people
And what they did on these two days
He said to go down...for they'd become corrupt
And had taken up pagan ways

God was very angry and was going to destroy them
But Moses began to pray,
"Lord if you do *that*...after bringing them from Egypt
What will their enemies say?"

"The Egyptians will say that you brought out your people
Only to destroy them *here*"
Then he reminded God of His promises
And continued to persevere

The Lord changed His mind and let the people live
His wrath...He would postpone
Then Moses turned and started down the mountain
Carrying the tablets of stone

Joshua exclaimed, "It sounds like war in the camp!"
When Moses reached his location
"It is not the sound of triumph or defeat," said Moses
"It is the sound of celebration"

Then Moses saw the idol and the people dancing
When he finished climbing down
And he burned with anger and he threw the tablets
Smashing them on the ground

He seized the golden calf and threw it in the fire
And the people watched it melt
They had no idea what he would do next
But his anger…could be felt

Then Moses took the gold and ground it into powder
The people didn't know *what* to think
Then he took the powder…and put it in the water
And gave it to the people to drink

Then he said to the people, "Whoever is for God
Come and stand by me"
So those who chose God and those who did not
All could plainly see

Immediately all of the Levites stepped up
And crossed to Moses' side
Then he told them to kill the idol worshipers
And three thousand people died

The next day Moses said to the people,
"You've committed a terrible sin
I will go back on the mountain and pray to the Lord
To obtain forgiveness from Him"

So once again Moses climbed up the mountain
And prayed in that same place
And God said of those who sinned against Him
Their names…He would erase

Then He struck the people with a plague
Because of the calf of gold
They had sinned against Him and worshiped it
So they saw His wrath unfold

THE NEW TABLETS

Sometime later the Lord told Moses
To come up on the mountain alone
And He gave him the Ten Commandments again
Carved on two tablets of stone

When Moses came down…his face was radiant
And he called the people near
But only Aaron and the leaders came
The others stayed back in fear

Finally all of the people gathered around
And Moses gave to them
The Ten Commandments and the Laws
That God had given him

From that day forward…Moses wore a veil
Covering his face
He removed it whenever he met with the Lord
In the Holy Place

Putting Up the Tabernacle

When the Israelites completed the Tabernacle
Moses anointed Aaron and his sons
For God had said they would serve as priests
They were His *chosen* ones

On the first day of the first month of the second year
The Tabernacle was complete
With the Ark, the tables, the altar, the lampstand
And a basin to wash their feet

Then the cloud came and covered the Tabernacle
And the Glory of the Lord came down
And Moses could not *enter* the Tabernacle
Or set foot on such holy ground

After that, the cloud was over the Tabernacle by day
And fire was in the cloud at night
So during their travels the cloud could be seen
By every Israelite

INSTRUCTIONS FROM THE LORD

One day Moses was in the Tent of Meeting
When the Lord called and spoke to him
The Lord gave him instructions for the Israelites
Which Moses gave to them

Instructions about offerings and sacrifices
Instructions about purification
And also about priests and food and cleanliness
And forbidden sexual relations

Instructions about health and consulting mediums
And observing holy days
All the instructions were for the good of the people
To guide them in their ways

Then the Lord told Moses they would be rewarded
If the people simply obeyed
But if they refused and *rejected* His commands
Then punishment...would be paid

REWARD FOR OBEDIENCE AND PUNISHMENT FOR DISOBEDIENCE

God said if they follow His decrees and commands
He will send rain in season
And the ground and the trees will yield their crops
And then He gave them *more* reason

From harvest to harvest the people will have plenty
And in safety they will live
He'll grant peace in the land and they won't be afraid
And even *more*...He will give

He'll remove the savage beasts and enemy swords
Will not pass through the land
And when His people pursue their enemies
Their enemies will not stand

"I will look on you with favor and increase your numbers
And keep my covenant with you
While you are still eating last year's harvest," He said,
"You will have to make room for the new

"I will put my dwelling place among you," He said
"I'll walk with you and be your God
And you will be my people," He promised
And His commandments were not hard

"I am the Lord your God, who brought you out of Egypt,"
Declared His voice from the sky
"I broke the bars of your yoke and enabled you
To walk with heads held high

"But if you will not listen to me and obey my commands
And you violate my covenant
Then I will do *this* to you," promised the Lord
And warned of their punishment

"I will bring upon you sudden terror," He said,
"Disease that will drain away your life
You will plant in vain for your enemies will eat it"
Then He described more strife

"I will set my face against you and you will be defeated
And be under your enemies' rule
And you will *flee* when *no* one," said the Lord,
"Is even *pursuing* you

"And if after all of this you will not listen to me
Seven times over will I punish you for your sin
I will break down your stubborn pride," said the Lord
This was a *promise* from Him

"I will make the sky like iron and the ground like bronze
Your strength will be spent in vain
For your soil and your trees will not yield their harvest
If hostile toward me you remain

"I will multiply your afflictions seven times over
As your sins deserve
Wild animals will rob you of your children and cattle"
From His word...He will not swerve

"And if you do not accept my correction," He warned,
"And continue to be hostile to me
I will be hostile to you and will afflict you for your sins
Seven times over...you will see

"And to avenge the breaking of the covenant
Upon you I will bring the sword
And when you withdraw into your cities
I will send plague,"...said the Lord

"You will eat the flesh of your sons and daughters"
Then He warned of other things
"I will pile your dead bodies on your lifeless idols
And reject the sacrifices you bring

"I will lay waste to the land and I will scatter you
Among the other nations
Your cities will lie in ruins for years"
He spoke of generations

"And you who are left in the land of your enemies
Their hearts will be so filled with fright
That the sound of a leaf being blown in the wind
Will send them into flight

"They will run...though no one is pursuing them
As though fleeing from the sword
They will stumble over each other and they will fall,"
Declared the Almighty Lord

"The lands of your enemies will devour you
In their lands you will waste away
Because of your sins and your fathers' sins
But if you *confess* your sins and *pray*

"And confess the sins of your fathers
Their *hostility* against *me*
When hearts are *humbled* and they *pay* for their sins
Then the people will see

"I will remember my promises to Jacob," He said,
"And Isaac and Abraham
And while you are in the foreign countries
I will remember the land

"They will *pay* for their sins for rejecting my laws
And despising my decrees
Yet I will not abhor them to destroy them completely
While in the land of their enemies

"And for their sake I will remember my covenant
With their past generations
Who I brought out of Egypt to be their God
In the sight of all the nations"

Wandering in the Desert

Although the Lord led the people from Egypt
And always took care of them
Time and again they grumbled and complained
Some even *rebelled* against Him

Many who rebelled were killed by the Lord
Some swallowed in the earth below
Moses prayed to the Lord to not destroy them *all*
Even though they angered Him so

Then God said of those who grumbled against Him
In the desert their bodies would fall
Only Caleb and Joshua would enter the land
The rest would not enter at all

So for forty more years in the wilderness
God led the Hebrews around
He gave them water and He gave them food
Called manna, which fell to the ground

And when the elder generation had died
Their children entered the land
The land that flowed with milk and honey
Given them by God's hand

Joshua

THE LORD COMMANDS JOSHUA

Moses died at the age of one hundred and twenty
God made Joshua the leader after him
God told him to cross the Jordan with the people
And leave the land where they had been

"I will give you every place where you set your foot
As I promised Moses too
And as I was with Moses," continued the Lord,
"So will I also be with you

"Be strong and courageous and lead the people
And they will inherit the land
Meditate on my Word both day and night"
Joshua was led by God's hand

RAHAB AND THE SPIES

So Joshua told the people to prepare to leave
And he then selected two men
He told them to go and look over the land
And report back to him again

In Jericho, they went to the house of a prostitute
Named Rahab, were they took a room
But the king of Jericho heard they were there
And he feared for Jericho's doom

He sent a message to Rahab to bring them out
For he heard they had come to spy
But Rahab hid them on the roof of her house
And told the messengers a lie

She told them that the men had left the city
At dusk…the end of day
"If you go quickly you can overtake them," she said
So they immediately went away

Then Rahab told the two men on the roof,
"The people are afraid of you here
I know that the Lord has given you this land
And our hearts are all melting in fear

"We have heard how the Lord had dried up for you
The waters of the Red Sea
So now…please swear to me by the Lord
You'll show kindness to my family

"Give me a sign that you will spare the lives
Of my father and my mother
And you will save all of those who belong to them
And all of my sisters and brothers"

The men responded, "Our lives for your lives!
If you do not tell of our plan
We will treat you kindly and faithfully
When the Lord gives us the land

"But our oath will not be binding," they went on,
"Unless, when we enter the town
You have tied a scarlet cord in the window
Through which you let us down

"And your family must be in your house," they said
"For if anyone goes out
What happens to him…will be his own fault"
Of that, there was no doubt

"We will see that no harm comes to anyone
Who is in this house with you
But we will not keep our promise if you go out
And tell what we're going to do"

"Agreed," said Rahab to the Israelite men
"It *shall* be as you say"
Then they climbed down a rope through the window
And the men went on their way

When the two men told Joshua what had happened
Their message to him was clear
"The Lord has surely given us the land," they said
"The people are melting in fear"

Crossing the Jordan

Joshua had the priests carry the Ark of the Covenant
Into the Jordan River, which was deep
But as soon as the feet of the priests touched the water
It stopped flowing and piled up in a heap!

Then the priests who carried the Ark stood firm
On dry ground in the middle of the river
Until the whole nation completed the crossing
And again God's people were delivered

Then God told Joshua to have twelve men
One from every tribe
Each take a stone from the middle of the Jordan
And bring it to the other side

He had them make a pile, where they spent the night
For the stones were to serve as a sign
They would be a memorial to the people of Israel
Until the end of time

And in the future, when their children would ask,
"What indeed...could these stones be?"
They would say that God stopped the flow of the Jordan
Just as He stopped the Red Sea

The Fall of Jericho

Now when Joshua was approaching the city of Jericho
He looked up and saw a man
Who was standing in front of them, blocking the way
Holding a sword in his hand

"Are you for us or for our enemies?" called Joshua
Wondering where he was from
"Neither," he replied, "but as commander of the army
Of the Almighty Lord I have come!"

In reverence, Joshua spoke to the angel
As he immediately fell facedown
"What message does my Lord have for his servant?"
He asked with his face to the ground

Then the commander of the army of the Lord
Spoke to Joshua and said,
"Remove your sandals, for the place you stand is holy"
And as ordered...Joshua did

Now the wall around Jericho was tightly shut up
For fear of the Israelite men
No one dared to leave...from inside of the city
And no one was allowed to come in

Then the Lord spoke to Joshua and told him
He would *give* them Jericho
And He told him exactly what they must do
In order for it to be so

And after the Lord told Joshua precisely
How to destroy the city borders
Joshua called all of the priests and the people
And gave to them their orders

All of them were to march around the city
Lined up in a certain way
And if they followed God's plan, they would receive
A miracle...on the seventh day

The first in the line up was the armed guard
Then with trumpets...seven priests went
Behind them...more priests were marching
Who carried the Ark of the *Covenant*

Behind the Ark of the Covenant was the rear guard
And as the trumpets blew
They marched around the walls *once*...in silence
For that was what God said to do

After they marched, they went back to their camp
Where they spent the night...and then
The next morning and for five *more* mornings
They marched the same way *again*

During each march, the trumpets were sounding
But no war cries or words came out
For Joshua had told the people to be silent
Until he would tell them to shout

On the seventh day...they rose up early
Just at the break of day
And again they marched around the city
In the exact same way

But instead of going back to their camp after *that*
They marched around *again*
And *again* and *again*...Seven times 'round they went
With trumpets sounding...And then

The trumpets gave a long and very loud blast!
And Joshua commanded, "SHOUT!
FOR THE LORD HAS GIVEN YOU THE CITY!"
And at once...the people *cried out*!

They raised their voices 'til it seemed like thunder
The trumpets blared during that
And as the people all shouted...long and loud
The walls of the city...fell flat

Immediately the Israelites charged the city
And took it by the sword
And they *knew* that the miracle and the victory
Were given to them by the Lord

Samson

The Israelites were always God's people
But when their evil was severe
He delivered them into the hands of the Philistines
Where they remained for forty years

Now living in the small town of Zorah
Was Manoah and his wife
His wife was sterile and she remained childless
Until a miracle came into her life

The angel of the Lord appeared to her and said,
"You are going to have a son
Drink no wine and do not cut his hair"
For he would be a *special* one

"He is to be a Nazirite," continued the angel,
"And for God...he is set apart"
When the woman told Manoah what had happened
He prayed with all of his heart

When the baby was born they named him Samson
God blessed him as he grew
And the Spirit of the Lord began to stir him
To do what he must do

For Samson had a very special role
To play out in God's plans
He would begin the deliverance of Israel
From the Philistines' hands

As Samson grew, he became very strong
The strongest in the lands
And one day when he was attacked by a lion
He killed it with his bare hands

Samson's Marriage

Eventually, Samson met a Philistine woman
And they became engaged
But after they married...the Philistines killed her
And Samson...was enraged

The Spirit of the Lord came upon him
Filling him with power and then
Samson took the jawbone of a donkey
And killed a thousand men

Now Samson was the leader of the Israelites
For a period twenty years long
And everyone knew throughout the land
That *he*...was incredibly strong

One day in Gaza his enemies waited
Hiding by the city gate
For Samson was there and they wanted to kill him
For Samson...they did hate

But Samson walked up to the gate
And as everybody saw
Samson...in a feat of enormous strength
Just tore off each door

He lifted both doors to his shoulders
Including the posts and bar
And carried it all...out of the city
To a hill afar

Samson and Delilah

Sometime later, Samson fell in love again
With a woman he had met
Her name was Delilah...but she was evil
This love...he would *regret*

The rulers of the Philistines went to Delilah
And they proposed a plan
They would give her silver if she would tell them
The source of the strength of her man

"Tell me the secret of your great strength,"
To Samson, Delilah did ask
"I would be weak if tied with seven straps," he said
So she set about the task

In the night while Samson lay sleeping
This is what Delilah did
She tied him up with seven fresh straps
While the Philistines waited and hid

When Delilah was finished she called out to Samson,
"The Philistines are upon you!"
Then Delilah stepped back...watched and waited
To see what he would do

But Samson woke up and broke the straps
Then Delilah said, "You lied
You have made a *fool* of me," she whined
"*Tell* me how you can be tied!"

"I would be weak if I was tied," he answered,
"With ropes that have never been used"
So she used new rope...It snapped like thread
Samson was not even bruised

"You've made a fool of me again!" she whimpered
"Again to me, you've lied
Now *tell* me the secret of your strength!
TELL ME!" Delilah cried

"If you weave my seven braids," said Samson,
"To fabric...on a loom...with a pin
I would be as weak as any other man"
So she did *that* to him

As Samson slept and the Philistines hid
Delilah wove the braids on his head
But when Samson awoke...he was still strong
And he tore out the fabric instead

"How can you say you love me," cried Delilah,
"And lie to me this way?"
Delilah continued begging and pleading
And nagging him day after day

"How can you say you love me," she whined,
"When you won't *confide* in me?"
Delilah kept it up until finally Samson
Was as tired as he could be

At last...worn down...Samson told Delilah,
"No razor ever touched my head
I would lose my strength if my head was shaved"
So she waited...'til he went to bed

Then the Philistines crept into the room
As he slept...they shaved his hair
He awoke with no strength and Samson was seized
By all of the Philistines there

They shackled him and gouged his eyes out
And threw him in prison then
But after some time...Samson's hair
Began to grow...again

Now one day the Philistine rulers had a celebration
For Dagon...their god...to thank
"Our god has delivered our enemy Samson!" they shouted
They cheered...they ate...they drank

And while the Philistines were high in spirits
They shouted "Bring Samson here!"
They figured that Samson would be entertaining
And so...they brought him near

But what the Philistines had not realized
What they had not known
What they didn't notice when they brought him in
Was how much...his hair...had grown

Then Samson spoke to the servant
Who led him by the hand
"Put me where I can lean against the pillars
That make this temple stand"

And as he stood between the two main pillars
With a hand upon each one
The Philistines watched and laughed at him
Thinking it was fun

But all the while...Samson was praying,
"Lord, strengthen me once more"
Then he took a breath...and spread his legs
And braced his feet on the floor

Now the temple was very crowded that day
There were people from wall to wall
And as Samson pushed with all of his might
The temple began...to fall

Samson died with thousands of Philistines
When the temple came down that day
But he knew that that would happen
When he began to pray

Ruth

In the time when Judges were the rulers of Israel
There was a famine in the land
And a man named Elimelech and his wife, Naomi
Had to change their plans

So they took their sons, Mahlon and Kilion
And moved to Moab for a while
But that was just the start of Naomi's troubles
For *she* would face *many* a trial

After a time she was left alone with her sons
Her husband, Elimelech, had died
Then two Moabite women came into her life
As each of her sons took a bride

But once again tragedy struck the family
After they'd been there ten years
For Naomi's sons Mahlon and Kilion *both* died
Leaving the women…in their tears

Now left with Naomi were Orpah and Ruth
Naomi's two daughters-in-law
Naomi heard the Lord had provided food in Judah
And decided to go home once more

So they packed their possessions and left Moab
But when they were on the road
Naomi told both of her daughters-in-law
To go back to their mother's abode

"May the Lord be kind to each of you," she said,
"As you've been kind to your dead and to me
May He grant that you each find another husband"
She truly hoped that it would be

Then Naomi kissed them and they all cried together
Over what she wanted them to do
Then Orpah and Ruth both said to Naomi,
"We will go to *your* people with *you*"

But Naomi insisted...for she had concluded
What would be best for them
Orpah kissed her good-bye and went back to her people
But Ruth objected again

"Don't ask me to leave you and go back," she said
"Wherever you go...I will go
I'll live where you live...Your people will be mine"
She insisted that it would be so

"Your God will be my God," she continued
"Where *you* die...*I* will die
And may the Lord *punish* me if ever we separate
Except by death," she cried

When Naomi saw that Ruth was determined
She stopped urging her to go
And the two women left for Bethlehem
What awaited...they didn't know

NAOMI AND RUTH IN BETHLEHEM

The whole town was stirred when they arrived
"Can this be Naomi?" they said
"Call me Mara," said Naomi, "for the Lord Almighty
Made my life bitter instead

"When I left I was full but He brought me back empty
Why call me Naomi?" she said
"The Almighty Lord brought affliction upon me,"
She concluded as she lowered her head

Now they had arrived at the beginning of harvest
And Ruth came and told Naomi,
"I will go to the fields and pick leftover grain
Behind whoever is kind to *me*"

So Ruth followed behind the harvesters
In a field that happened to belong
To a relative of Elimelech...a man named Boaz
Whose standing in the city was strong

And while she was there, it happened that Boaz
Came out to the field to see
"The Lord be with you!" he greeted his workers
And then he said…"Who is she?"

"She is the woman who came back with Naomi,"
His foreman said to him
"She asked if she could gather behind the harvesters,"
The man continued then

"She's been working steadily since morning," he said
Then Boaz spoke to *her*
He told Ruth she should gather in *his* fields only
And *not* the fields of another

Ruth bowed to the ground before Boaz
And she exclaimed, amazed,
"*Why* have I found such favor in your eyes?"
But then Ruth…Boaz praised

"I've heard all about what you've done for Naomi
Since your *own* husband died
Leaving your parents and your people and coming here
May the Lord repay you!" he cried

"May the God of Israel richly bless you," he said
Then he invited her to dine
And he offered her roasted grain and bread
To dip in vinegar wine

Ruth ate all she wanted and had some left over
Then went back to work again
"Leave her some stalks…and don't *bother* her,"
Boaz ordered his men

So Ruth gathered in the field until evening
And then she threshed the grain
She went back to Naomi with about *twenty* quarts
And then she began to explain

For Naomi was surprised at how much she had
"Where did you work?" she exclaimed
So Ruth told Naomi about the man and his field
And said, "Boaz is his name"

"The Lord bless Boaz for showing kindness," said Naomi,
"To the living and the dead
This man, Boaz...is a close relative of ours
And a kinsman-redeemer," she said

Ruth told her that Boaz said to work in his fields
Until the harvest is through
"That is good," said Naomi, "for in *another* field
Who *knows* what might happen to you!"

So Ruth worked through the wheat and barley harvests
Beside the servant girls in the field
Then one day as Naomi was speaking to Ruth
A plan, Naomi revealed

"Shouldn't I find a home for you, my daughter," she said,
"Where you will be provided for?
Boaz is our kinsman-redeemer and this very night
He'll be working on the threshing floor"

Then Naomi told Ruth to wash and perfume
And put on her very best clothes
Then go to the threshing floor and hide while he eats
So she's there...but nobody knows

And when he's finished eating...she should watch
Where he goes to lay down to sleep
Then Naomi told Ruth she should then go to Boaz
And lay down...by his feet

So Ruth agreed and went to the threshing floor
And did exactly what Naomi said
And in the middle of the night, Boaz woke up
And sat up his makeshift bed

When Boaz saw her…he said, "Who are you?"
As he strained in the dark to see
"I am your servant Ruth," she answered humbly
"Put the corner of your covering over me

"For you are my kinsman-redeemer," said Ruth
"The Lord bless you my daughter!" he replied
"For this kindness that you are now showing
Is even greater than before," he cried

"For you have not run after the *younger* men
Whether rich or poor"
Then Boaz told Ruth that she shouldn't be afraid
For her future…was secure

Then he told her that there was another relative
Who was closer to her than he
And he would go to the man on the following day
To see which of them…it would be

In the morning Boaz filled her shawl with barley
And Ruth went on her way
She told Naomi what happened and Naomi responded,
"He won't rest…'til this is settled *today*"

Meanwhile, Boaz was waiting at the town gate
For the kinsman-redeemer to come around
When he saw him, he called, "Come here, my friend"
The man came over and he sat down

Boaz had ten elders sit down with them too
And then he said to the man
That Naomi, who came back from Moab
Was selling Elimelech's land

"I'm telling you for you have first right," said Boaz,
"So redeem it if you *want* to
But if you do not want it…then tell me," he said,
"For I'm next in line after *you*"

"I will redeem it," said the relative
But then Boaz let him know
That on the day he redeems the land
He also gets Ruth...the widow

But in light of that new information
The relative changed his mind
And in front of all of the witnesses there
The offer...he declined

Then Boaz announced to all of the people
That *he* would purchase the land
So he bought it from Naomi...and as for Ruth
In marriage...he took her hand

Now Boaz and Ruth had a son they named Obed
Naomi cared for him with joy
And one day this child would care for *her*
This wonderful baby boy

And after all Naomi and Ruth had gone through
And in spite of *everything*
Ruth's son grew up and had a son named Jesse
Who had a son named David...a king

Samuel

THE BIRTH OF SAMUEL

There was a certain man named Elkanah
Who had two wives...not one
Now his wife Peninnah had sons and daughters
But his other wife Hannah...had none

And every year...year after year
Elkanah went from his town
And traveled to Shiloh to worship the Lord
To sacrifice and bow down

And whenever the day came for him to sacrifice
He gave portions of the meat
To Peninnah and her children...but to *Hannah*
Elkanah gave *double* to eat

He did this because Elkanah loved Hannah
And he wanted her to know
That even though she didn't have any children
That he still loved her so

But Peninnah teased her for having no children
Year after year it went on
When Hannah went to worship...Peninnah would tease her
Although it was very wrong

Peninnah would tease her until Hannah cried
And couldn't even eat
And though Elkanah tried to comfort her
Her sadness...was complete

Now one day at the Temple of Shiloh
As Hannah prayed and wept
She made a promise to the God of Heaven
A vow she later kept

"Oh Lord Almighty...if you look at me in mercy,"
Began the prayer of Elkanah's wife,
"And give me a son...I will give him to you
For all of the days of his life"

The Lord heard Hannah and gave her a son
Samuel was his name
And when he was weaned, he went with his mother
And to the temple they came

Hanna presented Samuel to Eli the priest
And Eli took *charge* of him
He would raise the boy to minister in the temple
His training would now begin

And each year after that when Samuel's parents
Came to the Temple at Shiloh
Hannah brought a brand new robe for the boy
And in the Lord, he continued to grow

And since Hanna had kept her promise to the Lord
By giving *Him* her little one
The Lord blessed her with many *more* children
Three daughters and two more sons

Eli's Wicked Sons

Now Eli had two sons who were both very wicked
Their sins were grave in God's sight
They stole from the sacrifices made to the Lord
And did sinful things...day and night

Eli spoke to his sons about what they were doing
For he heard of each wicked deed
And he warned them about the wrath of God
But his words...they did not heed

Then one day a prophet of God came to Eli
And spoke of coming days
He said that God was going to punish his family
Because of his sons' evil ways

Then the prophet said...that in the space of a day
Both of Eli's sons would be killed
And then the Lord would raise up...a *faithful* priest
Who would do whatever God willed

Those left in Eli's family would go to *that* priest
Before *him* they would bow their head
And beg *him* for appointment to a priestly office
A piece of silver and a crust of bread

God Calls Samuel

As time went by, Eli's eyes grew dim
'Til finally...he could barely see
One night he laid down in his usual place
Where to sleep, he would always be

Meanwhile, as Samuel was lying in the temple
The Lord called out his name
Samuel jumped up and said, "Here I am,"
And into Eli's room he came

"Here I am...You called me," he said to Eli
"I did not call...go lay down"
So Samuel went back and laid down again
And again the Lord came around

"Samuel!" the Lord called out once more
Samuel went to Eli *again*
"Here I am," he said "You called me"
And Eli said to him then

"My son...I did not call you...Go back
Go lie down in your bed"
But when Samuel did...the Lord called *again*
"Samuel!" He said

So yet again...Samuel went into Eli's room
And for the third time he called out
"Here I am," he said "You *called* me"
Now Eli *figured*...what it was about

He realized it was the Lord who was calling the boy
And he said...with his eyes glistening,
"Go and lie down...and if He calls you again
Say, 'Speak Lord...your servant is listening.'"

So Samuel went back and lay down in his place
And the Lord came in and stood there
Then the Lord called out, "Samuel!...Samuel!"
And Samuel answered...like a prayer

"Speak Lord, for your servant is listening"
Then he listened to every word
The Lord told him what He was going to do
But Samuel *feared* what he heard

For the Lord said He was going to punish Eli
For what Eli's sons had done
Since Eli didn't *stop* them, the family would suffer
For generations to come

The next day Samuel was afraid to tell Eli
The things the Lord had said
And when Eli asked him about the vision
Samuel was filled with dread

For he was afraid to tell Eli of the vision
Not knowing what Eli would do
"May God punish you if you do *not* tell me," said Eli,
"What He said to you"

So Samuel told Eli all the Lord had said
Hiding nothing from him then
"He is the Almighty Lord God," said Eli
"Let Him do what seems good to Him"

Now the Lord was with Samuel as he grew up
Appearing to him time and again
And everyone in Israel knew he was a prophet
For he brought the Lord's words to them

THE PHILISTINES CAPTURE THE ARK

The Israelites went out to fight the Philistines
And as the battle spread
The Philistines won...and by the end of the day
Four thousand Israelites lay dead

The elders asked each other, "Why did this happen?
Let us bring up the Ark from Shiloh!"
They figured if they brought the Ark to the battle
It would *save* them...from their foe

And when the Ark of the Lord came into the camp
The Israelites raised such a shout
That all the ground shook...and the Philistines heard it
And wondered what it was about

When they learned that the Ark was in the camp
The Philistines were terribly afraid
For they knew the God of Israel struck Egypt
With every manner of plague

But they decided to be brave...and fight they did
Their battle was very skilled
And the slaughter of the Israelites was huge
Thirty thousand of their men were killed

A Benjamite man ran to Shiloh from the battle
His clothes torn and dust on his head
He said the Ark of the Covenant of God was *captured*
And thirty thousand men were dead

When the people heard about the Ark and the men
All of Israel cried
And also in the battle...as the prophet foretold
Eli's sons both died

When Eli heard about the Ark of the Covenant
He was sitting in a chair
He fell backward and his neck was broken
And Eli died right there

Now after the Philistines had captured the Ark
They brought it to Ashdod
They placed it in the temple of Dagon
Beside the statue of their god

But when the people of Ashdod rose the next day
They found Dagon…fallen on his face
Laying on the ground before the Ark of the Lord!
So they put him back in his place

But the following morning when the people arose
There was Dagon again…facedown
His head and his hands had been broken off
And laid in the threshold on the ground

The Lord's hand became heavy on the people of Ashdod
Their lives became very stark
He sent devastation and inflicted them with tumors
And they *knew*…they must get rid of the *Ark*

So they moved the Ark to the city of Gath
But the Lord's hand was against them *too*
With an outbreak of tumors, the city was in panic
Until they figured out what to do

They sent the Ark of the Lord to the city of *Ekron*
And Ekron's people cried out that day,
"They have brought the Ark of God here to kill us!"
And the leaders said, "Send it away!"

"Let the Ark go back to its own place!" they said
"Or it will kill us and our people," they cried
For everyone in the city was afflicted with tumors
And overwhelmed at how many had died

Then the leaders asked their priests and diviners
How to send it back to the Israelites
After seven months of having the Ark of God
And seven months of blights

"If you return the Ark of the God of Israel
Do not send it empty," they said
The Philistines listened... for they would do *anything*
To lift the hand of God from their head

"Send a guilt offering," the priests told the leaders,
"And you will be healed... and *then*
You'll *know* why His hand was not lifted from you"
"What offering should we send?"

"Make models of the tumors and the rats," they replied,
"Of which are destroying your land
And pay honor to the God of Israel," they said
"And perhaps He will lift His hand

"Hitch two cows to a new cart and detain their calves,"
The priests went on to say
"Place the Ark and a chest with the offerings upon it
And send it on its way"

"Keep watch for we'll know that the Lord brought disaster
If it goes up to its own land
If it doesn't... we'll know it was *chance* that struck us
And it was *not* His hand"

But the cows went straight up and kept on the road
Lowing all the way
As it approached Beth Shemesh, the people saw it
And rejoiced and made sacrifice that day

Saul

ISRAEL ASKS SAMUEL FOR A KING

Now Samuel was a righteous judge over Israel
He continued through all of his days
And when he grew old, he appointed his sons
But they did not walk in his ways

They accepted bribes and made false judgments
They were dishonest in everything
So the elders of Israel requested of Samuel,
"Appoint to us...a king"

Samuel was displeased with their request
And went to the Lord in prayer
The Lord told him to go back to the people
And to tell them...to beware

For a king would take their sons from them
And make them soldiers and *more*
Some would plow his ground and reap his harvest
And some would make weapons of war

He would take their daughters and make them cooks
Take a tenth of their crops and grain
Take their servants, their cattle and their flocks
Take a tenth of all of their gain

The people themselves would become his slaves
Then they would cry to the Lord and pray
But because they *now*...choose a *king* over God
The Lord will not answer that day

So Samuel went back and warned the people
But they refused to listen to a thing
"No," they said, "we want to be like *other* nations!
We want to have a king!"

So Samuel told the Lord what the people had said
Not knowing the reaction this would bring
But the Lord told Samuel, to listen to the people
And to give to them...a king

SAMUEL ANOINTS SAUL

Now there was a man of standing whose name was Kish
Who had a son whose name was Saul
And Saul was the most handsome man in Israel
Handsome and very tall

Kish sent Saul to find some lost donkeys
Saul searched from town to town
And though he and his servant had traveled far
The donkeys could not be found

They arrived in a town where Samuel was staying
And they figured that he might know
For he was a *prophet*...so he *knew* things
And could tell them which way to go

Now the Lord had told Samuel, the day before
That He was going to send him a man
To anoint him as leader and the man would deliver
The people from the Philistines' hand

The Lord spoke to Samuel when Saul approached
The Lord said, "This is the man"
And the following day, Samuel anointed him
And Saul's new life began

The Spirit of God came upon him and filled him
And when he went to his own town
The people were amazed because he prophesied
And they all gathered around

SAUL MADE KING

Samuel summoned all of the people of Israel
To gather before the Lord one day
And when all of the tribes were assembled
He told them what God had to say

That although the Lord had brought the Israelites
Out of Egypt in the past
And had always delivered them from their distresses
Their faithfulness...did not last

Because now their request was for a king
Who they wanted put in place
Which meant that they were rejecting the Lord
Instead...of seeking His face

Then Samuel had Saul brought into the crowd
He was a head taller than the rest
And Samuel told them that the Lord *chose* Saul
For as king...he was the best

Then all of the people began to cheer
They shouted "Long live the king!"
They were all excited and looking forward
To whatever the future might bring

Saul was a great king and a mighty man of war
From the time his reign had its start
But after a while...he disobeyed the Lord
Samuel came to him...heavy in heart

"Because you have rejected the word of the Lord," he said,
"He has rejected you as king"
Then Samuel went out and mourned for Saul
Who would soon...lose everything

David and Goliath

SAMUEL ANOINTS DAVID

One day the Lord sent the Prophet Samuel
To the town of Bethlehem
He was going there to see the sons of Jesse
For God chose *one* of them

That chosen son would save the Israelites
Of him, the people would sing
One day this man would rule their nation
For *he* would become their king

Now when Samuel saw the sons of Jesse
He picked Eliab at the start
Because man looks at the appearance
But God...looks at the heart

And as seven sons walked past Samuel
God rejected every one
Then Samuel spoke and asked Jesse
If he had *another* son

"The youngest is tending the sheep," said Jesse
"Send for him," Samuel said
And when David came...God said, "He's the one"
Samuel anointed him with oil on his head

Jesse's son David...was a fine looking boy
Handsome features and ruddy skin
And the Spirit of the Lord came on him in *power*
When Samuel anointed him

Saul was still king, but he had an evil spirit
It tormented him and wouldn't go away
And the only thing that would make it leave
Was when David...on his harp...would play

So David went back and forth to the palace
Playing harp, tending sheep and such
Saul made him one of his armor-bearers
And liked him very much

DAVID BATTLES GOLIATH

Meanwhile, the Philistine warriors were gathered
To battle the Israelites
But this time the battle would be very different
From all of their other fights

For the Philistines now had a champion
Goliath was his name
This man was more than nine feet tall
And Goliath had great fame

His armor weighed a hundred and twenty-five pounds
Fifteen pounds was the point of his spear
And when he shouted at the Israelite soldiers
They ran from him in fear

He would stand outside the Philistine camp
And call out in a rage
"Choose a man to fight me!" he demanded
"If I win…you'll be our slaves!"

Every day for forty days, Goliath came out
Twice a day, to take his stand
But no one was willing to fight against him
No one in all the land

For the Israelite soldiers were terrified
Whenever he came near
They knew no one could kill this giant
And they were gripped with fear

Now three of David's older brothers
Were in Saul's army at the time
And one day David brought them food
Up to the battle line

But as David was talking to his brothers
Goliath...he came out
And as he had done each day before
Goliath began to shout

Then David said, "Who is this *Philistine*
Who defies the army of *God*?"
But after David had posed his question
His brother Eliab...began to prod

"Why have you come here?" Eliab demanded
"And who did you leave with the sheep?
You're wicked...You came here to watch the *fight*!"
His anger...was very deep

When Saul heard about what David had said
Saul had him brought near
Then David told Saul that he'd fight Goliath
Though everyone else ran in fear

Saul responded..."You can not fight that Philistine!
You're a boy...That's a fighting man there!"
But David told Saul that while tending sheep
He had killed both lion and bear

He told him that the Lord had delivered him
From the bear and the lion's paw
And the Lord would deliver him from Goliath
Faith in God...was all he saw

So Saul dressed David in his own coat of armor
And put a bronze helmet on his head
David walked 'round the room with a heavy sword
"I can't go in these," he said

He took off all the armor...and grabbed his staff
Chose five smooth stones from a stream
And with them in his pouch...he got his sling out
To face this giant so mean

But when Goliath saw David was merely a *boy*
He *cursed* him as he drew near
David yelled…"I come against you in the name of the *Lord!*"
Showing Goliath no fear

Then David took a stone from his pouch and slung it
Striking Goliath in the head
Goliath fell…facedown in the dirt
Goliath the giant…was dead

When the Philistines saw that their champion was dead
They all began to run
The Israelites shouted and chased after them
And the battle was quickly won

Then David became a leader in the army
One day he would become the king
He had great success…for the Almighty Lord
Was with him in everything

David and Saul

On the day that David killed Goliath
Saul brought him to his home
From then on David lived in the palace
And his name became well known

King Saul gave David a high position in his army
And Jonathan, Saul's own son
Loved David as a brother and they made a covenant
Their friendship...was as one

SAUL BECOMES JEALOUS OF DAVID

Now David was returning from a battle with the Philistines
And the women came out to sing,
"Saul has killed thousands and David *ten* thousand"
But it raised jealousy in the king

Saul figured if the people thought David was greater
What would happen next?
"David will want my kingdom!" he thought
And this left him very vexed

The next day as David was playing his harp
An evil spirit came over Saul
He picked up a spear and threw it at David
"I'll pin him to the wall!"

But David avoided the point of the spear
Then Saul threw once again
Saul knew the Lord left him and now was with David
And was more afraid of him then

So he sent him away and gave him command
Over a thousand men
David led them in battle and the Lord was with him
And he won...again and again

One day Saul said, "Here's my eldest daughter Merab
I will give her to you as your wife
Only serve me bravely...fight the battles of the Lord,"
Hoping David would lose his life

But David said to Saul, "Who am I?
And who is my father's clan?
That I should be the son-in-law of the *king*?"
So Merab married *another* man

Now Saul's other daughter Michal loved David
At that...Saul was pleased
He figured he could kill David through Michal
His jealousy was like a disease

But David said, "I am too poor and insignificant
To marry the daughter of a king"
Saul said, "Kill a hundred Philistines for her hand"
Hoping his death, *this* would bring

But again David did not die in the battle
And *two* hundred Philistines he slew
Now Saul was more afraid of David than ever
For the Lord was with David, Saul knew

As Saul's jealousy and fear of David continued
He kept sending him off to war
And though David did nothing to deserve it
Saul tried to kill him several times more

Finally David went to Jonathan and asked him,
"Tell me what I have done
That your father is trying to take my life,"
He cried out to Saul's own son

"Never!" cried Jonathan "It is not so!
You are *not* going to die!
My father doesn't do *anything* without *me*!
So why would *this*, he hide?"

But David swore that it was as he had said
Then Jonathan learned it was true
So David left the city and he stayed away
There was nothing else he could do

David went to Nob and Gath and continued
To the cave of Adullam, and then
He was joined by his brothers and his father's household
And around four hundred men

But after David left, Saul went after him
Traveling from town to town
And anyone he found who might have helped David
Saul had them struck down

Now God told David to save the city of Keilah
From the Philistine men
David obeyed the Lord and saved the city
But Saul heard about it then

David was told that Saul was coming
He went before the Lord and was still
"Will Saul come down as your servant has heard?"
And God responded…"He will"

"Will the people of Keilah surrender me and my men?"
"They will," the Lord answered again
So David and his men left the city of Keilah
They were about six hundred men

DAVID SPARES SAUL'S LIFE

One day as Saul was searching for David
Whom he wanted to attack
Saul went into a cave to relieve himself
But he didn't go all the way back

Meanwhile, David was in the back of the cave
Hiding out with his men
He snuck up and cut off a piece of Saul's cloak
He could have killed him right then

But David wouldn't allow his men to attack
And felt guilt over this thing
He came out of the cave and David called out,
"Saul…my lord the king!"

When David called out…Saul stopped in his tracks
And when he turned around
David bowed down and prostrated himself
With his face upon the ground

"Why do you listen when men say I want to harm you?"
Saul listened as David spoke
Then David proved that he could have *killed* Saul
By showing him the piece of his cloak

Then Saul wept aloud and he said to David,
"You are more righteous than I"
He knew then that God would make David the king
And didn't let the opportunity go by

He asked David to swear to not cut off his descendants
Or wipe out his family name
David agreed and gave his oath to Saul
And Saul went home again

DAVID AND ABIGAIL

Now as David and his men were traveling
They saw some men shearing sheep
The men worked for a rich man named Nabal
But Nabal was very cheap

And when David sent ten men to ask Nabal
For food for his men to eat
Nabal *insulted* them…and insulted *David*
Instead of giving them meat

David was angry when his men told what happened
When they reported back
"Put on your swords!" he said to his men
For Nabal…they would attack

Now four hundred men were going with David
Two hundred would stay behind
They rode to a battle...which wouldn't have happened
If Nabal had only been kind

But meanwhile, one of Nabal's sheepherders
Told the story to Nabal's wife
Her name was Abigail...she was beautiful and wise
And perhaps...she could save Nabal's life

Abigail quickly loaded five cooked sheep on donkeys
And two hundred loaves of bread
And corn and raisins and figs and wine
And sent them on ahead

Then she rode a donkey and came upon David
Who was heading down for the battle
When they saw each other...Abigail stopped
And alighted from her saddle

She bowed down at the feet of David and said,
"Please hear what I have to say
Pay no attention to that wicked Nabal!" she cried
She was pleading for their lives that day

She said Nabal was a fool and that she herself
Had not *seen* David's men
She begged him to not avenge himself
And offered the food to him then

David was impressed with this beautiful, wise woman
And he confirmed that it was true
That he would have slain Nabal and his household
And David accepted the food

Then Abigail went back to Nabal, who was drunk
He was having a feast at home
The next morning she told him all that happened
His heart failed...and he was like stone

About ten days later the Lord struck Nabal
And took away his life
And when David heard that Nabal was dead
He made Abigail his wife

DAVID SPARES SAUL'S LIFE AGAIN

Saul went down to the desert of Ziph
With three thousand of his men
For Saul had heard that *David* was there
And wanted to try to kill him again

When David heard where Saul was camped
He snuck in while they slept
And though Saul was surrounded by his soldiers
Right up to him David crept

There was Saul's spear…stuck in the ground
And a water jug near his head
David picked up the spear and the water jug
And walked past Saul in his bed

Then David went some distance away
And stood on top of a hill
And yelled to Saul's army that someone had been there
And that Saul could have easily been killed

"As surely as the Lord lives, you and your men
Deserve to die," he said
"Where are the king's spear and his water jug
Which were near his head?"

Then Saul recognized it was David's voice
"Is that your voice my son?"
"Yes my lord…but why do you pursue me?" said David
"Tell me…what have I done?"

Then Saul realized again that he was wrong
And called out, "I have sinned
Because you considered my life precious today
I will *not* try to harm you again"

Then Saul blessed David and went back to the palace
And David went on his way
But David was thinking, "I will be destroyed
By the hand of Saul one day"

DAVID AMONG THE PHILISTINES

Since David believed that if he stayed in the region
He would be killed by Saul's hand
He decided it would be best that he should leave
And he fled to the Philistines' land

Six hundred men went with him to Achish
The son of the king of Gath
They settled in Ziklag, each man with his family
And David chose a new path

And while David lived in Philistine territory
Four months and a year
He and his men raided cities and towns
Both far away and near

SAUL AND THE WITCH OF ENDOR

Again the Philistines and Israel gathered to battle
But Saul was greatly afraid
He inquired of the Lord…but the Lord didn't answer
Even though he prayed

So he said to his servants, "Find me a medium"
"There is one in Endor," they said
He disguised himself and went to the medium
To raise up a spirit from the dead

The woman asked Saul, "Who shall I bring up?"
"Bring up Samuel," he said
When the medium described the spirit she saw
To the ground, Saul bowed his head

Samuel asked, "Why have you disturbed me?"
Saul answered, "I don't know what to do
The Philistines make war and God has turned away
So I have called on you"

But Samuel said, "Why ask *me*, seeing as the *Lord*
Has become an enemy of *you*?"
Then Samuel told Saul...as he had done in the past
What the Lord was going to do

He said the Lord has given the kingdom to David
Saul's disobedience...the reason why
And that the following day the Philistines would win
And Saul and his sons would die

ACHISH SENDS DAVID BACK TO ZIKLAG

Now the Philistines were gathered for the battle
But they didn't trust David and his men
"He must *not* go with us into battle," they said,
"For he will turn *against* us then"

Achish did not want to, but he had to tell David
That he could not be in the fight
He told him that he must go back to Ziklag
At the following dawn's first light

DAVID DESTROYS THE AMALEKITES

In three days David and his men reached Ziklag
But when they arrived, they found
The Amalekites had been there and raided it
And burned it to the ground

Their wives and sons and daughters were gone
When the men returned that day
For the Amalekites had captured them
And taken them all away

Among the captives were David's two wives
Ahinoam and Abigail
David and his men broke down and cried
Everyone wept and wailed

Then David found strength in the Lord his God
And asked Him, "Shall I *pursue*?
Will I overtake them?"...And God answered him,
"You will succeed in the rescue"

When David and his men reached the Besor Ravine
Some of them stayed behind
Two hundred were too weak to continue on
In the search for the captives to find

So David and four hundred men continued on
Then they found an Egyptian in a field
They fed him and when David questioned the man
Some information...he revealed

He said he was the slave of an Amalekite
But his master had abandoned him
Because he became ill, three days before
He went on to tell David then

He said the Amalekites had raided several cities
And Ziklag they had burned
David asked if he could lead them to the Amalekites
After this news he had learned

The man said to David, "Swear to me before God
That you will *not* kill *me*
Nor give me to my *master*...and I will lead you"
And David granted his plea

Now the Amalekites were celebrating their victory
Scattered on the countryside
David fought them from dusk until the next evening
And most of the Amalekites died

David recovered all that was stolen from them
Everything and everyone
And they returned to the men at the Besor Ravine
With every wife, daughter and son

Now some of David's men didn't want to share
The plunder that they brought back
With the men who had been too weak to go on
And had not fought in the attack

But David told them they must *not* hoard the plunder
For the *Lord* had given it to them
And that everyone's share would be the same
And the men agreed with him

David sent some plunder to the elders of Judah
After he arrived home
And to Bethel, Racal and many other places
Where he and his men had roamed

SAUL TAKES HIS LIFE

When Saul and his men fought the Philistines
The men of Israel fled
The Philistines chased them and continued to fight
Until all of the Israelites were dead

Saul's three sons were killed in the battle
Along with his other men
His sons, Malki-Shua and Abinadab
And even Jonathan

Saul was critically wounded by Philistine archers
For he was abandoned by the Lord
But rather than allow himself to be captured
He fell on his own sword

David Hears of Saul's Death

Now a man from Saul's camp came to David
With his clothes torn and dust on his head
He bowed to the ground to pay honor to David
And said, "Saul and Jonathan are dead"

David and his men mourned and wept and fasted
For Saul and Jonathan, his son
And for the army of the Lord and the house of Israel
In the battle that the Philistines won

In the course of time, David went to Hebron
Because he asked the Lord what to do
The Lord told him to go, so he took his two wives
And his men and their families too.

David Is Made King

After they were settled, the men of Judah came
And they made David their king
And though many fought battles against David
His victory God did bring

After seven years of reigning over Judah
The other tribes of Israel
Came to King David and made him the king
Over all of them as well

All together King David reigned for forty years
He started at thirty years old
He asked God for direction and David was blessed
For he did as he was told

And when David marched on Jerusalem
It was said...they would never get in
But his army captured the fortress of Zion
And renamed it after him

Then he took up residence in the City of David
He was king of all Israel
The people loved him and the Lord God blessed him
And David and the people fared well

When the Philistines came against him, David prayed,
"Will you hand them over to me?"
"Go," said the Lord, "I will surely hand them over"
And gave David the victory

Then David brought up the Ark of the Lord
From the house of Obed-Edom the Gittite
And as they carried the Ark, David went before it
And danced…with all of his might

DAVID AND MEPHIBOSHETH

After King David was settled in his palace
And the Lord had given him rest
He looked for an heir from the house of Saul
And found Mephibosheth

Mephibosheth was the son of Jonathan
Who was David's dearest friend
And since Jonathan had died, David took his son
And cared for him 'til the end

David and Bathsheba

In the springtime King David sent his army to war
With his general, Joab, to lead
But David stayed behind in Jerusalem
And committed a terrible deed

One evening when David was on the palace roof
He looked down from the roof and saw
A beautiful woman who was taking a bath
And David watched in awe

He wanted to know who the woman was
So he sent a man to inquire
"She is Bathsheba, the daughter of Eliam," he said
"And she is the wife of Uriah"

At that time, Uriah was away in the army
Fighting and risking his life
But David did not care about Uriah's safety
David wanted his wife

So he sent for Bathsheba and they had an affair
They knew... it should not have been
For not only had they both betrayed Uriah
What they did was a grievous sin

And because of their sin, Bathsheba got pregnant
So to hide what they had done
They needed her husband to come home to her
So it would appear... that *he* was the one

David sent a message to Joab to send Uriah back
Joab sent him without knowing
David asked Uriah about Joab and the army
And how the war was going

Then David told Uriah to go to his home
After they drank and ate
But Uriah did not go home that night
He slept at the palace gate

For Uriah was indeed an honorable man
And while the nation was at war
He would not go home and be with his wife
So he slept at the palace door

Then David told Uriah to stay another night
Uriah didn't know what for
But yet again...he slept at the palace gate
Then David sent him back to the war

David gave Uriah a letter to give to Joab
"Put Uriah in the front line," it read,
"Where the fighting is fierce...Then withdraw from him
So Uriah will be struck down dead"

So Joab sent Uriah to a place in the battle
Where the enemy were the most skilled
And when the enemy came out of the city to fight
Uriah the Hitite...was killed

Joab sent David a full account of the battle
And to the messenger he said,
"After you have given King David this report
Tell him...Uriah is dead"

When Bathsheba heard that Uriah was killed
She mourned for the loss of his life
But when the time of her mourning was over
She became David's wife

NATHAN REBUKES DAVID

The Lord was now displeased with David
Because of David's sin
So the Lord sent Nathan the Prophet
Who told a story to him

"There were two men living in a certain town
One rich and one poor," he began
"And while the rich man had many sheep and cattle
The poor man had just one lamb

"The man raised the lamb like one of the family
With his children, the lamb grew up
It slept in his arms and was like a daughter
Shared his food...and drank from his cup

"Now one day it came to pass," he continued,
"That a traveler came to town
And the traveler went to the rich man's house
He came in...and they sat down

"But the rich man didn't use one of his own sheep
Or cattle...for the meat
He took the poor man's lamb and killed it
And prepared it for the traveler to eat"

David became angry when he heard the story
"The man who did this deserves to die!
He must pay for the lamb, four times over
For doing such a thing!" he cried

"You are the man!" Nathan exclaimed
David gasped in fright
"The Lord God has given you so much," said Nathan
"Why did you do evil in His sight?"

"*You* killed Uriah!" Nathan continued
"*You* took Uriah's life!
You used the swords of the soldiers of Ammon
And then you took his wife!"

"I have sinned before the Lord," said David
And David hung his head
Then Nathan continued as David listened
To every word he said

"The Lord has taken away your sin
And you shall not die," he said
But what Nathan told David after that
Filled David's heart with dread

He said the Lord's enemies show utter contempt
Because of David's sin
And now what the Lord was going to do
Was take David's son from him

Then the son of David and Bathsheba fell ill
David fasted and lay on the ground
Even the elders couldn't get him to eat or get up
Though they were all gathered around

Yet even so . . . the child died
On the seventh day
Then David saw his servants whispering
Because they were afraid

David asked them . . . "Is the child dead?"
"Yes," they replied "He is dead"
Then David got up . . . washed and got dressed
And put lotion on his body and head

He went to the house of the Lord and worshiped
Then he went to his house and ate food
"Why are you acting this way?" asked the servants
They couldn't understand his mood

"While the child was still alive I fasted and wept
I thought, who knows?" he said
"The Lord may be gracious and let him live
But now my child is dead

"So why should I fast? . . . Can I bring him back?"
The servants began to see
"One day I will go to him," David continued,
"But he will not return to me"

Then David comforted his wife Bathsheba
And soon she had another son
The Lord loved this child that was born to them
And they named him . . . Solomon

Solomon

Solomon Asks God for Wisdom

David was succeeded as the king of Israel
By Solomon...his son
Who went one day to worship the Lord
At a holy place called Gibeon

And while Solomon was staying in Gibeon
God appeared to him in a dream
"Ask for anything you want from me," said the Lord
His request...could be extreme

But Solomon answered, "O Lord my God
You have made your servant a king
But I am only a little child," he continued,
"And I don't know everything

"I am here among the people you have chosen
So give me a discerning heart
To govern your people and know right from wrong"
He asked for *wisdom*...from the start

God was pleased with his request and told him so
And because he asked for *this* thing
Instead of wealth or long life or victory in battle
That *wisdom*...God would bring

He would give him a wise and discerning heart
Like no one ever had before
And like none would ever have in the future
And then He told him more

God told Solomon He would also give him honor
Riches and many other things
So much so, that in Solomon's lifetime
He would have no equal in kings

"And if you walk in all of my ways," said the Lord,
"And obey my laws and commands
As did your father...I will give you long life"
His future...was in God's hands

A Wise Ruling

Now two women came before the king
When Solomon's reign was new
The first said, "We live together and I had a baby
Three days later...*she* had one too"

"During the night while I slept, her baby died
And she switched the babies, you see"
The other woman said, "No! The dead one is *hers*!
And the live one belongs to *me*!"

And so the women argued back and forth
Until King Solomon said,
"Both of you are saying, 'My son is alive
And yours is the one who is dead!'"

Solomon turned and said, "Bring me a sword"
What his plan was, no one knew
But when they brought him the sword...Solomon said,
"Now cut the child in two!

"Give half to one...and half to the other"
But the first mother cried..."I beg you!
Do not kill him my lord...give *her* the baby!"
While the other said, "Cut him in two!"

"Give the first woman the child," said Solomon
After he heard her cries
"Do *not* kill the baby...*She* is his mother"
The Lord had made him wise

The Building of the Temple

During the fourth year of Solomon's reign
He began building a temple for the Lord
It was ninety feet long and thirty feet wide
The finest that riches could afford

The Temple was designed with a very wide porch
And narrow windows of light
It was made of stone and had many rooms
Forty-five feet was its height

The stones were made ready before they arrived
So no hammer or chisel was heard
The walls and the ceilings were covered with cedar
And the floors with planks of fir

Solomon had the inner sanctuary prepared
And covered it with pure gold
It would contain the Ark of the Covenant
And be amazing to behold

In the inner sanctuary, stood a pair of angels
Of olive wood...fifteen feet tall
Covered with gold...their wings outstretched
They reached from wall to wall

The walls and the doors were carved with flowers
Palm trees and cherubim
And all of them were covered with gold
For the Lord...to honor Him

The altar itself and the vessels upon it
All were made of gold
And by the time the Temple was finished
It was already seven years old

Then Solomon assembled the elders of Israel
And the heads of every tribe
So they could bring the Ark of the Covenant
To the Temple and place it inside

They brought the Ark into the House of the Lord
And all of the holy men bowed
Then the Glory of the Lord came down on the Temple
And the Temple was filled with a cloud

THE LORD APPEARS TO SOLOMON

When Solomon completed the temple of the Lord
The Lord appeared to him again
"I heard your prayer and chose this place for myself"
And the Lord continued then

"When I shut up the heavens so there is no rain
Or send locust to devour the land
Or send a plague among my people," He said
Continuing to reveal His plan

"If my people...who are called by my name
Will humble themselves and pray
And seek my face," continued the Lord,
"And turn from their wicked ways

"Then I will hear from Heaven and forgive their sin
And I will heal their land"
Then the Lord told Solomon to walk in His ways
And to obey His commands

But the Lord also said...that if they turn away
And forsake His decrees and commands
And serve other gods...then He will uproot them
And remove them...from His lands

THE QUEEN OF SHEBA VISITS SOLOMON

When the Queen of Sheba heard about Solomon
And his relation to the Lord's name
She wanted to visit him to see for herself
If he truly lived up to his fame

She planned to ask him difficult questions
To put Solomon to the test
She brought a great caravan of laden-down camels
With gold and jewels and the rest

And when the Queen of Sheba arrived in Jerusalem
She met with Solomon, the king
She asked him all the questions she had on her mind
And he answered everything

None of her questions were too difficult
For Solomon to explain
The queen was astounded by all of his wisdom
And very glad she came

When the queen saw the palace Solomon had built
And the offerings to the Lord, he did render
His officials and his servants and his lavish food
She was overwhelmed by the splendor

"The reports I had heard in my country," she observed,
"Of your achievements and wisdom are true
But I would not believe them until I saw for myself
So I came to meet with you

"And behold! The *half* of it was not told to me!
In wisdom and wealth you *far* exceed
And how happy are your men and your servants
Who always *hear* your wisdom, indeed!

"Praises and blessing to the Lord your God
He has *delighted* in you
And He has *placed* you...on the throne of Israel
For His love of Israel too"

Then the Queen of Sheba gave her gifts to the king
Woods and precious stones and more
She gave to Solomon more than four tons of gold
And more spices than anyone before

And King Solomon gave to the Queen of Sheba
Anything she wanted...and then
She took her servants and her gifts from Solomon
And went back to her country again

THE WEALTH AND SPLENDOR OF SOLOMON

Solomon received about twenty-five tons of gold
Each year, brought to his hand
Plus the revenue from merchants and traders
And rulers and kings of the land

In his royal palace he made a great throne
Inlaid with ivory...overlaid with gold
With lions beside it and twelve more on six steps
No other throne...as great to behold

All of his goblets and utensils were gold
He had a fleet of ships at sea
And every three years the ships returned
With animals, gold and ivory

Solomon was greater in wisdom and riches
Than any other king from the start
And all of the world sought Solomon's presence
To hear the wisdom God put in his heart

Year after year, his visitors brought gifts
Of silver, gold and jewels
And clothing and weapons and spices
Gifts of horses and mules

Solomon had fourteen hundred chariots
Twelve thousand horses and men
Which he kept in the chariot cities
And with him in *Jerusalem*

KING SOLOMON'S WIVES

But King Solomon loved many foreign women
From nations where the Lord had said,
"They will surely turn your hearts to follow their gods"
Yet these women...Solomon wed

With seven hundred wives and three hundred concubines
His wives led him astray
And his heart was no longer devoted to the Lord
In his father David's way

He followed Ashtoreth and Molech and Chemosh
And other abominations
And he built high places for the gods of his wives
These women from other nations

Then the Lord became angry at Solomon
For his heart had turned away
And He said He would tear away Solomon's kingdom
But not during Solomon's day

"For the sake of David and Jerusalem, which I chose
I will tear it from the hand of your *son*
Not the whole kingdom...I will give him one tribe"
Which happened in days to come

Elijah

Now when King Ahab ruled over Israel
He did terrible, evil things
In fact, he did more to provoke the Lord God
Than *all* of the other kings

So the Lord sent Elijah the Prophet of Gilead
To tell Ahab what was to be
"As the Lord God lives, there'll be no rain or dew," he said,
"Without a word from me"

After that, Elijah again heard from God
Telling him what to do
"Hide in the Kerith Ravine," said the Lord,
"And the ravens will bring food to you"

So Elijah did as the Lord had commanded
And the ravens fed him, twice a day
They brought bread and meat and he drank from a brook
And Elijah survived that way

And it came to pass that the brook dried up
For there was no rain in the land
Then God told Elijah to go to Zarephath
Guided again by God's hand

God told Elijah there was a widow in Zarephath
Whom He had spoken to
He said He told the widow to feed Elijah
While he was passing through

When Elijah arrived at the town gate in Zarephath
There was a widow walking about
Elijah saw her gathering sticks to make a fire
And to the widow, he called out

"Would you bring me a little water in a jar
So I may have a drink?" he said
As the woman went to get it…Elijah added,
"And please…a piece of bread"

"As surely as the Lord God lives," said the woman,
"I have no bread...just handful of flour
And a little bit of oil" and then she told Elijah
What she was doing...that very hour

"I am gathering some sticks to take home," she said
Her voice was almost a cry,
"To make one last meal for myself and my son
That we may eat it...and die"

But Elijah said to her, "Do not be afraid
Go home and do as you said
But first make a small cake just for me," he continued
"Then make for yourselves your bread

"For the Lord God says...the flour will *not* run out
And the oil will not run dry
You will have flour and oil until the Lord sends rain"
And the widow and her son didn't die

Many days then passed and they all had food
For they had obeyed the Lord
And the Lord God provided the flour and the oil
Which they otherwise could not afford

But then the woman's son grew gravely ill
And she cried "What have I done?
Man of God, did you come to remind me
Of my sin and to kill my son?"

"Give me your son," Elijah said to the woman
He took him to the loft where he stayed
Then Elijah placed the boy upon his own bed
And cried out the Lord and prayed

"O Lord my God, did you bring tragedy on this woman
By causing her son to die?"
Then he stretched himself out upon the boy three times
And to the Lord he cried

"O Lord my God, let his life return to him!"
Elijah prayed and grieved
And the God of Heaven heard Elijah's prayer
And the child...began to breathe

Then Elijah brought the child back to his mother
He said..."Your child is alive!"
"Now I *know* you are a man of God!" she exclaimed
For she saw her child revive

Elijah and the Priests of Baal

In the third year during the time of the famine
Elijah was directed by God's hand
"Go and present yourself to Ahab," said the Lord,
"And I will send rain on the land"

When the king saw Elijah he asked him,
"Are you the man who troubles Israel?"
"Not I...but you and your fathers," said Elijah,
"For leaving God and worshiping Baal

"Summon the people from all over Israel," he said,
"To meet on Mount Carmel
And bring the false prophets of Asherah and Baal
Who eat with Queen Jezebel"

When everyone was assembled on the mountain
Elijah spoke to them all,
"How long will you waiver between two beliefs?"
For they worshiped God *and* Baal

"Now I am the *only* prophet of God," said Elijah,
"The only one who is left
But Baal has four hundred and fifty," he said
And then he proposed a test

"Get two bulls and let Baal's prophets choose one
And put it on the wood
But do not set it afire and I will do the same"
His plan...no one understood

"Then you call on your god…and *I'll* call on the *Lord*,"
The prophet said with a nod
Then Elijah concluded his challenge by saying,
"The god who answers by fire…*is* God!"

Then the people spoke up and they all agreed
This would be a very good test
So the prophets of Baal and Asherah got busy
While Elijah took a rest

He let them go first…they prepared their bull
And then they began to pray
They called on Baal from morning to noon
They pleaded for half of the day

But at noon Elijah began to taunt them
"Shout louder!" Elijah said
"Surely he is a god…but perhaps he is busy
Or traveling…or asleep in his bed!"

The prophets shouted louder and cut themselves
Using their swords and spears
But they still had no response by evening
Confirming…their greatest fears

Then Elijah spoke to all of the people
"Now come near to *me*"
And as they all watched, Elijah prepared
Now the power of *God* they would see

Elijah walked up to the altar of the Lord
Which *had* been broken down
And according to the number of the tribes of Israel
He took twelve stones from the ground

With the stones he gathered, he built a new altar
Then around it he dug a trench
He arranged the wood and prepared the bull
And laid it on the bench

"Fill four large jars with water," he said,
"And pour them on the bull"
Elijah had the people do it two times more
Until the trench was full

And when it was time for the evening sacrifice
Elijah stepped forward to pray
"Lord God of Abraham, Isaac and Israel," he said,
"Let it be known today

"That *you* are the God of Israel and I am your servant
And have done this at your command"
Elijah was praying that the Lord God of Heaven
Would show the people His hand

"That this people may *know* that *you* are the Lord
That you turn their hearts again"
Then the people watched…but nothing happened
All was silent…and then

Fire from Heaven *rained* down before them!
Consuming the bull on the bench
It burned up the wood and the stones and the soil
And licked up the water from the trench

When all the people saw it, they fell on their faces
"The Lord *He is* God!" they said
Then Elijah shouted, "Seize the prophets of Baal!"
And by nightfall the prophets were dead

Then Elijah said to Ahab, "Go eat and drink
For there is the sound of a heavy rain"
Then Elijah climbed to the top of the mountain
And as he prayed…clouds came

THE STILL SMALL VOICE

When Ahab told Jezebel all that had happened
All that Elijah had done
Jezebel was furious and sent Elijah a message
For she was an evil one

"Let the gods do to me and even more," she said,
"If by this time tomorrow I fail
To take your life…as you took the lives
Of all of the prophets of Baal"

Elijah was afraid when he heard the message
And for his life he fled
But when he came to the desert, he sat neath a tree
And prayed that he would be dead

Then Elijah laid down and he fell asleep
And an angel awoke him and said,
"Arise and eat," and Elijah saw before him
A jar of water and a cake of bread

So he ate and he drank and went back to sleep
The angel woke him again as before
And Elijah ate again and was fortified then
And traveled forty days and nights more

He arrived at Mount Horeb and slept in a cave
Where the voice of the Lord he heard
"What are you doing here Elijah?" asked the Lord
Then Elijah answered God's word

But his heart was heavy as he responded,
"I have cared *greatly* for the Lord
But the children of Israel have forsaken your covenants
And slain your prophets with the sword

"I'm the only one *left*…and they're trying to kill me,"
God heard Elijah cry
"Go forth and stand on the mountain," said God,
"For the Lord is about to pass by"

So Elijah went out and stood upon the mountain
And a powerful wind God did send
It tore apart the mountains and smashed the rocks
But the Lord wasn't *in* the wind

And after the wind there was a great *earthquake*
Moving mountains lower and higher
But the Lord was not *in* the earthquake
Nor in the following *fire*

But after the fire...came a still small voice
Elijah hid his face...for he knew
This was the voice of the Lord God of Heaven
Telling him what to do

God told him to anoint Hazel as king of Syria
And also to anoint Jehu
To be the king of Israel and then anoint Elisha
To be a prophet too

So Elijah departed and found Elisha
Plowing a field...the soil to turn
Then Elisha became the attendant of Elijah
Under Elijah...he would learn

ELIJAH IS TAKEN UP TO HEAVEN

As the years went by, Elisha traveled with Elijah
Everywhere Elijah would go
And one day they went from Gilgal to Bethel
Then on to Jericho

The followers of the prophets of Jericho
Came out to Elisha and cried,
"Do you know the Lord is going to take your master?"
"Yes I know," Elisha replied

Then Elijah said to Elisha, "Stay here
For the Lord has instructed me
That I must go to the Jordan River," he said
But Elisha would not let it be

"As the Lord lives and as your soul lives," he said,
"I will *not* leave you"
So they went together and stood by the Jordan
Fifty followers watched them too

Then Elijah took off and folded his cloak
And with it...he reached down
He struck the waters...and they were parted
And they crossed *over* on dry ground

"What can I do for you before I'm taken?" asked Elijah
But Elisha already knew
"Let a double portion of your spirit be upon me"
Then he pled, "I beg of you"

"You have asked a difficult thing," said Elijah,
"But nevertheless," he went on,
"If you see me when I'm taken...you shall have your wish"
For Elijah would soon be gone

"But if not...you shall not have it," said Elijah
And as they were walking then
A chariot of *fire* and horses appeared
Sweeping apart, the two men

Then Elijah was taken...in a whirlwind
Up to Heaven...out of sight!
Elisha watched and cried, "My father! My father!"
Tearing his clothes with all his might

Then he took Elijah's cloak and struck the water
As he stood by the shore bereft
And he said, "Where is the Lord God of Elijah?"
And the water parted...to the right and the left

When he crossed the river, the people were waiting
And as they gathered around
They said, "The spirit of Elijah rests on Elisha,"
Bowing themselves to the ground

Now Elisha continued on with the work of Elijah
And became a great man of God too
Healing and prophesying and serving the Lord
In whatever God told him to do

Esther

QUEEN VASHTI IS DEPOSED

The kingdom of King Xerxes was very large
From India to Cush was his reign
And in the third year of his reign, he gave a banquet
And everyone of importance came

The military commanders of Persia and Media
And nobles and princes were there
For a hundred eighty days, he displayed his kingdom
His wealth was seen everywhere

At the end of those days, the king held the banquet
The banquet was a seven-day feast
It was presented in the palace garden for the men
From the greatest to the least

The garden had curtains of white and blue linen
With purple and white linen cord
Which were tied to silver rings on marble pillars
The finest that wealth could afford

The guests reclined on beautiful couches
Made of silver and gold
Set on tile of marble and mother of pearl
Magnificent to behold

The royal wine was served in goblets of gold
Each one different from the rest
Each guest was served as much as they wanted
And the wine they poured was the best

Meanwhile, the women had a banquet *in* the palace
Which was hosted by the queen
And on the seventh day, the king *sent* for her
For he wanted her to be seen

He wanted to display her beauty to his guests
He wanted her to wear her royal crown
But the king was shocked…and so were the people
When the queen turned his invitation down

The king became furious and burned with anger
But he didn't know what to do
So he consulted with his closest noblemen
To find out if *they* knew

"According to law, what must be done?" he asked
To save face he would need a plan
For the queen had chosen to disobey the king
The answer came from Memucan

"Queen Vashti has done wrong," said Memucan,
"Not only against the king
But *also* against *all* of the *nobles* and the *people*"
This was a *very serious* thing

"Her conduct will be known to all of the women
They'll despise *their* husbands, every one
They'll say, 'The king commanded that the *queen* come in
But *she* refused to come!'

"And the Persian and Median women of nobility
Who have heard of her conduct this day
Will respond to *all* of the king's noblemen
In the very same way!

"There will be no end of disrespect and discord
Therefore, if it pleases the king
Let him issue a royal decree," said Memucan
Who had figured out everything

"Let it now be written into the law
Which cannot be repealed," he said,
"That Vashti never enter the presence of the king"
She would lose the crown from her head

"Also let the king give her royal position to another
Someone better than she
Then all of the women will respect their husbands
When the king issues this decree"

The king and his nobles were pleased with this advice
So he did what was proposed
And he issued a decree that proclaimed every man
Was the ruler of his own household

ESTHER BECOMES THE QUEEN

Later on, the attendants of the king proposed
That they search every city and town
And bring to the palace, the beautiful young women
So a *new* queen could be found

They suggested that all of the women be brought
To the harem at the Susa citadel
And Hegai, who was in charge of the harem
Would ensure they were treated well

Beauty treatments would be given to them all
And the one who *pleased* the king
Would become the new queen...replacing Vashti
They had thought of everything

Their advice appealed to King Xerxes
And so the search began
Beautiful young women were brought to the palace
From all across the land

Now in the city of Susa, there lived a Jew
By the name of Mordecai
And Mordecai had a cousin named Esther
Who was pleasing to the eye

Mordecai had raised his young cousin Esther
For her father and mother had died
And now *Esther* was taken to the palace
And entrusted...to Hegai

Hegai liked Esther and immediately he ordered
Beauty treatments and special food
Esther won the favor of everyone who saw her
For her beauty and attitude

Each of the women went through a beauty plan
Before going to the king's room
They each had six months of oil of myrrh
And six of cosmetics and perfume

When it came time for Esther to go to the palace
She was the finest the king had seen
So he set the royal crown upon her head
And made Esther...his new queen

But she had not revealed her family background
For Mordecai told her not to tell
Because if they knew...that Esther was a Jew
For her...it might not go well

MORDECAI UNCOVERS A CONSPIRACY

Mordecai would walk back and forth by the harem
Outside by the courtyard each day
To find out what was happening with Esther
And make sure that she was OK

One day Mordecai was sitting at the palace gate
When he overheard a plan to kill the *king*
Two guards were conspiring...Mordecai listened
Then he told Esther...*everything*

Queen Esther immediately told King Xerxes
Giving the credit to Mordecai
When the report was investigated and found to be true
The two guards were condemned to die

HAMAN'S PLOT TO DESTROY THE JEWS

Sometime later, the king honored Haman
Son of Hammedatha the Agagite
The king elevated Haman to a seat of honor
Raising him in everyone's sight

All of the other nobles had to now kneel down
When Haman walked through the gate
But Mordecai would not kneel or honor him
So Mordecai…Haman did hate

He learned that Mordecai's people were the Jews
And he wanted to kill them all
So he went to the king and he told him a lie
To set up the Jews for a fall

He said there were people throughout the kingdom
Who disobey the laws of the king
And he convinced the king to issue a decree
And seal it with his ring

So a proclamation was sent across the land
And everyone heard the news
That on a certain day, in a certain month
They were going to kill all the Jews

The women and children, the young and the old
They were all going to die
And in the city of Susa, the people were bewildered
For no one could understand why

When Mordecai heard of it, he tore his clothes
Put sackcloth and ashes on
Then he went through the city, wailing loudly
His spirit was nearly gone

And in every province of the kingdom
To which the order came
There was great mourning among the Jews
And they all reacted the same

Now when Esther heard about Mordecai
She was greatly distressed
She sent him clothes to replace the sackcloth
But Mordecai refused to get dressed

Then Esther told her servant to go and find out
What was *wrong* with *Mordecai*
When the servant asked him about his behavior
Mordecai told him why

Then Mordecai gave a message to the servant
And a copy of the order to bring
He told him to urge Esther to plead for the people
Directly to the king

The servant went back and reported to Esther
All that Mordecai had said
But if Esther did what Mordecai wanted
She could easily end up dead

For as everyone knew, if Esther obeyed
The request of Mordecai
And approached the king *uninvited*
The *law*...was for her to die

There was only *one* exception to this law
For anyone, even his wife
If the king extended the golden scepter
That would spare her life

But it was thirty days since the last time Esther
Had been called before the king
So Esther sent her servant back to Mordecai
Giving him *that* message to bring

Mordecai Responds to Esther

"Don't think because you're inside the king's house,"
The response of Mordecai read,
"That you alone out of all of the Jews, will escape"
His words were filled with dread

"For if you remain silent at this time," it continued,
"Relief and deliverance for the Jews
Will surely arise from another place"
Would Esther still refuse?

"But you and your father's family will all perish"
Left unsaid, he would have been remiss,
"And perhaps you have come to a royal position
For such a time...as *this*"

Esther responded, "Gather the people and fast for me,"
Telling Mordecai what to do
"Do not eat or drink for three days, day or night
And I and my maids will fast too

"When this is done, I will go to the king," she continued,
"Even though it opposes the law
And if I perish...I perish," her message concluded
She would *be*...the ambassador

On the third day, she entered the hall of the king
A move that was very bold
But when the king saw Esther, he was pleased
And held out...the scepter of gold

Then the king asked, "What is it Queen Esther?
What is your request?
Up to half of the kingdom, I will give you"
But she invited him to be her guest

"If it pleases the king," replied Queen Esther,
"Let the king and Haman too
Come today to a banquet that I have prepared
Especially for you"

By his quick response it was obvious to all
That for Esther the king deeply cared
And the king and Haman went to the banquet
That Esther had prepared

"Now what is your petition," he said "I will grant it!
And what is your request?"
And again the king offered her half of his kingdom
For he would be content with the rest

But Esther invited them to yet *another* banquet
To be held on the very next day
"*Then* I will answer the king's question," she said
He agreed it would happen that way

Haman was happy when he went home that day
He bragged to his friends and his wife
About all that he had and how the king honored him
And his elevated station in life

"And that is not all," Haman boasted
"*I* am the *only one*
That Queen Esther invited to a banquet with the king"
His bragging was overdone

"But all of this gives me no satisfaction," he said,
"As long as I see that Jew
Mordecai…sitting at the gate of the palace"
Then his friends suggested what to do

"Have a gallows built," said his wife and his friends,
"Seventy-five feet high!
Then go to the king in the morning and ask him
To *hang* the man, *Mordecai*!

"Then go to the dinner with the king and be happy"
Haman loved this suggestion
He had the gallows built and he was confident
The king would do it…without question

But that same night, the king could not sleep
So he ordered the record of his reign
His attendants brought it in and read it to him
After that…*everything* changed

For when Mordecai had exposed the plot to kill the king
The story was recorded there
The king asked what honor Mordecai had received
But nothing had been done *anywhere*

In the morning…Haman entered the outer court
To see the king about *Mordecai*
But little did he know…when he arrived at the palace
His plan…would go terribly awry

For when the king had Haman brought before him
The king said, "What should be done
For a man the king would delight to honor?"
And Haman thought *he* was the one

He thought, "Who else would the king want to honor?
Who else, rather than me?"
And he was thrilled that he even got to suggest
What that honor could be

"For the man that the king would like to honor
Have them bring a royal robe," he said,
"One the king has worn…and a horse the king rode
With a royal crest on its head

"Then let the robe and the horse be entrusted
To the king's most noble prince"
Haman was planning a display that was better
Than any before or since

"Robe him and lead him on the horse through the streets
And have the prince proclaim,
'This is the man the king delights to honor!'" he said
This plan would bring Haman much fame

"Go at once!" said the king "Get the robe and the horse!"
Telling *Haman* what to do!
"And do *everything exactly* as you have suggested
For *Mordecai*, the *Jew!*"

Haman was stunned…but he had to go and do it
After that, he went home in grief
He told his wife and his friends what had happened
They listened in disbelief

While they were talking, the king's servants arrived
And hurried Haman away
To go to the banquet with the king and the queen
Which was *also* happening that day

ESTHER'S BANQUET

"Now what is your petition?...What is your request?"
The king asked Esther again
"Up to half of the kingdom will be granted," he said
It was time for her to answer then

"O king," Queen Esther humbly began,
"If I have found favor with you
And if it pleases your majesty...grant me my life"
What *was* she *referring* to?

"That is my petition," Esther continued,
"And spare my people...is my request
For I and my people have been sold for destruction"
Then she told the king the rest

"If we were merely sold as slaves, I would have kept quiet,"
Esther softly said,
"For no such distress would justify disturbing you"
Now Haman began to feel dread

King Xerxes responded, "Who is he?" he demanded
"The man who dared such a thing?"
"The adversary is *Haman!*" Esther answered
And this *enraged* the king!

The king stormed out to the palace garden
Haman was terrified
He was begging Queen Esther for his own life
Staggering...he cried

And just as the king returned to the hall
Haman was falling on the couch
Where Esther reclined...and the king exclaimed,
"He even assaults the queen in my house!?"

Then one of the king's servants spoke up and said,
     "A gallows seventy-five feet high
     Stands just outside of Haman's house
     He had it built for *Mordecai*!"

"Hang him on it!" the king commanded
     He had several reasons why
Then he gave the estate of Haman to Esther
     And elevated Mordecai

Then the king changed the law and saved the Jews
     All across the nation
It was a time of happiness for all of the people
     With feasting... and celebration

Job

In the land of Uz lived a man named Job
Who was honest and upright
He reverently feared God and avoided all evil
And was blameless in God's sight

He had seven sons and he had three daughters
And Job had so much more
For Job was a man of wealth and standing
With servants and livestock galore

Job's camels numbered three thousand
He had seven thousand sheep
Five hundred oxen and five hundred donkeys
And his sons and daughters would feast

Taking turns in their homes, the brothers would gather
The sisters would be there too
And when the feast was over, Job had a custom
A cleansing that he would do

He would have each of his children purified
Lest any of them were in sin
He would offer a burnt sacrifice to the Lord
For every one of them

THE FIRST TEST

One day the angels came before the Lord
And Satan came with them too
The Lord said to Satan, "Where did you come from?"
Though of course, He already knew

"From roaming round the earth," Satan answered
For he'd been throughout the globe
Then the Lord looked at Satan and asked him,
"Have you considered my servant Job?

"No one on earth is like him," said the Lord
"He is blameless and upright
He is a man who respects God and shuns evil"
But the devil began to incite

"Why wouldn't he respect you?" Satan taunted
"You've blessed the work of his hand
You protect him and his household and all he owns
So his herds are spread through the land

"But if you stretch out your hand," he challenged,
"And take everything away
He will surely curse you to your face," he said
Satan had made his play

"All right," said the Lord, "all he has is in your hands"
Giving permission for a test
"But do not lay a finger on Job himself"
Satan nodded his head...and left

Then as Job's sons and daughters were feasting
A practice that was common with them
One of Job's servants...who was clearly upset
Rushed in with news for him

"We were plowing the fields with the oxen," he said,
"While the donkeys were grazing nearby
When the Sabeans attacked and stole all of the animals
And killed all of the servants but I!"

While *he* was *still* speaking, *another* servant came
He shouted, "Fire from the sky!
Fire came down and burned all of the sheep!
And burned all the servants but I!"

While *he* was still speaking, *another* servant came
"The Chaldeans raided!" he cried
"They swept down on your camels and stole *all* of them
And killed all of the servants but I!"

And while *he* was speaking…a *final* servant came
From the house of Job's eldest son
"A great wind came and collapsed the house," he cried
"Your children are dead…every one"

When Job heard these words, he tore at his clothes
And then he shaved his head
And then…not in rebellion but in worship
He fell to the ground and said

"I came here naked from my mother's womb
And I'll be naked when I depart
The Lord has given and taken…May His name be praised"
Though Job was grieving in his heart

THE SECOND TEST

On another day, the angels came before the Lord
And Satan came with them *again*
"Where have you come from?" asked the Lord
And Satan responded then

"From roaming back and forth throughout the earth"
And again God began to probe
He looked down at Satan and again He asked,
"Have you considered my servant Job?"

"No one on earth is like him," He said
"He is blameless and upright
He respects God and shuns evil," said the Lord
Holding Satan in His sight

"He has maintained his integrity," He continued,
"Though you incited me against him
To raise my hand without reason and ruin him"
And Satan said, "Skin for skin!

"A man will give all he has to save his own life"
Satan again pled his case
"But stretch out your hand and strike his *health*
And he will curse you…to your face"

"Alright then," said the Lord "He is in your hands
But you can't take his life," He said
Then Satan left and afflicted Job with painful boils
From the bottom of his feet to his head

Job scraped his skin with a piece of broken pottery
His wife looked at him and cried,
"Do you *still* try to hold on to your integrity?
Why don't you curse God and die!"

"You're talking like a foolish woman," said Job
"Do we accept good from God but not bad?"
And still Job would not curse...or sin against God
Holding on to the faith he had

Then three of Job's friends who heard of his troubles
Came to comfort and sympathize
But as they approached and saw him from a distance
They could barely recognize

They began to weep and they tore their clothes
They each put dust on their head
Then they sat on the ground with Job for a week
And not a word was said

When seven days passed, Job began to speak
And he cursed the day he was born
"I no longer have peace, only turmoil," he said
He was totally forlorn

Then one by one, his three friends spoke
He answered each one in turn
Back and forth they encouraged, debated, accused
Each one trying to discern

What had Job *done* to *deserve* all of this
All that had happened to him?
But in his own eyes...he was innocent and righteous
No matter *what* was said by them

Job's Final Discourse

In Job's final discourse to his three friends
He laid out his whole case
"I never would agree that you were right," he said
As he looked into each face

"God denied me justice and made my life bitter
Though I do not understand why
Yet as long as God continues to give me breath
I will never speak evil or lie

"I will maintain my integrity and righteousness
I know the wicked will meet their fate
And though men can't comprehend the wisdom of God
The wisdom of God is great

"I long for the days when God blessed me," he said,
"When I was prosperous and had respect"
Job spoke of his good deeds and the standing he held
As he continued to reflect

"*Now* young men of no stature mock me," he said
"They detest me and keep their distance
They spit in my face and lay snares for my feet
And resent my very existence

"And now as the very life ebbs out of my body
In days filled with *suffering*
I cry out to God…in all of my anguish
Yet no answer do my cries bring

"Yet if I had walked in dishonesty," he reasoned,
"Or had *evil* in my heart within
Then may *others* eat the crops that *I* have grown
If God has found me in sin

"If I had been enticed by another *woman*
Other than my wife
Then may my wife go and sleep with other *men*"
But neither was *that* in his life

"If I had dealt unjustly with my servants," he said,
"Or did not help the needy
If I had not clothed the naked or fed the hungry
But rather had been greedy

"Then may my arm be broken off at the shoulder
But *this* was not the case
For I *dreaded* the destructive punishment of God
So such behavior I would *never* embrace

"If I had put my trust in my riches," he continued,
"Or gave homage to the moon or sun
Those would *also* be sins to be judged by God
For being unfaithful to the Almighty One

"If I had gloated over an enemy's misfortune
Over trouble that had caused them strife
But I never allowed myself to sin in such a manner
Or speak a curse into someone's life

"If the people in my household had never said,
'Who hasn't had his fill of Job's meat?'
And my door was always open to the traveler
So no stranger had to sleep in the street

"If I had concealed my sin . . . as men often do
And hidden my guilt," Job cried,
"Because I dreaded the contempt of my neighbors
And would not go outside

"If only I had someone who would hear me out!
Let the Almighty *answer* me!
Let my accuser put His indictment in writing!
Stating what my sin would *be*!

"I would wear the indictment on my shoulder
Wear it like a crown on my head
Then I would give him an account of my every step
Like a prince I would approach Him," he said

"If my land cries out against me," he continued,
"Or if my tenants I have hurt
Then thorns and weeds, instead of wheat and barley
Should come up from the dirt!"

ELIHU SPEAKS

There was then no response from Job's three friends
Eliphaz, Zophar and Bildad
For Job was still righteous in his own eyes
And a rebuttal...no one had

Then a young man named Elihu became very angry
With many thoughts he wished to convey
For Job had justified *himself*...rather than God
Now Elihu had much to say

But Elihu was not only angry at Job
He was angry at Job's friends
For they hadn't been able to refute what Job said
Though Job, they *had* condemned

Now Elihu had been waiting before speaking
For they were all older than him
But when he saw that no one had anything to say
His tirade...would begin

He said that although he was young in his years
Not only the old are wise
For the breath of the *Almighty* gives understanding
They listened in their surprise

Then addressing the four men, Elihu continued
Dissecting all they had to say
He *expounded* on God's greatness and power
And His goodness in every way

THE LORD SPEAKS TO JOB

Then the Lord finally spoke and answered Job
In the middle of a storm,
"Who questions my wisdom by words without knowledge?"
Now Job…the *Lord* would inform

"Stand up like a man," He demanded of Job
"Now *I* will question *you*
And you will *answer* me" said the Lord
His words…strong and true

"Where were you when I laid the earth's foundation?
Answer if you understand
Who measured it out?…Surely you know!"
Of course it was by God's hand

"On what were its footings set?" He asked
"Who laid its cornerstone?
As morning stars sang and angels shouted for joy"
He made His feelings known

"Who put doors on the sea when it burst from the womb
Gushing forth in its might?
Who made the clouds for its garments?
And wrapped it in darkness at night?

"When I set its limits and made its boundaries,"
He spoke of the great seas of salt,
"I said, 'This far you may come and no farther
And here your proud waves halt.'

"Have you ever given orders to the morning?
And caused the dawn to know its place?
That it might hold the edges of the earth and shake it
For wickedness to erase?

"As the dawn approaches, the earth takes shape
As clay pressed under a seal
The light disturbs the wicked and stops their hands
For their evil is revealed

"Have you traveled to the springs of the ocean
Or walked its deepest breadth?
Or have you ever gone out and seen the gates
The gates of the shadow of death?

"Do you understand the vastness of the earth?
Do you have this knowledge to give?
Tell me how to travel to the home of light
And where does darkness live?

"Can you take the light and darkness to their places?
Do you know the roads to their dwelling?
Surely you do...for you've lived for so long!
And *now*...is the time for telling

"Have you been to the storehouses of the snow?
Or been where the hail is stored?
I reserve them for the times of trouble
Times of battle and war

"How do you get to where lightning comes from?
Or the origin of the wind of the east?
Who cuts the channels for the downpours of rain?
Or the course for the storms released?

"Rain sent to water...where no one lives
Rain...on a desolate land
To make a desert without people...sprout with grass
Tell me...by whose hand?

"Does rain have a father?" the Lord asked Job
"Who fathers the drops of dew?
Who gives birth to frost? From whose womb comes ice?
When water turns hard as stone too

"Can you catch the beautiful Pleiades?
Or make Venus look your way?
Can you bring forth the constellations in their times?
Or bring the Bear and her cubs out to play?

"Do you know the laws of the heavens?
Can you set up their rule upon earth?
Can you call on the clouds to release their rain
To cover with a flood your girth?

"Do you send out the lightning bolts on their way?
Do they say to you...'Here we are?'
Who is wise enough to count...all of the clouds?
And tip Heaven's water jar?

"When the dust of the earth is dry and thirsty
It is watered by *whose* design?
And *who* gave to man...a heart of wisdom?
And understanding to his mind?

"Do you help the lioness to hunt her prey?
As she waits in the thicket and sod?
Who is it who provides the food for the raven
When its young cry out to God?

"Do you know when the wild goats give birth?
Do you watch the doe bear her fawn?
Do you count the months until they are due?
Do you know the hour they are born?

"Who released the wild donkey and set him free?
Who untied his leads?
I gave him the wasteland to have as his home
And the hills on which he feeds

"Will a wild ox allow you to tame it?
At night, will it stay in your stall?
Can you hitch a wild ox to your plow?
Will it plow your field at all?

"And though the ostrich flaps its wings in joy
To a stork's feathers...it can't compare
Yet she leaves her eggs to warm in the sand
Unmindful of them there

"I did not give her wisdom for her young
She treats them as though not her own
And yet when she runs...she laughs at the horse
And any rider known

"Did you give to the horse his strength?
Or adorn his neck with hair?
Did you make him able to leap and snort
Striking terror everywhere?

"Before riding into battle, he paws at the ground
And rejoices in his strength
Afraid of nothing, he laughs at fear and charges
His rider's weapons upon his flanks

"Unable to stand still when he hears the trumpet
He snorts out his reply
He catches the scent of battle in the distance
And hears the battle cry

"Does the hawk head south for winter by *your* wisdom?
Do eagles soar at *your* command?
Do they know to build their nests on cliffs so high
By direction of *your* hand?

"From his stronghold the eagle looks for his food
His eyes see it from afar
His young ones eagerly feast on the blood
He will *be* where the carcasses are

"Will the one who argues with the Almighty correct Him?
Let him answer *now!*"
Then Job said, "I am unworthy...How can I speak?
I put my hand over my mouth

"I spoke once before but I *have* no answer
No twice...but I'll say no more"
Then again the Lord spoke to Job from the storm
Repeating what He said before

"Stand up like a man!" demanded the Lord
"Now *I* will question *you*
And you will *answer* me," He said again
His words still strong and true

"Would you discredit my justice or condemn me
For yourself to *justify*?
Is your arm like God's...Can *your* voice thunder?
Is this what you imply?

"Then with glory and splendor be adorned
Clothed in honor and *majesty*!
Release your furious wrath to humble the proud
And crush the wicked...wherever they be

"Crush and bury them all in the dust together
Then *I* will admit to *you*
That by *your right hand*," continued the Lord,
"*Yourself*...you *can* save too

"Consider the behemoth that I *also* created
And though he feeds on grass
His strength is massive, his limbs are as iron
And he ranks...*first* in his class

"While all of the wild animals can *play* near him
In the shadow of the lotus he lies
He can stand in the raging Jordan without fear
Can he be captured if he sees you with his eyes?

"Can you use a fishhook to catch a leviathan?
Or a rope to tie his tongue?
Can you put a ring in his nose or a hook in his jaw?
Will you hear begging from this one?

"Will he agree with you...to be your slave?
Can you make a pet of him?
If you touch him...you'll never forget your struggle
And never do *that again*!

"Will merchants barter and divide him up?
Can you fill his hide with spears?
Any hope of overcoming him is truly false
The mere *sight* of him causes fears

"No one is so fierce that he dares to rouse him
Who then...can stand against *me*?
To whom do I owe a debt...that I must pay back?
Everything is *mine* you see"

Then the Lord spoke more about the leviathan
He spoke about his limbs
His enormous strength and his graceful shape
"Who can strip the hide off of him?

"Who would try to bridle the leviathan?" He asked,
"Or open his mouth...Who would dare?
He has terrifying teeth and shields on his back
Sealed together there

"When he snorts, he throws out flashes of light
His eyes like the first light of day
Smoke billows from his nose like a boiling pot
And from his mouth...a firey spray

"When he breathes, his breath sets coals afire
Because his mouth spews flame
His chest like a rock...When he thrashes about
Men retreat...from whence they came

"When he rises up, even the mighty are terrified
They become frozen in fear
If they strike him with a sword, it does nothing
Nor does the javelin or spear

"Clubs and iron are straw...He laughs at the lance
And arrows don't make him run
His jagged armored underside leaves a trail in the mud
Like a threshing sledge when it's done

"He makes the depths appear as though boiling
A glistening wake *follows* him
Unequaled on earth, he reigns fearless over the proud
And he looks *down* on them"

Job Replies

"I know that you can do all things," replied Job,
"No one can foil your plan
You asked who questions your wisdom without knowledge
I spoke of things I did not understand

"Things too wonderful for me to comprehend
When my ears had only *heard* of you
Now I repent in dust and ashes and despise myself
For now my eyes have *seen* you too"

The Lord Rebukes Job's Friends and Reinstates Job

Then the Lord addressed Eliphaz, "I am angry with you
And your two friends," He said,
"For not speaking rightly about me...as Job did"
And Eliphaz bowed his head

"Now bring seven bulls and seven rams," He said
Telling Eliphaz what to do
"Bring them to my servant Job for a burnt offering
And Job will pray for you

"I will accept his prayer and for what you did
Your punishment I will spare"
So the three men did as He told them to
And the Lord accepted Job's prayer

Then the Lord prospered Job and gave him double
Double what he had before
His old friends and relatives came and ate with him
And *they* all gave him more

They consoled Job about what the Lord had done
Over his troubles and everything
Then each one of them gave him a piece of silver
And each gave him a golden ring

The Lord blessed Job for the rest of his life
Job had fourteen thousand sheep
Six thousand camels and a thousand donkeys
All for Job to keep

Job also had a thousand yoke of oxen
So much more than when he'd begun
But best of all, Job had three more daughters
And he had seven more sons

Job's daughters were so beautiful...it was well known
They were more beautiful than any others
And Job gave each of them an inheritance
Along with their seven brothers

After this, Job lived a long and prosperous life
Of a hundred forty years duration
And he lived to see his children and their children
Down to the fourth generation

Ecclesiastes

EVERYTHING IS MEANINGLESS

These are the words of the Son of David
The Teacher...Jerusalem's king
Meaningless, meaningless...utterly meaningless
Meaningless is *everything*!

What does man gain from all of his labor
At which he toils under the sun?
For the earth continues on forever
Generations go and come

The sun rises and sets and it rises again
The wind blows south and north
Round and round and round it goes
Returning on its course

All of the streams flow into the sea
And yet they fill it...never
And where they came from, they return
Again and again...forever

And though everything in life is wearisome
More than one can say, yet still
The eye can never see enough
Nor the ear ever have its fill

What has happened before, will happen again
Done before, will again be done
Can anyone say, "Look! This is something new!"
There is *nothing* new under the sun

There is no remembrance of men of old
And of those who are yet to come
They will be forgotten by those who follow
Remembered again...by none

Wisdom Is Meaningless

I was the king of Israel, living in Jerusalem
And myself...I devoted
To study and explore *everything* done under Heaven
And in the end...I noted

That God has placed a heavy burden on man
It is all meaningless, I discovered
What is twisted cannot be made straight
The missing cannot be recovered

I told myself..."Look, I've grown and I'm wiser
Than any of the rulers before"
Then I applied myself to understanding wisdom
And madness and folly and more

But I learned that this *too*, is chasing the wind
With much *wisdom*...comes much sorrow
And I found that the more knowledge one has gained
All the more grief will follow

Pleasures Are Meaningless

I told myself..."I'll sample the good things of life
And test myself with pleasure"
But this also proved to be meaningless
What is accomplished in leisure?

I tried drinking wine and embracing folly
But with wisdom guiding me
In the short time of life...what is *worthwhile* to do
Was what I wanted to see

I built myself houses and planted vineyards
Made reservoirs to water trees
I built parks and planted magnificent gardens
All for the eye, to please

I had slaves and owned more flocks and herds
Than anyone in Jerusalem before
I amassed the things that delight men's hearts
Treasures and a harem and more

I became greater than anyone in Jerusalem before
And through it all...I remained wise
I denied myself nothing that I desired
Anything before my eyes

I refused my heart no pleasures
I took delight in all I had done
Yet when I looked at it all...it was meaningless
Nothing gained under the sun

I thought to compare wisdom with madness and folly
Who could do this better than I?
As light outweighs darkness...wisdom outweighs folly
And of course...I reasoned why

A wise man will see where he is going
While a fool will walk in the dark
But I came to realize...that on the same fate
Both of them...will embark

The fate of the fool will be my fate also
So what do I gain by being wise?
This *too* is meaningless...for we'll both be forgotten
After each one of us dies

WORK IS MEANINGLESS

So I hated life and all the things I had worked for
For I will leave it to *another* one
And the one after me...may be wise or a fool
When all is said and done

Yet he will have control over all of my work
Into which I have poured my heart
I began to despair...for work is meaningless too
What *does* one gain from the start?

Man works his whole life in pain and grief
And at night...no rest for his mind
He can do no better than to enjoy food and drink
And in his work...satisfaction find

I realized these pleasures are from the hand of God
Who can enjoy *anything* without *Him*?
To those who please *Him*...He gives wisdom and joy
But to the sinner...it is more grim

For the sinner's task is to work and store wealth
But it is only a façade
It is *meaningless*...for he must hand it all over
To the one who pleases God

A Time for Everything

There is a time and a season for everything
For every activity
There is a time to be born and a time to die
Whenever that time may be

There is a time to plant and a time to harvest
A time to kill and a time to heal
There is a time to tear down and a time to build
And each time is right and real

There is a time to weep and a time to laugh
A time to mourn, a time to dance
And there is a time for scattering stones
And a time to gather and enhance

There is a time to embrace...and a time to refrain
A time to keep...and to throw away
There is a time to search and a time to give up
And each has its perfect day

There is a time to tear and a time to mend
A time to be silent...a time for speech
There is a time to love and a time to hate
A time for war and a time for peace

God has made everything beautiful in its time
He set eternity in the hearts of men
And yet they cannot understand what He has done
From the beginning to the end

But I know that there is nothing better for man
Than to be happy and to do good
We eat, drink and work...which are gifts from God
This much I understood

I know everything He does, endures forever
Nothing can be added or taken away
And He does it all so that men will revere Him
Because...that is His way

Whatever is happening now has happened before
What will be...has already been
For God makes history repeat itself
Over and over again

I saw that in the courts of judgment and justice
Wickedness was there
But I believe that to *both* the righteous and the evil
God will bring judgment to bear

I also think that to show us we are like animals
God is testing men
For both men and animals share the same fate
They both go to dust again

For who *really* knows if our spirits go up
And animals' spirits go down?
But the best thing we can do, is enjoy our work
For who *knows* what next comes around?

OPPRESSION, TOIL, FRIENDLESSNESS

I saw all of the oppression in the world
And I saw the people's tears
No one comforted them...and their oppressors
Held the power to *cause* their fears

I have decided that the dead are better off
Than those who are still alive
But those not yet born, are better than both
For they haven't seen evil thrive

I saw that labor and achievement spring from envy
But this *too* is meaningless
Better is one handful of work with tranquility
Than two handfuls with stress

There was a man all alone, who did nothing but work
Yet he was never content
Finally he said, "Who am I working for?
And why deny myself enjoyment?"

And as for whether people should be alone
Two are better than one
If one falls down, his partner can help him
But pity the man with none

They lay down together and keep each other warm
True, though perhaps unspoken
One can be overpowered, but two can defend
A cord of three strings...not easily broken

Advancement Is Meaningless

I learned it is better to be a poor but wise youth
Than an old and foolish king
For the youth may rise and become the *new* king
The ruler of *everything*

I've seen everyone follow the youth...the new king
Yet he does not retain his success
For the next generation follows yet *another* youth
So *advancement* is meaningless

STAND IN AWE OF GOD

Be careful when you go into the house of God
Go to *listen*...not to speak
And when you make a vow to God...fulfill it
Don't make promises you can't keep

For God does not take pleasure in fools
Don't *let* you mouth lead you to sin
Why give God reason to become angry at you?
Just stand in awe of Him

RICHES ARE MEANINGLESS

Don't be surprised that the poor are oppressed
Denied their justice and rights
For their rulers are directed by those above *them*
And above *them*, to the highest heights

Whoever loves money will never have enough
Though over his income, he obsesses
What does it benefit the owner except to view
All that he *possesses?*

And while the sleep of a worker is sweet
Whether he eats a little or a lot
The burden of abundance hinders sleep
And so the *rich* man...sleeps not

I have seen wealth hoarded to the point of harm
Or through misfortune...lost and grieved
Naked a man comes from his mother's womb
And naked he will leave

So the man who works only to chase the wind
What then does he gain?
He spends his life in frustration and darkness
In anger he complains

But if a man enjoys his work, his food and his drink
And God *chooses* to give him wealth
The man spends no time brooding over the past
God keeps him busy *enjoying* himself

WORDS OF WISDOM

A good reputation is better than fine perfume
That anyone has worn
And the day of your death...is far better
Than the day that you were born

It is better to go to a funeral, than to go to a feast
For everyone must depart
For death is the destiny that everyone shares
And the living should take this to heart

The wise man considers death quite often
While *good* times, the *fool* will seek
Better to listen to the criticism of a *wise* man
Than the praises a *fool* will speak

Extortion will turn a wise man into a fool
A bribe will corrupt the heart
The end of a matter is better than its beginning
When the matter had its start

Remember that patience is better than pride
Patience...a far better tool
And do not be quickly provoked to anger
For anger resides in a fool

Do not ask if the old days were better
It is not wise to ask such a thing
Remember wisdom is a shelter like money
A saved *life*...wisdom can bring

And whether times are good or times are bad
Remember God has made it so
So whatever will happen in a man's future
A man can never know

A seductive woman is a trap...more bitter than death
Of *her*...men should beware
The man who pleases God will escape her
But the sinner...she will ensnare

I ask now...who is like the wise man?
Who knows the meaning of things?
Wisdom will soften a man's appearance
A bright face...wisdom brings

When a sentence for a crime is not quickly carried out
People think it is safe to do wrong
But the evil will not prosper...for they do not fear God
Their days will not be long

I learned that no one has the wisdom to comprehend
All of the works of God
Even though a wise man may *claim* to understand
It is really much too hard

A COMMON DESTINY FOR ALL

After reflecting on all of this...I concluded
That everything is in God's hands
And everyone shares a common destiny
No matter what their plans

So go and eat your food with gladness
Drink your wine with a merry heart
Enjoy life with your wife whom you love
We know not...when we will depart

And always anoint your head with oil
Always be clothed in white
And whatever you find to do with your hands
Do it with all of your might

I have seen that the race is not to the swift
Or the battle...to the strong
Nor wealth to the brilliant or favor to the learned
For time and chance...occur all along

No man knows when his hour will come
As fish are caught in a net
Men are trapped by unexpected and evil times
This...we must *not* forget

Wisdom and Folly

It is better to listen to the quiet words of the wise
Than the shouts of a ruler of fools
And wisdom is better than weapons of war
Wise words are *far* better tools

But one sinner is able to destroy much good
And as dead flies give perfume a bad smell
A little bit of folly outweighs wisdom and honor
As far as *I* can tell

The heart of the wise inclines to the right
But the fool's heart to the left
If a ruler is angry at you...stand your ground
Calmness...can lay error to rest

Whoever digs a pit may fall into it himself
A stone cutter may be hurt by a stone
And while the words of a wise man are gracious
A fool is consumed by his own

When the rulers of a country are of noble standing
Their country they will bless
But woe to the land whose rulers party all night
And rule in drunkenness

When a man is lazy and idle, the roof will sag
And eventually fall to the ground
A feast is for laughter and wine makes life merry
But money makes the world go 'round

Do not talk about your leaders even under your breath
Or curse the rich in your home
For a little bird of the air may carry your words
And he may make them known

CAST YOUR BREAD ON THE WATERS

Cast your bread on the waters for after many days
It will come *back* to you
Be generous in your charity for you *never know*
What a disaster may do

As no one can fathom the path of the wind
Or in the womb, how new life springs
No one can fathom either...the work of God
Creator of all things

Sow your seeds and do not let yourself be idle
For you don't know which one will succeed
Maybe this thing or that thing will be successful
Or maybe *both*...indeed

REMEMBER YOUR CREATOR WHILE YOU ARE YOUNG

Daylight is pleasing...It is good to see the sun
Rejoice in every day of your life
But also remember the past days of darkness
Days of pain and strife

Be happy young people and follow your hearts
And the things you see in your youth
But know God will judge you...for all that you do
Always remember this truth

Banish anxiety from your heart and your mind
And throw your pain away
For youth is fleeting and meaningless
And doesn't last for many a day

While you are still young...remember your Creator
Before the days of trouble come
When you will say..."I no longer enjoy the years,"
And light is like the setting sun

When the keepers of the house will tremble
And the once strong men are bent
And the grinders cease because they are few
And their vision has been spent

When the sound of birds grows faint to the ear
And yet they rob the sleep
When men become afraid of heights
And dangers in the street

When the hair turns white as almond blossoms
And old men drag their feet
With no more desire...they will go to their rest
As mourners come down the street

Remember your Creator, before the cord of life is cut
Before the pulley is broken at the well
When the dust returns to the ground it came from
The spirit returns to God to dwell

The Conclusion of the Matter

The Teacher is wise and has shared his knowledge
His writings...upright and true
But be warned of studying too many *other* books
For they can *weary* you

Now all has been heard and here is the conclusion
Revere God and keep His commands
For *this* is the foundation of all happiness
And the whole duty of man

For God will bring every deed into judgment
Every...single...one
Including everything hidden...whether good or evil
That was ever done

Isaiah

God gave visions to the prophet Isaiah
During the reign of Uzziah
And during the reigns of three other kings
Jotham...Ahaz...Hezekiah

THE SINFULNESS OF JUDAH

Hear O heavens!...Listen O earth!
For the Lord has spoken you see
"The children I have raised and cared for," He said,
"They have rebelled against *me*

"The donkey knows his owner's manger
And the ox, his master's hand
But my nation Israel...it does *not* know
My people do not understand"

Ah, sinful nation...people heavy with guilt
They have forsaken the Lord
They have rejected the Holy One of Israel
Turned their backs and ignored

So now your country is desolate
Your cities burned with fire
Your fields are stripped by foreigners
Your situation dire

"Your abundant sacrifices," says the Lord,
"What are they to me?
I have more than enough burnt offerings
And *detestable* is what I see

"I *hate* your evil assemblies and New Moon festivals
And the appointed feasts you do
And when you spread your hands in prayer
I will hide my eyes from you

"I won't listen while your hands are full of blood
Take your evil deeds from my sight
Make yourselves clean and stop doing wrong
And learn to do what is right

"Begin to seek justice and be an encouragement
To those who are oppressed
Stand up and plead the case for the widow
Defend the fatherless

"Come now... let us reason together
Though your sins are scarlet red
They shall be white as snow and wool"
This... the Lord has said

"If you are willing and obey, you will eat the best,"
Says the Almighty Lord,
"But if you resist and you turn against me
Destroyed you will be by the sword"

The Last Days

The mountain of the Lord's temple will be established
In the latter end of days
"Let us go to the Lord's mountain," many will say,
"And He will teach us of His ways"

For the law shall go forth out of Zion
From Jerusalem, the word of the Lord
He will judge between the nations and settle disputes
They will beat into plows their swords

And the nations will no longer train for war
They will no longer take up sword
O come house of Jacob and let us walk
Walk in the light of the Lord

THE DAY OF THE LORD

The day of the Lord's judgment is coming
He will punish the lofty and proud
The arrogance of man will be humbled
Their idols no longer allowed

Men will run and hide in holes in the ground
To caves in rocks they will flee
In terror these men will hide from the Lord
And the splendor of His majesty

They made and worshiped idols of silver and gold
But when He shakes the earth that day
They will throw their idols to rodents and bats
They will throw their idols away

JUDGMENT AGAINST JUDAH AND JERUSALEM

The Lord is taking from Judah and Jerusalem
All of their support and supplies
Their food, their water, their judges and prophets
Right before their eyes

He is taking their soldiers and their heroes
Counselors and fortune tellers
Their craftsmen and their astrologers
Governors and elders

I'll make youth their leaders and children will rule
And each other, the people will oppress
For their words and their actions are against the Lord
But the righteous will be blessed

My people, your guides are leading you astray
Turning you from the path
The Lord will judge the elders and leaders
And they will face His wrath

"The daughters of Zion are haughty," says the Lord,
"Walking with outstretched necks
With deceiving eyes and anklets that jingle
They walk with dainty steps

"Therefore the Lord will make their scalps bald
And sores on their heads will be"
And in that day, the Lord will strip them
Of all of their finery

Their headbands and necklaces of the crescent moon
Headdresses, veils and rings
Their sashes, bangles, earrings and bracelets
Perfumes and other things

And instead of glory and might in battle
Your men will fall by the sword
And Zion will mourn and sit destitute
Declares the word of the Lord

The Promise of Restoration

The Branch of the Lord will be beautiful
And glorious in that day
And the filth of the women of Zion
The Lord will wash away

And those left in Jerusalem will be called holy
The fruit of the land will inspire
He will cleanse the bloodstains of Jerusalem
By spirits of judgment and fire

Then the Lord will create over all of Mount Zion
Over all who assemble there
A cloud of smoke by day and fire by night
A sheltering canopy in the air

ISAIAH'S VISION OF THE LORD

During the year that King Uzziah had died
I saw the Lord seated on a throne
He was high and lifted up...His train filled the temple
Angels with six wings I was shown

"Holy, holy, holy is the Lord God Almighty,"
They called to one another
"The whole earth is full of His glory," they said
As they sang out to each other

At the sound of their voices the doorposts shook
The temple was filled with smoke
"Woe to me, I'm unclean and have seen the Lord!"
I cried out when I spoke

Then one of the angels came with a coal in his hand
Touched it to my lips and said,
"Your guilt is taken away and your sin atoned for"
I stood and bowed my head

Then I listened and heard the voice of the Lord
"Who shall I send?" said He
"And who will go for us?" asked the Lord
"Here I am!" I said "Send me!"

"Go," said the Lord "And say to the people,
'You hear but do not understand
You look and look but never perceive,'"
He continued His command

"Make the hearts of these people be calloused
Dull their ears and close their eyes
Or they might see and hear and understand
And turn and be healed otherwise"

"How long, O Lord?" I asked of Him
"Until the cities lie ruined," said He
"And the Lord has sent everyone far away
And the land...forsaken shall be

"Though a tenth remain…it will be invaded again
Invaded and burned to the sand
But as a tree leaves a stump when it is cut down
The holy seed will be a stump in the land"

A Virgin Will Give Birth to a Son

When King Ahaz was the king of Judah
The Lord spoke through Isaiah of a sign
It was a promise for the house of David
Concerning a future time

"A virgin will be with child," said Isaiah,
"And she will give birth to a Son
And she will call Him Emmanuel," he said
Speaking of…the One

Then he went on to speak of other things
That would happen *before* this birth
He spoke of war and pestilence and terrible times
For those upon the earth

Then the Lord spoke of the virgin birth *again*
And He said He will call in Uriah
Who will be a reliable witness for Him
Along with Zechariah

Then He said that because the people rejected
The gently flowing Shiloah waters
He will bring a mighty flood…the king of Assyria
Flowing across their borders

It will sweep into Judah, swirling over the top
Covering the breadth of the land
Distant lands prepare for battle but are shattered
Their offenses will not stand

FEAR GOD

The Lord warned me not to follow the people's ways
And do not fear what they fear
"Regard the Lord Almighty as the one who is holy
The one you should revere

"He is the one you are to fear and dread
And a sanctuary you can call
He'll be a stone for Israel, that causes men to stumble
And a rock that makes them fall

"And for the people of Jerusalem
He will be a trap and a snare
Many will stumble...fall and be broken
Snared and captured there"

Bind the testimony and seal the law in my disciples
I will wait for the Lord 'til then
He is hiding His face from the house of Jacob
I will put my trust in *Him*

When people tell you to consult with mediums
Why consult with the dead?
If they don't speak *this* word...they have no *light*
Inquire of *God* instead

Distressed and hungry they will *roam* the land
Enraged...their anger they will rent
They will curse God...and see fear and gloom
Into darkness...they will be sent

A SAVIOR IS BORN

In the past He humbled the land of Zebulun
And the land of Naphtali too
In the future He will honor the Galilee of the Gentiles
Where the Jordan to the sea, runs through

People walking in darkness have seen a great light
In the land of the shadow of death
You increased their joy, they rejoice before you
You increased the nation's breadth

You have broken the yoke that burdens them
You broke the oppressor's rod
As you did in the day of Midian's defeat
The mighty hand of God

Every warrior's boot that was worn for battle
All of the bloodstained attire
Every piece will be used for burning
Fuel for the fire

For unto us a Child is born
To us is given a Son
And the government will be on His shoulders
He will be the One

His name is called Wonderful…Counselor…Mighty God
Everlasting Father…Prince of Peace
And of His government…there will be no end
It will ever increase

He will rule with righteousness and justice forever
From His ancestor David's throne
And this will happen by the zeal and passion
Of the Lord Almighty alone

PUNISHMENT ON ISRAEL

The Lord sends a message against Israel
Against *them* He raises His hand
Because the people are ungodly and wicked
Destruction will be on the land

Woe to the ones who make unjust laws
Or issue oppressive decrees
Where will you run on the day of reckoning?
You will cringe down on your knees

ASSYRIA

"Woe to the Assyrian…the rod of my anger
The club of my wrath in your hand
I send you against the ones who anger me
A godless nation in the land"

When His work is finished against Mount Zion
And against Jerusalem, He will say,
"Now I will punish the king of Assyria
For his pride and his haughty way

"For he says he has done this by his own hand
But does the ax swing by its own expertise?"
So the Lord will send on the Assyrian soldiers
A terrible wasting disease

And under the pomp of the Assyrian king
The Lord will kindle a fire
The Light of Israel a fire…their Holy One a flame
Consuming the thorns and brier

In one day the splendor of his forests and fields
The fire will completely destroy
And the trees that remain will be so few
They can be numbered by a boy

Now in that day…the remnant of Israel
And the house of Jacob who survive
Will no longer depend on the ones who struck them
But on the Holy One of Israel rely

And only a *remnant* of Jacob will return to God
Though Israel be as numerous as the sand
So the Almighty Lord will bring righteous destruction
Decreed upon the whole land

"Do not be afraid of the Assyrians," says the Lord
"Soon my anger against *you* will end
And my wrath will be directed against *them*
Their destruction…I will send"

A BRANCH FROM THE ROOT OF JESSE

A shoot will come up from the root of Jesse
A branch bearing fruit will come
And the Spirit of the Lord will rest upon *Him*
Wisdom and understanding in this One

With a Spirit of counsel and power and knowledge
He will delight in the fear of the Lord
He will not judge...by what He sees or hears
But justice...He will afford

With the rod of His mouth...He will strike the earth
Slay the wicked with His lips
Righteousness will be the belt 'round His waist
Faithfulness...the sash round His hips

In that day the wolf shall live with the lamb
And the leopard and kid lie down
And the lion and calf and farm animal together
And a child shall lead them around

The cow and the bear shall feed side by side
Their young shall lie down together
And the lion will be eating straw like the ox
And the snake hurt the baby...never

The child shall put his hand into the viper nest
But no harm shall come to he
For the earth will be full of the knowledge of the Lord
As the waters cover the sea

In that day as a banner before the people
The Root of Jesse will stand
And the place of His dwelling will be glorious
The nations will rally to His hand

He will reclaim the remnant for the second time
From wherever they may be
Reaching out to the countries all around
And the islands of the sea

The Lord will gather the exiles of Israel
And a flag among the nations, unfurl
He will assemble the scattered people of Judah
From all around the world

The enemies of Judah will be cut off
Ephriam's envy...turned away
They will plunder Philistia, Edom and Moab
And the Ammonites will obey

The Lord will dry up the gulf of the Egyptian Sea
Over the Euphrates, wave His hand
A mighty wind will divide it into seven streams
So men can walk over the land

He will make a highway for the remnant
Who from Assyria come
As He did long ago for Israel
When Egypt...they came from

And in that day...you will say to the Lord,
"O Lord...I *will* praise *you*
Your anger has turned away from me
And you have *comforted* me too"

You'll say, "God is surely my salvation
I will trust...I will not fear
For the Lord, He is my strength and song
And my salvation here"

And with much joy...you will draw water
From the *fountain* of salvation
You'll thank Him and tell what He has done
To every other nation

Proclaim to the world that His name is exalted
For glorious things He has done
Sing for joy Zion people...for in your midst
Is the Great...and Holy One

Babylon

An oracle of Babylon was given to Isaiah
A message that spoke of their fates
Raise a flag on a hill and call out the order
To enter the rulers' gates

I have ordered my holy ones and called my warriors
To carry out my wrath
Listen!...Hear the noise on the mountains
Of a multitude so vast

It is the noise and shouting of many nations
Brought together by the Lord's hand
He will use them to carry out His anger
And they...will destroy the land

Scream in terror for the day of the Lord is here
Destruction from Shaddai
Every arm is paralyzed in fear
Hearts melting...terrified

Pangs of anguish will grip them and they will writhe
As a woman whose labor came
They will look in shock at each other
As their faces are aflame

Look!...The day of the Lord is coming!
With wrath...the day will begin
He will make the land desolate in His anger
And destroy the sinners within

The stars of heaven and their constellations
Will not show their light
The sun will be darkened when it rises
And the moon won't shine at night

I will punish the world for its evil
And the wicked for their sin
I will crush the arrogance of the proud
And humble the ruthless men

I will make the heavens tremble
And the earth shake from its place
The burning wrath of the Almighty Lord
And His anger they will face

Like hunted gazelle or sheep with no shepherd
Each to their land will flee
And all of the ones who are captured
Killed by the sword shall be

Their babies will be dashed to pieces
Right before their eyes
And their houses will be looted
Raped will be their wives

Look, I will stir up the Medes against them
For gold and silver...The Medes don't care
They will strike down the young men with their bows
And show no mercy for the babies there

And Babylon...the jewel of kingdoms
The glory of their pride
Will be overthrown by God Almighty
As when Sodom and Gomorrah died

Babylon will never again be inhabited
Lived in...never again
No Arab pitch a tent or shepherd rest a flock
Only wild animals then

The Lord will have compassion on Jacob
As once again Israel He favors
The Lord will settle them in their own land
Joined by alien neighbors

Other nations will bring them to their *own* place
Israel will possess the Lord's land
And *they* will rule *over* their oppressors
Given them by God's hand

On that wonderful day when the Lord gives you rest
You will taunt the Babalonian king
"How the oppressor has come to his end!" you will say
"And his fury has ceased!" you will sing

The Lord has broken the staff of the wicked
Which struck with unceasing blows
And subdued the nations in unrestrained fury
And every nation knows

Finally the earth is at rest and at peace
And the underworld *welcomes* you
Now maggots are spread as your mattress
And worms are your blanket too

O shining star…how you've fallen from Heaven
Son of the morning unfurled!
You have been thrown…down to the earth
For destroying the nations of the world

"I will ascend to Heaven and set *my* throne
Above the stars of God," you said
"I will be the Most High in the highest heavens"
But you're brought down to the pit instead

Those who see you, stare and ponder and ask,
"Can this man be the one
Who shook the earth and made kingdoms tremble
And destroyed the world when done?

"The one who made it into a wasteland
The greatest cities demolished?
The one who showed no mercy on captives
And entire peoples abolished?"

While kings lie in stately glory in tombs
You'll be thrown *out* of *your* grave
You'll descend to the pit for the slaughter you wrought
And neither will your descendants be saved

ASSYRIA

"As I have planned, so it will happen," says the Lord
"As I decided, so it will stand
On my mountains I will trample the Assyrian
I will crush him in my land

"I will remove his burden from my people
For the whole earth I have a plan"
For now the Lord Almighty has purposed
And who...can stop His hand?

THE PHILISTINES

An oracle came in the year King Ahaz died
"Do not rejoice, you Philistines," it said,
"That the rod that had struck you is broken
And the king who attacked is dead"

For a viper will spring up from the root of that snake
A venomous serpent he will be
Though your poor and needy will find food and rest
Your root and survivors are slain by me

Wail and cry and melt away you Philistines
A smoke cloud from the north comes this way
But the Lord's afflicted people have a refuge in Zion
The northern envoys will learn that day

MOAB

Many cities in Moab have been ruined
Destroyed in just one night
Their waters dried up and vegetation gone
Their survivors weeping in flight

The waters of Dimon are full of blood
Yet still more will come by my hand
A lion will be upon the fugitives of Moab
And those remaining in the land

The women of Moab are crossing the river
Like birds cast from a nest
They sent gifts of lambs to Jerusalem
Sanctuary...their request

When the oppressor and destruction come to an end
A throne of love will be
The Man upon it...from the house of David
Faithful and righteous is He

Damascus and Ephraim

Damascus and the fortified city of Ephraim
Will be only ruinous sites
And the remnant of Syria will be the same
As the glory of the Israelites

In that day the glory of Israel will fade
Its body will waste away
And as when a harvester gathers the grain
A few will remain that day

Then at last the people will look to their Creator
God of Israel...the Holy One
They will no longer look to their idols
And creations their *hands* have done

And the same strong cities they abandoned before
Will all be desolation
For you have *forgotten*...the Rock of your strength
The God of your salvation

Cush

Woe to the land that is shadowed by wings
Which sends envoys over the seas
Beyond the rivers of Ethiopia
In boats of papyrus reeds

Sent to a tall and smooth-skinned people
A people feared far and near
An aggressive nation, divided by rivers
People of the world... listen here

When a trumpet sounds, all on earth will hear it
A flag on the mountains they will see
"I will quietly watch from my dwelling place,"
The Lord has said to me

Then just before they begin their attack
Just when their plan is ripe
The Lord will cut their spreading branches
And their new growth... He'll swipe

Their mighty army will lay dead in the fields
For animals and birds of prey
And the tall, smooth skinned people will carry gifts
To the Lord Almighty that day

EGYPT

See the Lord riding on a swift cloud to Egypt
Their idols tremble before Him
The hearts of the Egyptians are melting inside
His plan for them is grim

"I will stir up Egyptian against Egyptian
And brother against brother
And neighbor against neighbor," says the Lord,
"And kingdoms against each other

"I bring their plans to nothing and they will lose heart
They'll consult idols and spirits of the dead
And I will hand them over to a cruel and fierce king
And *he*... will rule over their head"

The waters of the river will stop flowing
The bed will be parched and dry
The canals will stink... the streams dry up
The reeds and rushes die

The fields by the Nile will all become parched
And no more...will they be
The fishermen of the Nile will lament and groan
For no fish...will they see

There will be no flax for the harvesters
For the weavers...no more threads
All of the workers will be sick at heart
And they will hang their heads

The advice of the wise men is worthless
Stupid and wrong what they say
The officials of Zoan and Memphis are fools
The leaders led Egypt astray

For the Lord sent a spirit of foolishness on them
Whatever they do will fail
Egypt can do nothing...and all are helpless
From the head down to the tail

And under the upraised fist of the Lord
They will cower in fear
Just the name of Israel will terrorize them
The plan of the Lord is clear

In that day five of the cities of Egypt
Will swear allegiance to the Lord
With an altar to the Lord in the heart of Egypt
He'll be worshiped and adored

When they cry to the Lord because of their oppressors
A savior He will send
And the Lord will make Himself known to them
And He will heal them then

EGYPT AND CUSH

Assyria's king will take prisoners from Egypt and Cush
Barefoot and naked they will walk
And they will be afraid...who trusted in Cush
And spoke of Egypt with boastful talk

BABYLON

Disaster is roaring like a whirlwind upon you
From the desert a coming invader
A terrifying vision of the destroyer destroying
Betrayal by the betrayer

You Elamites and Medes, attack and lay siege
He will make an end
To all of the groaning that Babylon caused
In anguish, I comprehend

Great pain in my loins as a woman in labor
I am troubled by what I see
I tremble with fear...and the twilight I desired
Has become a terror to me

They *feast*...but should be preparing the shields
For the Lord has said to me,
"Post a watchman on the wall and have him report
Whatever he may see"

Then day after day the watchman looked out
And finally...a chariot sound
The man shouted, "Babylon is fallen, is fallen!
All their idols lie broken on the ground!"

EDOM AND ARABIA

"Watchman, how much longer until dawn?"
Someone from Edom calls to me
"Morning is coming, but night soon returns
Come back...ask again and see"

Within one year all the pomp of Kedar
Will all come to an end
The surviving soldiers of Kedar will be few
This word...the Lord did send

JERUSALEM

Why are you all running to the rooftops?
What *is* this that I see?
Your dead were not killed in battle
In this city of *revelry*

Your leaders have fled and been captured
The people are captured too
Leave me alone and don't try to console me
As I watch and weep for you

What a day of terror and crushing defeat
That by the Lord was brought
The walls of Jerusalem have been broken
Is here a lesson taught?

You gathered your weapons and stored up water
Inspected all of your walls
But you didn't turn to the One who *made* it
Or cry out any calls

In that day the Lord of Heaven's armies
Called you to repent and weep
But instead there is joy and dancing and drinking
Feasting on cattle and sheep

This iniquity will not be purged from you
Until your dying day
The Lord Almighty has *revealed* this to me
This…the Lord did say

TYRE

The Lord gave Isaiah a prophecy against Tyre
The nations will mourn when they hear
That the great trading city of Tyre is destroyed
In ruin for seventy year

After that it will be a world trading port
But her profit will be set apart
For food and fine clothes for all of the people
Who live with the Lord in their heart

THE DEVASTATION OF THE EARTH

The Lord is going to devastate the earth
Its people He will scatter
Whether priest or prince, master or servant
Their status...will not matter

The people have broken the Covenant of God
The guilt, the people must bear
And therefore a curse consumes the earth
Laid waste and plundered there

The inhabitants of earth will be burned up
Very few will be left
The revelry will cease...gaiety is banished
But not so...in the west

Their voices raised, they shout for joy
For the *Lord* in His *majesty*
Let the God of Israel be exalted in the east!
And in the islands of the sea!

But I spoke up and said, "Woe to me"
I exclaimed, "I waste away!
With treachery the treacherous
The treacherous betray!"

Awaiting you O People of the earth
Is terror, pit and snare
And those who flee at the *sound* of terror
Will fall and be captured there

The floodgates of Heaven will be opened
The earth's foundations will shake
The earth will reel like a drunkard
Split asunder...in the quake

And in that day the Lord will punish
The powers in the heavens on high
Together with the kings of the earth below
Their punishment...draws nigh

The moon will be bewildered
The sun will be ashamed
Before the elders in Mount Zion and Jerusalem
The Lord Almighty will reign

Praises to the Almighty

O Lord, you are my God, I will exalt you
Your holy name I will praise
You did wonderful things...planned long ago
The fortified city you razed

The stronghold of foreigners now lays in ruin
Never to be built again
So the city of ruthless nations will fear you
You'll be honored by strong men

You've been a stronghold for the poor and needy
A shelter from the storm
The uproar of foreigners is silenced by you
You still their boastful song

The Lord will prepare a feast for the people
Upon the mountain high
And the richest of foods and finest of wines
The Almighty Lord will supply

And He will remove the cloud of gloom
On the earth through years gone by
And the Lord will swallow up death forever
And wipe every tear from their eye

He will remove the disgrace of His people
And the mockery of His land
The people will say, "Surely...this is our God
He saved us...by His hand

"This is the Lord . . . in whom we trusted
Let us rejoice in His salvation!"
His blessings on Jerusalem . . . but not so on Moab
Trampled will be *that* nation

As straw is trodden on the manure pile
Their pridefulness will be crushed
And He will lay down . . . their fortified walls
Down . . . into the dust

In that day, Judah will sing His praises
Of how He makes salvation
How He keeps in peace those who trust Him
Enter the righteous nation

He humbles the proud and brings down the city
The lofty city to the dust
Where the oppressed and poor will trample it
He is a God . . . who is just

He smoothes out the path for the righteous
We show trust by obeying His ways
My soul yearns to be with you during the night
My spirit longs for you in the days

And when your judgments come upon the earth
Though to the wicked . . . you show grace
In a righteous land, they continue their evil
And do not seek your face

Let them see your love for your people
So they will be put to shame
Consume them in the fire awaiting your enemies
Their fate . . . will be the same

Lord, you gave us peace and all of our works
Have been done for us by you
And though only *your* name . . . do we honor
Over us . . . other gods *did* rule

But they are now dead, they live no more
Their spirts will not rise
They were inspected and destroyed by you
Their memory wiped from our eyes

You have expanded the nation O Lord
Glory for yourself you did gain
When you disciplined your people, they came to you
As a woman in birthing pain

But when we gave birth...it was only to wind
Not salvation to the land
But your people who died will live again
Raised up...by your own hand

Wake up and sing...you who dwell in the dust
The dew of morning on your head
Wake up and shout...shout for joy
The earth will give up her dead

Hide in your rooms and shut the doors
Until His anger has passed
For the earth will show the blood of her slain
Revealing it at last

Then the Lord will take His terrible, swift sword
And the dragon of the sea He will slay
And the Lord will speak of the fruitful vineyard
Which He guards both night and day

EPHRAIM

Woe to the proud city...the city of Samaria
Israel's drunken people's pride
For the Lord will throw it down to the ground
Trampled underfoot...cast aside

In that day the Lord will be a glorious crown
For the remnant who are His
A spirit of justice to Him who sits in judgement
And strength to the warriors He gives

But now the leaders and priests are drunk with wine
Stumbling from too much beer
All of the tables are covered with vomit
Not a clean place anywhere here

The Lord tried to teach them about the *resting* place
To make them understand
But they didn't listen...so He'll bring oppressors
From a foreign land

Therefore, you scoffing rulers in Jerusalem
Listen and hear the Lord's word
For you said, "We have made a covenant with death
Coming destruction will be deterred

"We made a lie our refuge...in falsehood we hide"
So the Lord sent words of His own
"Look...I am laying a foundation in Zion
A precious cornerstone

"Justice the measuring line...righteousness the plumb
The trusting will never feel dismay
Your hiding place will flood and your refuge, the lie
Hail will sweep away

"Your bargain to cheat death will be cancelled
Your deal with the grave will not hold
You'll be trampled and carried away by an enemy,"
The word of the Lord foretold

WOE TO THE CITY OF JERUSALEM

I will besiege Jerusalem and she will mourn
She will mourn and lament
I will prepare an attack on her from all sides
The city will be rent

Brought low...your voice will come from the dust
As a whisper from the ground
Suddenly in an instant...the Almighty Lord will come
With earthquake and great thunder sound

In windstorm and tempest and devouring fire
Against the attacking nations
And as a hungry man dreams he is eating
It is gone when he awakens

But the Lord has blinded your understanding of this
As words that are sealed in a scroll
And if you were to give it to someone to read
He would not see…what is foretold

"These people say they are mine," says the Lord,
"And they honor me with their lips
But their hearts are far away and their worship
Is man-made rules and scripts

"And so once more I will astound them with wonders
The wisdom of the wise will pass away"
Woe to those who hide their evil work from the Lord
"Who sees us and who knows?" they say

You people are turning things upside down
As though the potter was the clay
"*He* didn't make me…He doesn't understand,"
To the creator the created say

In a short time Lebanon will become a fertile field
Looked upon as a forest it will be
In that day the deaf will hear the words of the Book
And out of darkness, the blind will see

The humble will be filled with joy in the Lord
The poor rejoice in the Holy One
For the evil one and the mockers will be no more
Those of iniquity…will be done

Therefore the Lord says to the house of Jacob,
"No longer will they feel shame
When they see my blessings upon all of their children
They will sanctify my name"

JUDAH'S WORTHLESS TREATY WITH EGYPT

"Woe to the obstinate children," says the Lord,
"Pursuing *their* plans…not mine
Going to Egypt for protection without consulting *me*
Will only bring disgrace and decline"

So go now and write this all down in a book
So the record will all be there
For this is a rebellious and deceitful generation
They don't listen to God…They don't care

"Don't tell us what is right," they say to the prophets
"Turn aside from the way
Tell us pleasant things and prophesy illusions
Don't confront us with the Holy One," they say

"So because you reject this message," says the Lord,
"And you rely on oppression and deceit
This sin will become as a bulging cracked wall
With sudden destruction…complete

"Your strength is in quiet and trust," said the Lord
"You'll be saved in repentance and rest
But you were not willing…you said, 'We will flee,'
And became your enemy's quest"

And yet the Lord rises to show you compassion
He longs to be gracious to you
For the Lord our God is a God of justice
Blessed are all who wait for Him too!

People of Zion, who are living in Jerusalem
You shall weep no more
When you cry for help, He will be gracious
As soon as He hears you implore

THE COMING KINGDOM OF RIGHTEOUSNESS

A king will come who will reign in righteousness
And rulers who rule will be fair
And each one will be as a shelter in a storm
Or water in a desert bare

Then the ears of those hearing will listen
And the eyes that are open will see
The heart of the rash, will understand knowledge
Stuttering tongues will speak fluently

No longer will the vile man be called noble
Nor the scoundrel highly esteemed
For the methods of the scoundrel are wicked
He devises evil schemes

The mind of the vile is kept busy with evil
Ungodly are his ways
He spreads false teachings about the Lord
The hungry and thirsty he dismays

The scoundrel destroys the poor with his lies
Even if right is the case they bring
But the noble man makes noble plans
And stands up for a noble thing

THE JUDGMENT OF GOD

Woe to the one who is the destroyer
Who has not yet been destroyed
Woe to the one who is the betrayer
Betraying *you*...was never employed

A time will come when you *stop* destroying
Then *that* will be done to *you*
A time will come when you stop *betraying*
Then *that* will be done to you *too*

Please favor us Lord, we have waited for you
Give us new strength every day
And in times of distress...be our salvation
You *are* the only way

When they heard your voice thunder...the people ran
When you stood...the nations fled
Then the nations' plunder was pounced upon
As if a swarm of locust fed

The Lord is exalted for He lives on high
He fills Zion with righteousness
He's the sure foundation, wisdom and salvation
Those who fear Him...He will bless

Ambassadors of peace weep bitter tears
Brave men cry in the street
The treaty is broken, the highways deserted
His disrespect of men...complete

The land is mourning and languishing
Lebanon ashamed and aching
Sharon has withered and become a wilderness
Bashan and Carmel are shaking

"Now will I arise," says the Lord God
"Now I am exalted," says He
"And your breath shall devour you as fire
And the people...burned shall be"

Those far away...hear what I have done
Acknowledge my might...those near
"Who of us can live with the consuming fire?"
The sinners cry out in fear

But he who walks rightly and speaks what is right
And despises oppressors' gain
And refuses to hear plans of murder and evil
Shall live safely on the high plain

The high fortresses of rock shall be his retreat
Food will be given to his hand
Your eyes shall see the King in His beauty
You shall *see*...the far off land

Your heart will meditate on the terror
"Where is the one?" you will say
"Where is the one in charge of the towers
The one who counts and weighs?"

No more will you see the fierce people
Whose speech you don't understand
Now look upon Zion, the city of our meetings
And see Jerusalem...a peaceful land

A quiet habitation...a tent not taken down
It's ropes will not be broken
And Mighty Jehovah will be there for us
The Word of the Lord has spoken

For He is our Judge, our Lawgiver and King
And He will save us still
Then the sins of those living in Zion are forgiven
And none there...will be ill

THE NATIONS WILL BE JUDGED

Now all of the nations and all of the people
Everyone...draw near!
All in the earth...and all that come from it
Pay attention and hear!

For the wrath of the Lord is against the nations
And the armies they deployed
They will be given over...to total slaughter
And they will be destroyed

Their bodies will cause a stench to rise up
As His anger takes its toll
Blood soaked mountains...the stars will dissolve
The sky will roll up like a scroll

For my sword has been bathed in the heavens
And down upon Edom it falls
For an animal sacrifice to the Lord in Bozrah
And a great slaughter in Edom, He calls

Vengeance for the Lord and recompense for Zion
Edom will be paid this way
Its streams and ground will be covered with fire
Not quenched... night or day

And it shall lie desolate forever and ever
None will pass through again
Her princes will vanish and her noblemen
Will have no more kingdom then

THE RANSOMED OF THE LORD

The wilderness and the dry land shall be glad
The desert will blossom as a rose
The honor of Lebanon will be given to it
As the majesty of Jehovah shows

Strengthen the feeble hands and steady the knees
Speak to the fearful heart
"Be strong, do not fear, your God will save you
And vengeance... *He* will impart"

Then the eyes of the blind will be opened
The ears of the deaf will hear
The tongue of the mute will shout for joy
The lame will leap like deer

For in the wilderness will be bodies of water
In the desert, streams will flow
And in the former habitation of jackals
Grass and reeds will grow

A highway called the Way of Holiness
Will be there in that day
But the unclean shall not tread upon it
Only those who walk in the Way

Neither will ferocious beasts be there
Only the redeemed walk thereon
And the ransomed of the Lord will enter Zion
In happiness and song

Their heads will be crowned with everlasting joy
They'll be overcome with gladness
Their sorrow and sighing shall flee away
And there shall be no sadness

Comfort for God's People

Comfort you my people, says your God
Tell the heart of Jerusalem
Her sin is paid for...and from the hand of the Lord
She received *double* for her sin

A voice is crying out in the wilderness
"Prepare the way for the Lord," says he
"Make straight in a desert, a highway to our God
Valleys raised and mountains low shall be

"Rough places will be plains and the crooked straight
And the glory of the Lord revealed then
And all of mankind will see it together
The mouth of Jehovah has spoken"

Men are like grass and their glory like flowers
Grass withers and flowers fall
For the breath of the Lord blows down upon them
But His word stands forever for all

You who bring good news to Jerusalem and Zion
Go up on a mountain high
Lift your voice without fear and shout to Judah
"Here is your God!" loudly cry

Behold the Lord Jehovah will come with power
And for Him...His arm shall rule
He will bring His rewards and will tend His flock
Which He'll feed...as a shepherd would do

He will gather the lambs with His arm
And carry them close to His heart
And those with young…He will gently lead
So they will not drift apart

Who has understood and measured the dust of the earth?
Or the waters in the hollow of His hand?
Who has weighed the hills and mountains on scales?
And meted out the heavens by a span?

Who has portioned out the *Spirit* of Jehovah?
Or counseled the Lord before?
Who did *He* consult to learn understanding
And judgment and knowledge and more?

The nations are no more than a drop in a bucket
Or dust on a scale in His hand
All Lebanon's beasts…not enough for an offering
The islands are a handful of sand

The nations are as *nothing* before Him
So who will you *compare* Him to?
And what likeness do you compare to *Him*?
An *idol* that a craftsman would do?

Do you not know?…Have you not heard?
Declared since the earth began
It is *He* who sits above the circle of the earth
And as grasshoppers are…so is man

He stretches out the heavens like a canopy
As a tent in which to dwell
He reduces princes and rulers to *nothing*
Even when rooted well

"To whom will you liken me…or shall I be equal?"
Inquires the Holy One
Look to the heavens and see His creation
The work that He has done

He brought out by number, the starry host
He called each one by name
And by the greatness of His might and power
Each one of them remain

Do you not know?...Have you not heard?
The Lord God does not tire
And no one can fathom His understanding
He lifts the weak and weary higher

Those who hope in the Lord will renew their strength
And soar on wings as *eagles* do
They will run and will not grow weary
They will walk and not faint too

God's Help for Israel

"You islands...keep silent before me
Let the people renew their power
They will come near, and then they will speak
We draw near...to the judgment hour

"Who stirred up from the east a righteous one
And gave Him kings and nations
Giving them as dust and stubble to His sword and bow
Unscathed in His quest's duration?

"Who has done this since the beginning of time
Calling each generation to be?
It is I, the Lord...with the first of them
And with the last...I am He"

The islands see and fear, the earth ends tremble
Each one helps the other
They approach...and they come forward
"Be strong!" they tell their brother

The idol builders encourage each other
They work together all
And when it is finished they nail it down
So the idol will not fall

"But you O Israel, whom I chose as my servant
I gathered you from every land
Fear not, for I am with you... I am your God
I uphold you with my righteous right hand

"All who rage against you will be put to shame
They will perish and be no longer here
For I am your God, who takes your right hand
And says to you... 'Do not fear'

"Fear not you worm Jacob, you men of Israel
For I will help you," the Lord does say
"I will make you a sledge and you'll winnow them
And the wind will blow them away

"And you will rejoice in the Lord Jehovah
And boast of the Holy One
The poor and the needy will search for water
And yet... they will find none

"But I, the God of Israel, will answer them
And them I will not forsake
I'll form rivers on high places and springs in valleys
Pools of water in the desert I will make

"I will put in the desert... the cedar and acacia
The myrtle and the olive tree
Pines in wasteland... fir and cypress together
So that the people will see

"So they may consider and act wisely
And they may understand
That the Holy One of Israel *created* this
That it was by *my* hand

"Present your case and state your arguments,"
Says Israel's holy King
"Bring in your idols to reveal the past
Or what the future will bring

"Do good or do evil so we'll be astonished
Then *together* we will see
That you are gods...But you're less than nothing
And detestable, your followers be

"I have stirred up one from the north...and he comes
He calls my name from the rising sun
He treads on rulers as though they were clay
And no one foretold of *this* one

"I give one who proclaims good tidings
I give one to Jerusalem
And I look and see that there is no man
No counselor among them"

THE CHOSEN SERVANT OF THE LORD

"Here is my servant, whom I uphold
He is my *Chosen* One
I give Him my Spirit and upon the nations
His judgment will be done

"He'll not shout or cry out to be heard in the street
Nor will He break a bruised reed
A flickering candle...He will not snuff out
He will judge in *truth*...indeed

"And until He sets His judgment in the earth
He won't become weak or bruised
And the islands wait with hope for His law
Wait for His law to be used"

Hear the word of God who created the heavens
Created and stretched them out
Who spread out the earth and all it produces
And gave life to all who walk about

"I the Lord have called you in righteousness
And I will take hold of your hand
I will preserve you and make you a covenant
For the people of the land

"I will make you a light for the nations
To open the eyes of the blind
To bring out the captives from the prisons
Those sitting in darkness you find

"I am Jehovah...That is my name
I *will not* give my glory to another
Nor my praise to graven images," He declares
Because there *is* no other

"Look, the former things have come to pass
And new things I declare
Before they spring forth, I tell you of them
So you will be aware"

A Song of Praise to the Lord

Come sing unto the Lord a new song
Sing praises from the ends of the earth
You who sail the seas or live on distant isles
Sing for all you're worth

The wilderness and the cities lift their voices
And also the villages of Kedar
The inhabitants of Sela, all cry out for joy
From the mountaintops afar

They give glory to the Lord Jehovah
His praises in the isles they declare
Jehovah will go forth...as a mighty man of war
Against His enemies there

"For a long time I have kept silent
Kept silent and held back my rant
But now I cry out like a woman in childbirth
All at once...I gasp and pant

"I will lay waste, the hills and the mountains
Their vegetation, I will dry
Turn rivers to islands...lead those who are blind
Putting light before their eye

"I will not forsake them...But as for the others
Who do not follow my name
Who tell graven images, 'You are our gods,'
They'll be turned back...in shame"

Israel Is Deaf and Blind

"You who are deaf, listen and hear," says the Lord
"You who are blind, look and see
Who is as blind as the servant of Jehovah?
As deaf as the messenger sent by me?

"You saw many things but you paid no attention
What you heard...you did not take in"
The Lord handed over Israel for plunder
For against Him, we did sin

And no...they would not follow in His ways
They did not obey His law
So he poured out His burning anger on them
In violence of war

Surrounded by fire, yet they did not understand
The lesson He tried to impart
And though they were consumed by it
They took it not...to heart

Israel's Only Savior

But now O Israel, the Lord your Creator
Says, "Fear not, for I have *redeemed* you
I have called you by name and you are mine"
And the Lord says further, too

"When you go through the waters, I'll be with you
And when you go through a river
It will not sweep over you," declares the Lord
For you...He will deliver

"When you go into the fire, you will not be burned
And the flames will not consume you
For I am your God, the Holy One of Israel
And I am your Savior too

"I have appointed Egypt to be your atonement
Cush and Seba in your place
You're precious and honored and I love you,"
The Lord's redeeming grace

"Fear not, for I am with you," says the Lord,
"And your children I will bring,
Bring from the east and gather from the west,"
So says the Almighty King

"You are my witnesses...my servant whom I chose
So you know and understand, I am *He*
And before *me*...no god was ever formed
And none will be *after* me

"I am the Lord and there is no other Savior
I declared and saved and proclaimed
I...and not some foreign god among you
You are my *witnesses* to my name

"Yes, since the ancient days...I am He
No one delivers out of my hand
And when I work...who can hinder it?"
Hear now what He has planned

"For your sake I will send out the Babylonians
As fugitives...those I will bring
Even the Chaldeans, in all of their proud ships
I am the Lord, the Holy One, your King

"I make a way in the sea, a path in the water
Bring army and reinforcements together
And they will lay down there...extinguished
And they will rise up again...never

"Forget the former things, dwell not on the past
Behold...I am doing a new thing
Now it springs up, do you not perceive it?
A new way in the desert I bring

"I make rivers of waters for my chosen people
Yet you have not *called* upon me
Nor *honored* me but *wearied* me *instead* with your *sin*
State your case...do you not see?"

The Servant of the Lord God

"The Lord God gave me the ability to teach
So I can make the weary strong
Morning by morning He awakens me
I listen all along

"I offered my back to those who beat me
And my cheeks as they pulled my beard
I did not hide my face when they mocked me
Spit at me and jeered

"And because the Lord God gives me help
I will *not* be shamed
And so I set my face like flint
No disgrace upon my name"

Salvation for Zion

"Listen and hear me my people Israel
My law shall proceed from me
And I will establish my justice
A light to the nations it will be

"My righteousness is drawing near quickly
My salvation is on the way
And my arm shall bring justice to the nations
The isles wait in hope for what I say

"Lift up your eyes…up to the heavens
Look to the earth below
For as smoke…the heavens will vanish
And the earth wear out like clothes

"The inhabitants of earth will die like flies
But my salvation will last forever
My righteousness will not be broken
Will not be broken ever

"You people who have my law in your hearts
Fear *not* the reproach of men
And do not be terrified by their insults
The worm will *devour* them"

Awake, O arm of the Lord with strength
Long ago…was it not you?
The one who cut Rahab to pieces?
Piercing that monster through?

And when, for the crossing of the redeemed
Wasn't it *you* who dried up the sea?
And so the ransomed of the Lord will return
Entering Zion with singing and glee

Everlasting joy will be upon their heads
They will be filled with gladness
Sorrow and sighing will flee away
And there will be no sadness

"I, even I…am He that comforts you
Who are *you* that you fear mortal men
And forget your Creator who stretched out the heavens
And laid earth's foundation then?

"You fear every day, the fury of the oppressor
As he prepares his destruction spree
Where is the fury of the oppressor now?
The prisoners will soon be set free

"I am the Lord your God who makes the waves roar
The Lord Almighty is His name
I put my words in your mouth and I cover you
The people of Zion...I claim"

The Cup of the Wrath of the Lord

Awaken, awaken...arise O Jerusalem!
Who drank from the Lord's fury cup!
You who drained the goblet that makes men stagger
Making it hard to stand up

Of all of the sons she bore and raised
There were none to take her hand
Famine and sword and destruction and ruin
Can no one console you in the land?

Your sons lay dead at the heads of every street
As animals caught in a net
They are full of the fury of the Almighty Lord
The rebuke of your God...they met

Therefore, hear this, you afflicted and drunken
Drunken, but not from wine
Your Lord who defends you sends this message
Hear the words...of the Divine

"I am taking from your hand, the cup of my wrath
And from it, you will not drink again
I will give it to your oppressors who said to you
'Bow down so we can walk on you then'"

Awake O Zion and dress yourself in strength
Jerusalem...dress in splendor too
O Holy City...the uncircumcised and defiled
Will no longer enter you

Arise O Jerusalem and sit enthroned
O captive daughter of Zion
The bands have loosed themselves from your neck
Hear the word of the Judah Lion

"For you have been sold for nothing," He says
"And not by money are you redeemed
My people went to Egypt, but Assyria oppressed them
And my name is constantly blasphemed

"Therefore, my people will know my name
And that this was foretold by me
Therefore in that day, it is I who is speaking
Surely... I am He"

How beautiful on the mountain are the feet of those
Of those who bring good news
Proclaiming peace, good tidings and salvation
"Your God reigns," they tell the Jews

Your watchmen have lifted their voices together
Together in joyful cries
For on the day the Lord returns to Zion
They'll see it... with their own eyes

Break forth in songs of joy together
O ruins of Jerusalem
For the Lord is comforting His people
And He is *redeeming* them

And the Lord will lay bare His holy arm
Before the eyes of all the nations
And all of the people to the ends of the earth
Will see... our God's salvation

Turn aside, turn aside and go out from there
And touch no unclean thing
Leave from her midst and be pure, you who carry
The weapons of Jehovah the King

But you will not go out in haste or in flight
For the Lord will go before you
And the rear guard who protects your back
Is the God of Israel too

The Suffering and Exaltation of the Servant

My Servant acts wisely...is high and lifted up
And He has been exalted
So many were astonished at His appearance
So disfigured...so assaulted

He will sprinkle many nations...and regarding *Him*
Kings will shut their mouths in the land
For what they were not told...and have not heard
They will see...and understand

He grew as a tender plant before Him
As a root growing out of dry ground
Majesty or appearance to make us desire Him
These things...were not found

Despised...rejected...a Man of sorrows
Acquainted with illness extreme
And as one from whom...men hide their faces
Him...we did *not* esteem

Surely He has borne our infirmities
And He has carried our pain
And yet we considered Him plagued by God
Afflicted by God's disdain

But He was pierced for *our* transgressions
Bruised for *our* iniquity
And by His chastisement...and by His wounds
Are peace and healing for you and me

For all of us like sheep have wandered
Each turned to his own way
And the Lord laid on *Him* the punishment
For *all* of us...that day

Oppressed and afflicted...yet He did not speak
As a lamb to slaughter He was led
Plagued by the transgressions of my people
Standing in their stead

And He was assigned a grave with the wicked
Yet in His *death*...with the elite
Because *He* had done no violence
Nor in *His* mouth...deceit

Yet it *was* the Lord's will to bruise Him
And to subject Him to *suffering*
And though a guilt offering is made of His soul
He will *yet* see...His offspring

And the will of the Lord prospers in His hand
He'll see the fruit of His suffering there
And by His knowledge He will justify many
Their *iniquities*...He will bear

I will give a portion to Him among the many
He'll divide the spoils with the strong
Because *He* has exposed His soul to death
And the sins of many...He has borne

THE FUTURE GLORY OF JERUSALEM

"Sing childless woman...who never gave birth
Burst into joyful song
For more are the offspring of the desolate woman
Than the woman with a husband all along

"Enlarge the place of your tent," says the Lord
"Stretch the curtains wide
Lengthen your cords...strengthen your stakes
For you'll spread to the right and left side

"Your descendants will possess other nations
Making desolate cities live
Fear not, you won't be ashamed or confounded,"
So says the One who forgives

"For your Creator is your Husband
The Lord Almighty is His name
The Holy One of Israel...your Redeemer
God of all earth...the same

"I turned away in anger…and left you for a moment
But in mercy…will I *gather* you
And with everlasting loving-kindness
I'll have compassion on you too

"In the days of Noah…I swore an oath
That I would never flood the earth as then
So also have I sworn to not be angry with you
Or rebuke you…ever again

"Though mountains leave and hills are removed
My loving-kindness will not depart
Neither will my covenant of peace be removed,"
Says the Lord, with mercy in His heart

"Oh storm-tossed, afflicted, uncomforted city
I lay with sapphires…your foundation
I make your pinnacles of rubies…your gates of garnet
Your border…precious stones of variation

"And all of your children will be taught of the Lord
Abundant will be their peace
You will establish yourself in righteousness
Your oppression and fear will cease

"Whoever may attack you will surrender
A destroyer to destroy I prepared
No weapon formed against you will prosper
And words against *you*…will be snared

"This is the inheritance of the servants
The servants of the Lord
This is their vindication from me," He said
These…He will reward

"All who are thirsty, come to the waters
Even he without money to dine
Come buy and eat without money and price
Come buy milk and wine

"Why work for things that do not satisfy?
Listen diligently
Eat good and your soul will delight itself
Listen and come to me

"Listen to me...so your *soul* may live
A lasting covenant I'll make with *you*
My faithful love that I promised to David
I made *him* a witness too

"*He* was a leader and commander of people
You'll call nations you don't know
And nations who don't know *you*...will run to you
Because of the Lord your God, it is so

"For the Holy One of Israel has beautified you"
Seek Him while He can be found
For the Lord has mercy and pardons the repentant
Let the wicked turn around

"My thoughts are not your thoughts," says the Lord,
"And your ways are not my ways
My ways and my thoughts are *higher* than yours"
The words of the Lord amaze

"As the rain and the snow fall from Heaven
And neither return thereto
Without watering the earth and causing it to yield
And so my word does too

"So is my word...that goes out from my mouth
It will not return empty to me
But it will accomplish and it will achieve
What I sent it for *purposely*

"You will go out in joy and be led forth in peace
The hills go before you and sing
And all of the trees in the field clap their hands,"
So says the Almighty King

"Instead of the briar the myrtle tree will grow
Instead of the thornbush, the pine
And this shall happen for the Lord's renown
For an everlasting sign

"Be just and do what is right," says the Lord
"My salvation is close at hand
My righteousness will soon be revealed
And blessed will be the man

"Blessed will be the man who does this
The man who holds on tight
Who keeps from polluting the Sabbath
Does no evil...does what is right"

Do not let the foreigner who follows the Lord
Say, "The Lord will surely *exclude* me"
And do not let the eunuch complain to you
Saying, "I am but a dry *tree*"

For the eunuchs who keep the Lord's Sabbath
And keep His covenants too
And choose to do what pleases *Him*
The Lord has a promise for you

"I will give them a place in my house and a name
Better than a daughter or son
An everlasting name that will not be cut off,"
So says the Holy One

And He says to the foreigners who follow Him
Who serve Him and love His name
Who worship Him and keep the Sabbath
And His covenant...proclaim

"These I will bring to my holy mountain
And give them joy in my house of prayer
I will accept their burnt offerings and sacrifices
Upon my altar there

"My house will be a house of prayer for all nations,"
The gatherer of Israel declares
"And again I will gather still others to those
Already gathered there"

All of you beasts of the field and forest
Come here and devour
Israel's watchmen are blind and lack knowledge
Mute dogs...without power

Laying down and dreaming, they love to sleep
Greedy dogs who are never satisfied
Undiscerning shepherds who turn to their own way
Seeking what their gain will provide

They say, "Come, we'll get wine and fill ourselves
Much strong drink we will pour
And as abundant as today has been
Tomorrow...even more!"

The righteous die and no one thinks about it
They don't ponder it in their hearts
The devout are taken...but no one understands
They are spared before the evil starts

Those who are righteous enter into peace
And in their beds they rest
"But *you*...offspring of adulterers and prostitutes
Come *here*...you sons of a sorceress

"Who do you mock and stick out your tongue at?
You burn with passion 'neath the trees
Are you not the offspring of sinners and liars?
You slaughter *children* in the valleys

"You worshiped idols and sacrificed to them
Should I be *happy* with you?
You put your pagan symbols behind your doors
They are now your inheritance too

"You were tired from the multitude of idols you tried
But wouldn't say… 'It is of no avail.'
And you *did* find a renewal of your strength
And so your health didn't fail

"Who is it that you have so dreaded and feared
That you *forgot* me… and fail to see?
Is it because I have been silent for so long
That you do *not*… fear *me*?

"I will expose your works and righteousness
But they will do you no good
When you cry for help, let your idols save you!"
If the whole collection could

"The wind will come and carry them away
A mere breath will blow and take them
Yet the man who trusts *me*… will inherit the land
And possess my holy mountain"

And it will be said, "Build the road for my people!
Move the obstacles out of the way!"
For the One who lives forever, whose name is holy
This is what *He* does say

"I live in the high and holy place
And I also live with him
With he who has a contrite and humble spirit
To revive his spirit within

"For I will not fight against you forever
Angry I will not always be
For the spirit of all of the men I have made
They would grow faint before *me*

"He was dishonest for profit and so I was angry
I punished him for going astray
I hid my face from him in anger
Yet he continued his willful way

"But I will heal and guide and give comfort to him
His mourners' mourning will cease
But as the driven sea...the wicked cannot rest
For the wicked...there is no peace"

TRUE AND FALSE FASTING

"Shout it out loud and do not hold back
Like a trumpet, raise your voice
Declare to my people their transgression
The house of Jacob sins by choice

"As though they were a nation of righteousness
They seek me every day
And as though they did not *forsake* my commands
They desire to know my ways

"They ask me for righteous judgments
And desire for God to draw near
'Why have we fasted and you didn't see it?'
Are the questions that I hear

"But on the day of your fast you seek your own pleasure
And oppress the workers you enlist
Look...you only fast to quarrel and fight
And to hit with a wicked fist

"You can't fast this way and expect to be heard
Isn't the fast that is chosen by me
To loose the chains of injustice and undo the yoke
And the oppressed...to free?

"Is it not to feed the hungry and clothe the naked
And to bring the poor wanderers home?
And as to your family...your flesh and blood
To not turn away from your own?

"Then your light will break through like the dawn
Your healing...you'll quickly find
Your righteousness will go before you
The Lord will guard you from behind

"*Then* when you call...the Lord will answer
And He will say, 'Here am I.'
If you eliminate oppression and malicious talk
Then He will hear your cry

"If you work on behalf of the hungry
And the needs of the oppressed
Then your night will be like the noontime
For your light...will rise in darkness

"*Then* the Lord will guide you *continually*
And satisfy your spirit too
You will be like a well-watered garden
And He will *strengthen* you

"Your people will build up the ancient ruins
Which remained for generations
And you will be called rebuilder of walls
You will raise the old foundations

"If you keep your feet from breaking the Sabbath
Doing as you please on my holy day
If you honor the Sabbath and delight in it
Without going your own way

"*Then* you will find your joy in the Lord
I will cause you to ride high on the land
And give you the inheritance I promised to Jacob,"
So says...the Great I Am

Warning Against Sin

The arm of the Lord isn't too weak to save you
Nor His ear too deaf to hear your call
But your sins have *separated* you from God
He turned away...and won't listen at all

For your hands have been polluted with blood
Your fingers are filthy with sin
Your tongues are muttering wicked things
Your lips speak lies from within

No one calls for justice or uses integrity
Whenever they plead their case
They speak lies, trust vanity and conceive trouble
And birth evil in its place

They run to do evil and shed innocent blood
Their thoughts are thoughts of sin
Not knowing peaceful ways, they leave destruction
Wherever they have been

So we cannot find any justice among us
We know nothing of living right
We seek brightness...but walk in obscurity
And find darkness...when we seek light

Like the blind we feel our way along a wall
But we cannot see ahead
We stumble at noon as though it were twilight
In desolate places...as the dead

We growl like bears and moan like doves
We wait for justice...there is *none*
For our offenses multiply and our sins testify
And far from us...is salvation

In rebellion and treachery against the Lord
From God...we did depart
We speak oppression, revolt and falsehoods
Conceived and uttered...from the heart

So justice is driven backward
Righteousness not at the center
For truth has been feeble in the streets
And honesty cannot enter

Whoever shuns evil makes himself the *prey*
Truth is nowhere to be found
The Lord God looked and He was displeased
For no justice was around

He wondered that there was no intercessor
He saw that there was none
So by His own arm He brought salvation
And His righteousness upheld the One

He put on righteousness as a breastplate
A helmet of salvation on His head
He put on garments of vengeance for clothing
And wore zeal as a cloak instead

He'll repay wrath and retribution to His enemies
According to what they have done
From the west they will fear the name of the Lord
And His glory from the rising of the sun

When the adversary shall come in like a flood
God's Spirit will lift a banner against him
A Redeemer will come to those in Zion in Jacob
To those who repent of their sin

"This is my covenant with them," said the Lord
"My Spirit...who is on you
And my words that I have put in your mouth
Depart not...from your mouth too

"And also from the mouths of your children,"
The Lord went on to proclaim,
"And from your children's children...from now to the end,"
Said the One...who will forever reign

ZION'S GLORY

"Arise and shine for your light has come
And God's glory rises upon you
For behold...darkness shall cover the earth
Thick darkness on the people too

"But the Lord will arise upon you
On you, His glory will be seen
The nations will come to your light
And kings to your rising sheen

"See them gathering themselves together
Lift up your eyes and see
Your sons are coming from far away
Your daughters, carried will be

"Then you will look and you will be radiant
Your heart will throb and swell
The abundance of the seas shall be brought to you
And the wealth of the nations as well

"A multitude of camels shall cover your land
From Midian and Ephah they will come
They will come from Sheba bearing incense and gold
Proclaiming God, the Holy One

"All the flocks of Kedar will be brought to you
The rams of Nebaioth will serve you
They will be accepted as offerings on my altar
And my temple I will glorify anew

"The ships of Tarshish will bring your sons
Their silver and gold they will render
To the honor of your God, the Holy One of Israel
For *He* has endowed you with splendor

"Foreigners will come and rebuild your walls
Their kings will come and serve you
For though in my anger I have struck you before
In favor I have mercy on you too

"And your gates will always stand open
They will not be shut, night or day
The nations will bring you their wealth and serve you
Those who don't...will perish away

"The sons of your oppressors and all who despise you
Will come to you, bowing down
Saying, 'City of Jehovah, Zion of the Holy One,'
With their faces to the ground

"Instead of you being forsaken and hated
With no one traveling through
The joy of generations and forever excellent
I will make of you

"And you will drink the milk of nations
Nurse at breasts of royalty
You will know I am your Savior and Redeemer
And the Mighty One of Jacob is Me

"Instead of bronze, I will bring you gold
Instead of iron, silver you'll own
Instead of wood, I will bring you bronze
And iron in place of stone

"Peace will govern you and righteousness will rule
No more violence heard in your land
No more ruin or destruction within your borders"
All *this* by the work of God's hand

"The sun will no longer be your light by day
Nor the moon by night
For God will be your glory forevermore
And the Lord...your everlasting light

"The days of your mourning will be ended
And righteous your people will be
And they will possess the land forever
They're the shoot that was planted by me

"The work of my hands, that I may be glorified
The smallest will become a mighty nation
I am the Lord God...And when it is time
This...I will hasten"

The Good News of the Lord

The Spirit of the Lord is upon me
For He has *anointed* me
To preach the good news to the poor
And to set the captives free

To heal the brokenhearted
Release prisoners from the dark
To proclaim the year of favor of the Lord
And the day His vengeance will mark

To comfort the mourners and give them beauty
Beauty instead of ashes
Oil of joy instead of mourning…and a garment of praise
If in despair…their spirit crashes

He is calling them trees of righteousness
Plantings He created
And they will rebuild the ancient ruins
Restoring places…devastated

They will renew the ruined cities
Desolate for generations
Foreigners will work your flocks and fields
You'll feed on the wealth of nations

You will be called the "Priests of the Lord"
"Ministers of God"…your name
And my people will receive a double portion
Instead of confusion and shame

"For I, the Lord, love justice
I hate robbery and wrong
In my faithfulness I will reward them
With a covenant ever long

"Their descendants will be known among the nations
And the people will attest
All who see them will acknowledge them
As a people the Lord has blessed"

I delight in the Lord…my soul rejoices in my God
He clothed me in garments of salvation
He covered me with a robe of righteousness
As a bride and groom dress for celebration

For as the soil makes the sprout come up
And seeds grow in garden locations
So the Lord will make righteousness and praise
Spring up...before all of the nations

A New Name for Zion

For Zion's sake...I will not be silent
I do not rest...for Jerusalem's concerns
Until her righteousness shines out like brightness
And her salvation...as a torch that burns

And the nations will see your righteousness
Your honor all kings will know
And a brand new name will be given to you
That the Lord Himself will bestow

You'll be a crown of beauty in the hand of the Lord
And no longer called "Forsaken"
For the Lord will say, "My delight is in *her*"
And in marriage, your hand is taken

For as a young man marries a maiden
Your Builder will marry you too
And as a bridegroom rejoices over his bride
Your God will rejoice over you

I have posted watchmen on Jerusalem's walls
They won't be silent night or days
And you who call on the Lord...take no rest
Until He makes her worthy of praise

He has sworn by His right hand and mighty arm,
"I will never again give your grain
As food for your enemies...nor will they drink your wine
Your labor will not have been in vain

"For the harvesters will eat it and praise the Lord
And in my holy courts...drink the wine"
Prepare the way for the people and clear the highway
For the nations...raise a sign

God says to the world, "Tell the Zion daughters,
'Look…here comes your salvation!'
And for the redeemed of the Lord, He brings rewards"
And you *are*…the City not Forsaken

The Day of God's Vengeance

Who is this who is coming from Edom
His garments from Bozrah stained red?
Who is this who is glorious in His royal apparel?
In great strength…He moves ahead

"*I* who speak in righteousness, mighty to save"
But why are your garments red
Like those of one who treads in a winepress?
"For in the winepress…I have tread

"I have trodden in the winepress alone
Not one man from a nation with me
And I have trodden them down in my anger
Trampled them down in my fury

"Their blood is sprinkled upon my garments
And stained…my garments appear
For the day of vengeance was in my heart
And the year of my redemption is here

"I looked and was appalled that no one gave support
There was *no one* to be found
My own arm gave salvation and my wrath supported me
I poured the nations' blood on the ground"

Praises to the Lord

I will tell of the kind deeds of the Lord
For which He must be praised
The many good things He has done for Israel
His mercies and kindness amaze

"Surely they are my people," said the Lord,
"Sons who will not lie"
And He became their Savior and lifted them up
And carried them in days gone by

Yet they rebelled and grieved His Holy Spirit
So He became their *enemy*
Then the people remembered the days of Moses
Where is *He* who brought them through the sea?

Where is *He* who put His Holy Spirit among them?
Who sent His power to Moses' right hand
To make for Himself an everlasting name
By parting the seas for dry land

Who led the people through the depths
Like a horse in the wilderness?
They did not stumble...and as cattle in a valley
His Spirit gave them rest

Look down from Heaven and see from your throne
Where is your might and your zeal?
Do you withhold your tender mercies from us?
But you're our Father...*that* is real

Abraham or Israel don't acknowledge or know us
But you're our Father...just the same
And you O Lord...you are our Redeemer
Everlasting is your name

Why do you make us wander from your ways
And harden our hearts to not revere you?
Return to us for the sake of your servants
The tribes of your inheritance too

For a little while we possessed your holy place
But by our enemies...trampled it became
We were *always* yours...but them you *never* ruled
Nor *upon* them is your name

Oh that you would rend the heavens and come down
The mountains would tremble before you
Come and make your enemies know your name
And make the *nations* tremble *too*

When you *did* awesome things that we did not expect
The mountains *trembled* when you came
And since ancient times no one has seen nor heard
Of any God by any *other* name

No other god acts on behalf of His followers
Only *you* help those who do right
And though you get angry when we continue to sin
Yet...we are saved in your sight

We have all become...as one who is unclean
Our righteous acts are as garments in decay
We fade as a leaf...and our sins, like the wind
Have carried us away

Yet you are our Father...We're the work of your hand
You're the potter...We're the clay
Don't be angry or remember our sins forever
We're your people...Look at us we pray

Your holy cities and Zion became wilderness
Jerusalem...a desolation
Our glorious temple has been burned with fire
Our treasures lie in devastation

After considering all of this O Lord
Will you yourself restrain?
Will you punish us beyond all measure
As silent...you remain?

GOD'S RIGHTEOUS JUDGMENT

"I've been inquired of by those who did not ask
Found by those...not *seeking* me
And to a nation that was *not* calling in my *name*
I said, 'Here I am...I am He'

"I have held out my hands to an apostate people
Who walk in a way not good
They follow their own thoughts and provoke me
Rather than do as they should

"They burn incense on altars made of brick
In gardens they sacrifice
They sit among graves and spend their time
In secret vigil...in the night

"'Keep to yourself...Do not come near me
I've declared you unholy,' they say
These people are a smoke in my anger
A fire that burns all the day

"Look, it is written...I will not keep silent
In full...I *will* recompense
For your sins and the sins of your fathers
Past and present offense

"For they have made sacrifices on the mountains
And on hills they have defied me
I'll measure the full payment for their past deeds
And into their laps it will be

"As new wine is found in the cluster of grapes
'Do not destroy it!' they call
'There's a blessing inside!'...And so for my servants
I will *not*...destroy them all

"I will bring from Judah, possessors of my mountain
I will bring out from Jacob, a seed
And my chosen people will *possess* my mountain
My servants will dwell there indeed

"Sharon and the Achor Valley for flocks and herds
For my *people* who *have* sought me
But for those of you who *forsake* the Lord
I issue a *different* decree

"For those who forget my holy mountain,"
So says the Holy Lord,
"Who set a table for Fortune and wine for Destiny
I have numbered *you*...for the sword

"And you will all bend down for the slaughter
For you do evil in my eyes
I called, you didn't answer...I spoke, you didn't listen
And you chose...what I despise

"So my servants will eat but you will go hungry,"
The Holy Lord proclaimed
"My servants will drink...but you will go thirsty
They'll rejoice but you will be shamed

"My servants will sing from the joy in their hearts
But you'll cry from your heart's pain
You will wail from the breaking of your spirit
And you will *leave* your name

"You'll leave your name to my chosen as a curse
You'll be put to death by the Lord
But to the faithful servants of the Holy One
Another name He will award"

A New Heaven and a New Earth

"Behold I will create a new earth and new heavens
Remembered no more...the former things
A delightful new Jerusalem and a people of joy
So rejoice in the creation I bring

"And I myself will take delight in my people
In Jerusalem my joy will soar
And the sound of weeping and crying
Will be heard in it no more

"Never again will an infant live just a few days
Or an old man not live out his years
One who dies at a hundred will be thought of as young
And any *younger*...*cursed* he appears

"They'll live in houses they've built and eat the fruit
Of vineyards they plant in the lands
They will no longer build and plant for others
They'll enjoy the work of their hands

"They and their offspring will be blessed by the Lord
And they will not toil in vain
I'll hear them and answer while they are speaking
Before they call my name

"The wolf and the lamb will feed together
The lion like the ox, will eat straw
The serpent will eat dust...and on my holy mountain
They'll neither harm nor destroy anymore

"Heaven is my throne and the earth is my footstool
Where is the house you build for me?
All of these things came into being by my hand
Where will *my* resting place be?

"I favor one who is humble and trembles at my word
But he who kills an ox...kills a man
And like one who breaks the neck of a dog
Is the one who offers a lamb

"Like one who offers the blood of a swine
Is the one who offers an oblation
They chose their own ways and their souls delight
In their abomination

"And so I also...will choose their vexations
And bring on them what they dread
For I called and none answered and when I spoke
No one listened to what I said

"They do the things that are evil in my sight
And choose what displeases me"
Now you who tremble at the word of the Lord
Hear what is going to be

"Your brethren who hate you and exclude you
And cast you out because my name
Said, 'Glorify the Lord...so we can see your joy!'
But they will be put to shame

"A voice of tumult from the temple in the city
It is the voice of the Lord
He is rendering recompense to His enemies
Their terrible reward

"Before she goes into labor and feels any pain
She has given birth
Who has ever seen or heard of such a thing?
A nation born in one day on earth"

"Do I bring to the birth and not give delivery?
Do I close up the womb?
Rejoice with Jerusalem...all you who love her
And all who mourn for her in gloom

"For you will nurse and you will be satisfied
At her consoling breast
You will drink from the abundance of her glory
And you will be greatly blessed

"I will extend peace to her like a river
And as an overflowing stream
She will receive the honor of nations
Great is her esteem

"You will nurse and be carried on her side
And dandled on her knee
And I will comfort you in Jerusalem
And comforted...you will be"

Your hearts will rejoice and you will flourish
When all these things you see
The Hand of God will be shown to His servants
But fury...to His enemy

Behold...the Lord is coming with fire
His chariots...as a hurricane
He will punish with the fury of His anger
His rebuke...a fiery flame

For with His sword and with His fire
The Lord will judge all men
And when He executes His judgment
Many will be slain right then

Those sanctifying and cleansing themselves in gardens
And following Ahad in the midst
Who eat the sow, the abomination and the mouse
A declaration of the Lord is this

"Together they will be consumed," says the Lord
"Their works and thoughts are before me
I am coming to gather all nations and tongues
They will come and see my glory

"I'll set a sign among them...and send survivors
To nations who don't know my fame
To Tarshish, Libya, Greece and others
And my glory...they will proclaim

"And they will bring your brethren from all nations
To my holy mountain...Jerusalem
On horses and camels...on chariots and wagons
As a present to the Lord from them

"Then I will select Priests from the sons of Israel
And as before me shall remain
The new heavens and the new earth that I create
So shall your seed...and your name

"And from month to month and Sabbath to Sabbath
All mankind will bow before *me*
They'll go see the burning bodies of those who rebelled
And loathsome will be what they see"

Ezekiel

VISION OF THE LIVING BEINGS

Ezekiel the priest received the word of the Lord
Beside the River Kebar
The heavens opened and he saw a windstorm
Coming from afar

He saw a huge cloud with lightning flashing
Surrounded by brilliant light
The center was fire...then four living creatures
Began to come into sight

Their form was as men, but each had four faces
And each of them had four wings
They all had straight legs and gleaming calf feet
As he looked, he saw *other* things

Each creature had the face of an eagle
With the face of a lion on the right
And the face of an ox on the left
And wings spread up in flight

Fire flew back and forth among them
As the creatures sped straight ahead
They did not turn...yet followed the Spirit
Wherever the Spirit led

Each of the creatures had a wheel beside it
Which sparkled like chrysolite
Each wheel had a cross-wheel and without ever turning
They changed their course in flight

The rims of the wheels were awesome and large
And filled with eyes all around
The spirit was in the wheels and moved with the creatures
Whether up...or on the ground

Over the heads of the creatures was a vast expanse
Which sparkled as crystal would be
Their wings made a sound like rushing water
Like the voice...of the Almighty

As the creatures stood...with lowered wings
Above their heads he saw
A sapphire throne and the figure of a man
Ezekiel stood in awe

From the waist up He appeared as glowing metal
And as fire...from the waist down
Radiance shone round Him like a rainbow in a cloud
Ezekiel fell prostrate on the ground

Then a voice said, "Son of man, stand to your feet
And I will speak to you"
Ezekiel felt the Spirit enter and lift him
Then God *told* him what to do

"I am sending you to the Israelites," said the Lord,
"To a rebellious nation
They and their fathers have revolted against me"
He spoke of generations

"They are obstinate and stubborn," He continued
"Tell them what I say
Whether they listen or not, they'll know that a prophet
Was *there* with them that day

"Do not be afraid of them or whatever they say
Though thorns are *all* around you
Walk among the scorpions and tell them my words
But do not do what they do"

Then the Lord gave Ezekiel a scroll full of words
Words of lament and woe
He told him to go warn the house of Israel
But first...he must eat the scroll

The scroll was as sweet as honey in his mouth
Then the Lord said…"Go your way"
Ezekiel heard the rumble of the wheels and the wings
As the Spirit carried him away

He came to the exiles and sat among them
Overwhelmed, for seven days
Then the word of the Lord came and told him
To warn them to change their ways

The Lord *told* him that if he *doesn't* warn an evil man
As He had *sent* him to do
Then the man will die in his sin…and Ezekiel
Would be accountable *too*

But if Ezekiel warns the man and he pays no attention
Then he himself is saved
Likewise, if he warns *good* men who've gone bad
And in evil…have behaved

Then the Lord showed Ezekiel the siege of Jerusalem
And the people being led into exile
For they practiced idolatry and sacrificed their children
And the Temple they defiled

They were more evil than the nations around them
They rebelled against God's law
So He will do to them in front of the nations
What He had never done before

Then the Lord told Ezekiel to tell all the people
That because of their grave sin
That one third will perish by plague and famine
Because He will *turn* from them

Another third will be scattered to the winds
A third by the sword will fall
And the third who will perish by the sword
Will die outside of the walls

Then His anger will cease and His wrath subside
And the Israelites will know
That He is the Lord and He paid them for their sins
And it was *He* that struck the blow

Then over the years the Lord continued
Through Ezekiel to prophesy
And He told him that Israel would be restored
After many years went by

Prophecies Against the Nations

Sometime later God gave Ezekiel a vision
For the nations of the Middle East
That He would set His face against them
Both the largest and the least

To the nations to the North and South of Israel
He foretold what He would do
He spoke of the nations to the East and the West
And His words would all come true

Prophecy Against Ammon

"You rejoiced at the desecration of my Temple," He said
"And because you cheered with glee
Over Israel's destruction and the people's exile
I will give you to the people of the East

"They will set their tents and camps among you
And harvest the fruit of your land
I will make Rabbah and your nation into pastures
And you will know it was by my hand"

Prophecy Against Moab

"Because you and Seir said that Judah is the same
As all of the other nations
I will allow your border towns to be attacked
Overrun in their locations

"Starting with Jeshimoth, Baal Meon and Kiriathaim
Your nation will fall by the sword
I will *give* you to the people of the East as a possession
Then you will know that *I* am the Lord"

PROPHECY AGAINST EDOM

"Because you acted in revenge on the people of Judah
And are guilty for doing so
I will raise my hand against you," declares the Lord,
"And my vengeance you will know

"I will lay to waste the land of Edom
From Teman to Dedan
I will kill your men and your animals
By my people Israel's hand"

PROPHECY AGAINST PHILISTIA

"Because with vengeance and malice in your hearts
You Philistines did act
With ancient hostility you sought to destroy
And Judah...you attacked

"So I will raise my hand and destroy the Kerethites
And those remaining by the sea
When I punish them they will know I am the Lord
And the vengeance is from me"

PROPHECY AGAINST TYRE

After the fall of Jerusalem, the Lord told Ezekiel
About yet *another* nation
For when wealthy Tyre saw Jerusalem fall
They rejoiced in celebration

"I will bring many nations against you," said the Lord
"Your walls, they will tear down
I will sweep away the rubble so all that is left
Is bare rock upon the ground

"From the North I will bring Nebuchadnezzar
The king of Babylon
He will kill your people with the sword
Your city will be gone"

Then He spoke about the merchants of the world
Who had come to Tyre's port
To trade livestock, jewels, food and fabrics
And wares of every sort

The kings of the coast will shudder in fear
As they look upon Tyre's shore
The merchants of the world will be astounded
For Tyre will be no more

Prophecy Against Sidon

"I am against you and will gain glory within you
And you will know that I am the Lord
When I send a plague upon you O Sidon
And place all around you...a sword

"When I gather the scattered people of Israel
And bring them back by my own hand
They will know that I am the Lord their God
And they will live in their own land

"The land that I gave to my servant Jacob
They will plant and they will build
I will punish their neighbors who despise them"
His prophecy would be fulfilled

Prophecy Against Egypt

"When the people of Israel tried to lean on you
You were nothing but a broken staff
When they reached out to you for your support
You did nothing on their behalf

"I am against you O Pharaoh, king of Egypt
'I *own* the Nile,' you said
I will bring a sword against you," said the Lord
"Your men and animals will be dead."

"I will make the land of Egypt a ruin
From Migdol to Aswan
And as far as the border of Ethiopia
And no one will live thereon

"I will scatter the Egyptians among the nations
Your cities in ruin will lie
No one will pass through and no one will live there
Until forty years go by"

THE SHEPHERDS OF ISRAEL

"Woe to the shepherds of Israel," said the Lord,
"Who do not take care of the sheep
You haven't healed the sick or bandaged the injured
You haven't strengthened the weak

"You have not brought back the strays," He said,
"Or gone to look for the lost
You have ruled with a harsh and brutal hand
And my sheep have suffered the cost

"And without a shepherd they became scattered
For wild animals, they were plunder
You took care of yourselves instead of my flock
And they have gone asunder

"So I will hold you accountable," He continued,
"And remove you from your stations
And I will find and rescue my sheep *myself*
And bring them out of the nations

"I will bring them to graze on the hills of Israel
Bring them to their own land
I will bandage up the injured and heal them
By the touch of my own hand

"I will shepherd my flock with justice
And I will strengthen the weak
My flock will no longer be plundered
I will judge between the sheep

"And the fat and powerful... I will destroy
Is it not enough that you eat the best?
It is not enough that you drink the clearest water?
Must you also trample the rest?

"I will make a covenant of peace with my people
The wild beasts I will rid from the land
I will send showers of blessings upon them
And save them from enemy hands

"They will no longer be plunder for other nations
Now crops their land will afford
They will live in safety and know I am with them
Declares the Sovereign Lord"

Another Prophecy Against Edom

Again the Lord prophesied against Edom
Speaking of its doom
Because Edom had come against Israel
Edom would lay in ruin

He said because of their ancient hatred of Israel
They butchered them with the sword
So He will make them a desolate waste forever
Then they will *know*... that He is the Lord

Prophecy to the Mountains of Israel

Then the Lord prophesied to the mountains of Israel
Where the nations on every side
Had plundered them to take possession
Boasting in their pride

He spoke to the mountains and hills of Israel
The valleys and the ravines
The deserted towns and desolate ruins
And all of the land in between

He spoke against the surrounding nations
For with malice and with glee
They plundered His land to make it their own
And raised His jealousy

"I swear with uplifted hand," said the Lord,
"The nations around you will suffer scorn"
Then He spoke of restoring the nation of Israel
And how it would be reborn

"You will produce fruit for my people," He said,
"For they will soon come home
With concern and favor I will look upon you
You will be plowed and sown

"I will multiply the people of the house of Israel"
And then the Lord said more
"They will rebuild the towns and they will be
More prosperous than before

"Then you will know that I am the Lord," He said
"When my people possess the land
You will never again deprive them of their children,"
He continued to reveal His plan

"I am not doing this for your sake, O house of Israel
But for the sake of my holy name
For you have gone out among the nations," He said,
"And my name you have profaned

"And when I *take* you from the nations and *gather* you
And bring you back to your own land
Then the nations will *know* that I am the Lord
Who returned you by my hand

"I will cleanse you from your filthiness and idols
I will put a new Spirit in you
I will remove from you…your heart of stone
And replace it with a heart of flesh too

"I will put my Spirit in you to cause you to follow
My judgments and my law
And you will live in the land that I had given
To your fathers before

"You will be my people and I will be your God
And I will make you clean
I will bring grain and you will not have famine"
He continued to reveal the scene

"I will increase the harvest of fruit from your trees
And the harvest of crops in your field
So the nations can no longer scoff at your land
For its abundance will be revealed

"Then you will *remember* your wicked deeds
And the evil things you've done
And you will *despise* yourselves for your sins,"
Continued the most Holy One

"Remember I'm not doing this because you deserve it
For you should be ashamed
You should be disgraced O house of Israel,"
The Sovereign Lord proclaimed

"On the day I cleanse you, I will resettle your towns"
The Lord promised He will do it
"The land will be cultivated…no longer desolate
In the sight of all who pass through it"

They will say it is now like the garden of Eden
Where before it had lain in waste
And the remaining nations will know He rebuilt it
When with it they are faced

THE VALLEY OF DRY BONES

The Lord showed Ezekiel a valley of dry bones
And He questioned Ezekiel then
"Son of man, can these bones live again?" He asked
And Ezekiel answered Him

"You alone know, O Sovereign Lord," he said
Then the Lord said, "Prophesy
Tell the bones 'the *Lord* said, I will give you breath
And *you* will come to life

"'I will give you tendons and put flesh upon you
And cover you with skin
I will give you breath and you'll know I'm the Lord
When you come to life again.'"

Ezekiel did as he was told and as he prophesied
He heard a rattling sound
He saw tendons and flesh appear on the bones
As they laid upon the ground

Then the Lord said to prophesy to the breath
To come from all four winds
And breathe into the slain so they would live
So Ezekiel prophesied again

The bones came to life and a vast army stood up
Ezekiel stood and he looked on
God said they are the house of Israel who *say*,
"Our bones are dry and hope is gone"

Then the Lord told Ezekiel to prophesy to them
And to tell them then,
"'I will open your graves and bring you up,' says the Lord,
'And bring you back to Israel again'

"'Then *you* my people…will know I am the Lord
When I bring you up by my hand
I will put my Spirit in you and you will live
I will settle you in your own land'"

Israel and Judah United

Again the Lord God spoke to Ezekiel
"Take two sticks of wood," He said
"Write on one of them, 'The Kingdom of Judah'"
Ezekiel listened and nodded his head

"On the other stick write 'The Kingdom of Israel'
Join them together as one in your hand
Show the people and tell them, I will bring them home
To once again live in the land

"I will make them one nation in the land of Israel
With one king over them
They will never again be two nations divided
Or worship idols again

"They will no longer do things unacceptable to me
Their sins I will wash away
They will be my people and I will be their God"
Then the Lord went on to say

"Their king will be my servant David
One shepherd there will be
And they will be careful to follow my laws
And keep my every decree

"Generation after generation will live there forever
My covenant of peace with them
I will establish them and increase their numbers"
Ezekiel listened to Him

"My sanctuary will be among them forever
I will dwell within their midst
And the nations will know, I made Israel holy
When they see all of this"

A Prophecy Against Gog

The Lord told Ezekiel to prophesy against Gog
The chief prince of Mesheck and Tubal,
"I will turn you around and put hooks in your jaws
To war you will be called

"I will bring you out with your whole army
A fully armed great horde
Persia and Cush and Put will be with you
All of them brandishing sword

"Gomer and Beth Togarmah from the far north
The many nations with *you*
Be prepared and take command of them"
Then He said what they would do

"In future years you will swoop down on Israel
A land recovered from war
Whose people were gathered from many nations
To the land of their fathers before

"You will plan an attack on a peaceful people
With evil thoughts in your mind
And Sheba, Dedan and Tarshish will also
Have thoughts of a *similar* kind

"You will advance together on my people Israel
Like a cloud that covers the sky
I will bring you against them so the nations may know me
When I show myself before their eyes

"And when you attack the land of Israel
My hot anger you will awake
Then at that time…in my fiery wrath
There will be a great earthquake

"The fish of the seas and the birds of the air
Every creature on the ground
And all of the people on the earth will tremble
And every wall will fall down

"The mountains will overturn and cliffs will crumble
I will pour down torrents of rain
And I will call forth a sword against Gog
On the mountains and the plain

"Your men will raise swords against each other
And on the nations that were sent
Burning sulphur and hail I will pour out on them
With blood and plague I send judgment

"And when I do this, my greatness and holiness
To the nations will be shown
And then they will *know* that I am the Lord
For I will make it known

"I will turn you around and bring you from the North
And drag you across the lands
I will strike your bow...and make your arrows drop
From your left and your right hands

"You will fall on the mountains of Israel
Your troops and the nations with you
I will give you as food to the birds of the air
And to the wild animals too

"You will fall on the open field," He said,
"And on Magog I will send fire
And also on those living safely on the coast"
He continued to describe His ire

"The nations will know I am the Holy One of Israel,"
Declared the One from above
"This will surely take place...This is the day
That I have spoken of

"Then those in Israel will use their weapons for fuel
For seven years, their weapons, they'll burn
And they will plunder those who plundered them
Looting *them*...in return

"And I will make a graveyard for Gog in the valley,"
Continued the word from the Lord
"The valley that is east toward the sea will be called
The Valley of Gog's Horde

"It will take seven months for Israel to bury the dead
And to cleanse the land
And the birds and wild animals will eat the flesh
As though they were goats and rams

"And I will display my glory to the nations
And the punishment of my hand
They'll know that the Israelites were unfaithful
So they were exiled from the land

"I turned my face from them and handed them over
And they all fell by the sword
I punished them for their uncleanness and their sins,"
Declared the Sovereign Lord

"I will bring them from captivity and have compassion
I will be zealous for my holy name
They'll forget their unfaithfulness when they lived in safety
And they will forget their shame

"I will gather them to their own land," He said,
"Leaving none of them behind
I will pour out my Spirit on the house of Israel,"
These prophesies for all mankind

THE GREAT TEMPLE VISION

In the twenty-fifth year of their exile
Fourteen years after the fall
God took Ezekiel to a mountain in Israel
In a vision, where he could see all

As he stood on top of the mountain
And looked across the land
He saw a city and a man who appeared as bronze
With a measuring rod in his hand

The man said, "Son of man, look with your eyes
And listen with your ears too
And then tell Israel…for it is why you are *here*
Pay attention to all that I *show* you"

Ezekiel watched as the man measured the temple
He measured the gates and the walls
He measured the courts, the rooms, the sanctuary
Ezekiel *saw* him measure it all

The walls and floors of the portico and sanctuaries
All were covered with wood
With carvings of cherubim and palm trees
He saw it *all* from where he stood

The man brought Ezekiel to the gate facing east
Where the glory of God he was shown
And the land was radiant from His glory
His voice…a rushing water tone

Then the Glory of the Lord entered the temple
And Ezekiel fell face down
The Spirit lifted him and took him to the inner court
With the Glory of the Lord all around

Then Ezekiel heard a voice from inside the temple
"Son of man," he heard it say,
"This is the place of my throne and where I will live
Among the Israelites for always

"They will never again defile my holy name
By their spiritual adultery
As they did when they placed their lifeless idols
With just a wall between them and me

"In my anger I destroyed them," said the Lord
"Now let them put away
The idols of their kings and their spiritual adultery"
And He then went on to say

"Describe the Temple to the house of Israel
So of their sin they may be ashamed
If they are...then give them the design and the laws,"
The Sovereign Lord proclaimed

He said the surrounding area will be most holy
Then He described the altar
In minute detail He planned its construction
So the people would not falter

He directed the dedication of the altar
And the sacrifices on it
On the first day a bull and then for a week
Three animals a day upon it

Then Ezekiel was brought back to the outer gate
And directions were given to him
Concerning how the people would worship and live
Which Ezekiel would give to them

From the temple flowed a river which fed the fruit trees
And the creatures of land, sea and air
And from that time on, the name of the city
Will be "THE LORD IS THERE"

Daniel

DANIEL'S TRAINING IN BABYLON

Jerusalem was attacked by Nebuchadnezzar
The Babylonian king
When he saw the treasures in the temple of God
He stole most everything

Then Nebuchadnezzar gave an order to Ashpenaz
Chief official of his court
To take men from the Israelites' royal family
And noblemen...of a certain sort

They must be handsome, smart and quick to learn
The young men he was to bring
Men who had perfect bodies and minds
To serve in the palace of the king

Teach them the language and literature of Babylon
And train them for three years time
The men would be assigned a daily amount
Of Nebuchadnezzar's food and wine

Daniel, Hananiah, Mishael and Azariah
Were some of the men who came
They were from Judah and the chief official
Gave each of them a new name

Daniel's new name would be Belteshazzar
Hananiah was renamed Shadrach
Azariah would now be known as Abednego
And Mishael became Meshach

But Daniel would not defile himself
With the royal food and wine
So he asked the official if the four of them
Could have *another* way to dine

God made the official feel compassion for them
But he was also feeling dread
For if these four men looked worse than the rest
The king would have his *head*

So Daniel asked that they be tested for ten days
Given water and vegetables to eat
And then be compared to the rest of the men
Who were fed the king's wine and meat

Ten days later...they looked better than the rest
So the official changed *everyone's* food
God also gave these four men great knowledge
In all that they were schooled

And in accordance with the order of the king
They were presented three years later
In every matter of wisdom and understanding
No one in the land was greater

NEBUCHADNEZZAR'S DREAM

Now sometime later, Nebuchadnezzar
Had a troubling dream
He called his astrologers, wizards and magicians
To ask them, "What does it mean?"

But when he told them what it was that he wanted
To their very hearts they were chilled
They had to tell *him*...*what* he had dreamed
Or else...they would *all* be killed

Of course, no one was able to tell the king
What his dream was *about*
Let alone interpret it, so they all would die
Of that...there was *no* doubt

They appealed to him, "No man can do this!"
They cried out to the king,
"And no king, *however* great and mighty
Has *ever* asked such a thing!

"What the king is asking is *much* too hard!"
They pleaded with him then
"*No one* can do this except the *gods*!
And *they* don't live among *men*!"

But at this, the king became *very* angry
Furious at *all* of them!
And so the king ordered the execution
Of *all* of his wise men

Guards were sent to find Daniel and his friends
For they would be killed too
But Daniel asked the king for time and said,
"*I* will interpret for you"

He told Shadrach, Meshach and Abednego
What was going on
They prayed to God so they wouldn't be killed
With the wise men of Babylon

The mystery was revealed when Daniel had a vision
During a midnight hour
And he praised the God of Heaven for giving him
Such wisdom and such power

Then Daniel went to the chief of the guard
Saying, "Do not *execute* them!
Take me to the king…and I will *now*
Interpret his *dream* for him!"

"Are you able to tell me," asked the king,
What I dreamed…and interpret it too?"
"No wise man, enchanter or wizard," said Daniel,
"Can explain this dream to you

"But there's a God in Heaven who reveals mysteries
And He is the *only* One
God has shown you in your dream what will happen
In days that are to come"

Then he told the king all about the dream
And the future was revealed
The king was amazed and promoted Daniel
His position in the palace...was sealed

"Surely *your* God is the God of gods," said the king
For it was plain to see
"And the *Lord* of kings...for you were able
To reveal this mystery"

Then the king placed Daniel in a high position
Lavished gifts upon him and then
Made him ruler over the province of Babylon
In charge of *all* the wise men

And in addition...at Daniel's request
The king gave new jobs to do
To Shadrach, Meshach and Abednego
And made *them* administrators too

The Image of Gold and the Fiery Furnace

Now King Nebuchadnezzar made an image of gold
The statue was gigantic in size
At nine feet wide and ninety feet tall
It stretched into the skies

Then the king summoned all of his officials
And all of them were told
Whenever anyone hears instruments playing
They must worship...the image of gold

And anyone who *doesn't* fall down and worship
Will immediately raise the king's ire
They will be seized and they will be thrown
Into a furnace of fire

From then on, whenever the people heard
Any kind of music at all
They immediately began to worship
And on their faces they'd fall

But astrologers came forward and told the king
He was not obeyed by *all*
For Shadrach, Meshach and Abednego
On *their* faces...did *not* fall

Nebuchadnezzar was *furious* with rage
And he asked them, "Is it *true*?
You *don't* serve my gods or worship the image?
As all of the others do?

"Now if you're ready to fall down and worship the image,
The image I've made...very good!
But if not, I will *throw you into the furnace!*"
And everyone knew he would

"If you throw us into the furnace," they replied
The three men taking a stand
"The God we serve...is able to save us
And rescue us from your hand

"But even if He does not, O king
We *still* want you to know
That we will *never* serve your gods
Or worship the image of gold"

"*Seize them!*" shouted Nebuchadnezzar
Now he was *really* mad
He ordered them tied from head to foot
By the strongest soldiers he had

He ordered the furnace be seven times hotter
Than any other day
But Shadrach, Meshach and Abednego were calm
They just began to pray

When the soldiers took them, to throw them in
The furnace was *so* hot
The flames of the fire *killed* the soldiers
But the other three...it did not

And when the three men *fell* into the furnace
They were *firmly* tied
But then Nebuchadnezzar leaped to his feet
"Weren't there *three*?!" he cried

"Look!" he shouted "I see *four* men!
And they are *walking around*!
The fourth one looks like a son of the *gods*!
They're unharmed and they're unbound!

"Shadrach, Meshach and Abednego!"
He *shouted* to them, "Come out!"
Then he called them servants of the Most High God
And of this…he had no doubt

And when the officials gathered around them
There was no harm that they could tell
Their hair was not singed…their robes not scorched
Not even a fiery smell

Then the king began to praise the God
Of these three faithful men
Then he stood and faced all of the people
And said to all of them

"Praises be to the God of Shadrach
Meshach and Abednego
He sent an *angel* to *rescue* them!"
He wanted everyone to know

"They trusted their God and defied my command!"
King Nebuchadnezzar said
"They refused to worship any other god
They would rather have been dead"

Then he ordered that *anyone* would be killed
If they had *anything* bad to say
Against *this* God for *no other god*
Could save *anyone* this way

Nebuchadnezzar Has Another Dream

When Nebuchadnezzar had another dream
Which put him in great fear
Again no one else could interpret his dream
So he had Daniel draw near

He said, "I know that the spirit of God is in you
So interpret this for me
In the middle of the land and visible to all
I saw an enormous tree

"It had beautiful leaves and abundant fruit
Enough to feed *everyone*
It had birds in its branches and it sheltered beasts
And then I saw a *holy* one

"I saw the holy one come down from Heaven
And he shouted, 'Cut the tree down
Trim its branches and strip off its leaves
And scatter the fruit all around

"'Let the animals and birds flee from the tree
But the stump and roots that are bound
With iron and bronze, shall remain in the field
They shall remain in the ground

"'The angels bring this verdict of the Holy One
So everyone will know then
That the Most High God rules over earth's kingdoms
And can set over them the lowest of men

"'He shall be drenched with the dew of Heaven
And eat with animals in the field
And have an animal's mind for seven years time.'
Tell me Daniel, what *does* this *reveal?*"

Daniel was troubled about the dream for a while
In fact...he was terrified
"Daniel...don't be afraid of the meaning of the dream,"
King Nebuchadnezzar cried

Daniel said sadly, "If only it was about your enemies
But the tree you saw...is you
You are great and strong...but will be cut down
And drenched with Heaven's dew

"You will live in the fields with an animal's mind
Until seven years pass by
Until you learn that the One...who is sovereign over earth
Is the Lord Most High

"And that the stump be bound with iron and bronze
And then left in the ground
Means your kingdom will be restored to you
When your thinking turns around

"Therefore O king, if you accept my counsel
Then my advice to you
Is repent and change your life...and just *perhaps*
Your prosperity...will continue"

But the king didn't listen to Daniel's advice
And twelve months later, one day
The interpretation of the dream...came to pass
And happened...just that way

THE WRITING ON THE WALL

Years later...after Nebuchadnezzar had died
The king was Belshazzar, his son
He had a great feast for a thousand of his nobles
And drank wine with everyone

He gave orders to bring in the goblets
Of silver and of gold
The same goblets that his father had *stolen*
From the Jerusalem temple of old

They praised the gods of silver...gold and bronze
Iron, wood and stone
Then a hand appeared...and wrote on the wall
Where a light, from the lampstand shone

The king watched the hand as it wrote on the wall
His face turned pale and then
He was so frightened, that his knees knocked together
And his legs gave way under him

He saw the words, "Mene, Mene, Tekel, Parsin"
What did these words *mean*?
They were words of mystery written on the wall
That no one had ever seen

Then the king cried out for all his astrologers
Enchanters, soothsayers, wise men
To come to the palace *immediately*
And gather around him *right then*!

"Whoever tells me what this writing means
Written on the wall by the hand
Will be clothed in scarlet, have a chain of gold
And made highest ruler in the land"

But all of the men that he had brought in
Couldn't read the writing at all
Then the queen, who heard the voice of the king
Came into the banquet hall

"O king live forever!...Don't be alarmed!"
The queen began to say
Then she told him all about Daniel
And his interpreting way

So Daniel was brought before the king
Who offered the reward to *him*
But when Daniel turned and looked at the wall
The words he saw...were grim

"You may keep your gifts for yourself," said Daniel
"Give your rewards to someone else
Nevertheless...I *will* read the writing to you
So you will understand yourself

"God gave your father...Nebuchadnezzar
Majesty, greatness and splendor
But his heart was arrogant and hardened with pride
Honor to God...he did not render

"So his throne was taken away from him
His glory taken too
He lived with donkeys and grazed with cattle
And his body was drenched with dew

"When he finally acknowledged that the Most High God
Rules over the kingdoms of men
And that *God* puts in place...leaders *He* chooses
Nebuchadnezzar became king again

"But you...his son...O Belshazzar
Though all of this *you knew*
Instead of *humbling* yourself...*you* had the goblets
From the temple of God brought to *you*

"You had everyone drink from those goblets
And worship false gods too
Not the God who holds your *life* in His hand!
So He sent *this* message...to *you*

"Mene...God has numbered the days of your reign
And brought it to an end
Teckel...you've been weighed on the scales and found lacking"
And Daniel finished then

"Peres...Your kingdom is divided and given," he said,
"To the Persians and the Medes"
Then King Belshazzar rewarded Daniel
For his interpreting deeds

That very night...King Belshazzar was slain
And so his reign was through
And Darius the Mede took the kingdom
At the age of sixty-two

Daniel in the Lions' Den

Now King Darius set in place, over the kingdom
One hundred and twenty men
They were to rule...but each had to answer
To three rulers...higher than them

The king made Daniel the *leader* of the *three*
Because of his excellent mind
But the others were jealous and they decided
Some *fault* with Daniel they'd find

But the leaders could find no corruption in Daniel
He was an honest and loyal man
It would have to involve...his worship of his God
So they came up with a devious plan

They went to the king and asked him to sign
An order of law right then
That anyone who prayed over the next thirty days
Would be *thrown* into the *lions'* den

Daniel knew about the law, but he went to his room
Where he knelt down on the floor
In front of the window, he prayed and thanked God
As he had always done before

The leaders reminded the king of his rule
That *no one* was allowed to pray
Then said, "Daniel pays no attention to your law
He *still* prays three times a *day*"

When the king heard this...he was greatly distressed
For Daniel was his favorite one
He pondered all day on how he could save him
He thought 'til the setting of the sun

But the men said, "Remember O king...it's the *law*
That no law of the king can be changed"
So reluctantly, King Darius gave the order
And Daniel's execution...was arranged

The king spoke to Daniel before they took him
There was nothing else he could do
"May your *God*...whom you serve *so* faithfully
Come to rescue you"

Then the guards threw Daniel into the lions' den
The entrance was sealed with a stone
And King Darius spent the night in silence
Fasting...and alone

At the first light of dawn, the king got up
And hurried to the den
He cried out to Daniel in a sorrowful voice
All was quiet...and *then*

"O king...live forever!" Daniel shouted
"My *God* sent an *angel* to me!
He *shut* the mouths of the *lions*!" he said
"I'm not hurt...as you will see!"

"They didn't hurt me for I was found *innocent*!
Innocent in God's sight!
Nor have I *ever* done wrong before *you*!"
Daniel exclaimed with might

The king was overjoyed and gave the order
To lift Daniel from the den
And when he was lifted...all could see
No wounds were found on him

Then the king gave another order to his guards
To get the families and the men
Who came to him...and spoke against Daniel
And throw *them* in the lions' den

And before they reached the floor of the den
Amid their screams and groans
The lions overpowered all of them
Crushing all of their bones

Then King Darius wrote to the people
Issuing a decree
To fear and reverence the God of Daniel
Henceforth...it was to be

"For *He* is the living God," said the king
"His mercy endures forever
His kingdom *will not* be destroyed
His dominion will end...*never*!"

Daniel's Prophesies

DANIEL'S VISION OF FOUR BEASTS

In the first year of the reign of King Belshazzar
Daniel had a dream
And in specific detail...Daniel chronicled
The amazing things he'd seen

"I saw the four winds of Heaven," he wrote,
"Churning up the sea"
Then he described four beasts that rose from it
In detailed degree

"The first was like a lion with wings of an eagle
As I watched...a change began
Its wings were torn off...and it stood on two feet
And was given the *heart* of a *man*

"The *second* beast was like a bear raised up on its side
And as it stood upon its feet
It had three ribs in its jaws...and *this* beast was told
'Get up and eat much meat'

"Then I looked and saw the third beast," Daniel wrote
"This one looked like a leopard
It was given authority...and it had four heads
On its back...four wings like a bird

"The fourth beast I saw was terrifying and powerful
This one had large iron teeth
It crushed and ate its victims and whoever was left
It trampled under its feet"

"This beast was *different* from the others before
There were *ten horns* on this one
As I contemplated the horns, another *smaller* horn
Came up from among

"To make room for the little horn, three of the first horns
Were pulled out by the roots from their host
The little horn had eyes like the eyes of a man
And it had a mouth to boast

"I continued to watch as thrones were set up
Then the Ancient of Days took His seat
He had robes white as snow and hair white as wool
And His throne had *fire* at its feet

"It had wheels of fire and a *river* of fire
Which flowed out in *front* of Him
Ministering to Him were thousands and thousands
And He was ready... to begin

"Before Him stood ten thousand, times ten thousand
And the rest of the court was seated
As I watched I saw that the books were opened
Now judgment... would be meted

"The little horn was speaking boastful words
But then the beast was *slain*
And as I stared... its body was destroyed
And thrown into the flame

"Power was taken away from the other beasts
But they were allowed to live for a span
Then I saw before me... coming in the clouds
One... like a Son of Man

"And when He approached... He was presented
To the Ancient of Days
He was given honor, authority and sovereign power
And Him... the people praised

"His dominion will last forever and ever
It shall never pass
His kingdom can never be destroyed
It *will* forever last"

DANIEL'S DREAM IS INTERPRETED

"As I watched I was troubled in my spirit
At the visions in my mind
I questioned one who was standing there
So the meaning I could find

"He told me the four great beasts that I saw
Are kingdoms which will rise
But in possession of the *final* kingdom
Will be saints of the One Most High

"I wanted to know more about the fourth beast
The one with the iron teeth
The terrifying one that crushed and ate its victims
And trampled the rest with its feet

"And I wanted to know more about the ten horns
And the small one replacing the three
The horn with the eyes…that had the mouth
That spoke so boastfully

"I saw the horn was waging war against the saints
And I saw the horn was winning
Until the kingdom was given *to* the saints
By the One who *was*…from the beginning

"Then he explained to me that the fourth beast
Is a kingdom like none before
It will devour the whole earth and trample it
And then he told me more

"He said the ten horns that I saw are ten kings
Who from this kingdom will come
But then three of the kings will be subdued
By yet *another* one

"He will speak against God and suppress the saints
And attempt to change times and law
He will persecute the saints of the One True God
For three and a half years more

"But when the court of the Lord is called to order
The horn will be stripped of its power
And he will be completely destroyed forever
From that very hour

"Then all of the kingdoms will be handed over
To the saints of the Most *Holy* One
And all of the rulers will worship and obey Him
In His everlasting kingdom"

The Vision of the Ram and the Goat

In the third year, Daniel had another vision
Where he saw himself in Elam
While standing by the Ulai Canal he looked up
And Daniel saw a ram

"The ram that I saw had two horns," he wrote
"And one of the horns was greater
But the shorter horn was the one that grew *first*
And the longer horn grew later

"He charged to the west, then north, then south
Against him no beast could stand
I watched as the ram did whatever he wanted
As he became great in the land

"As I wondered about the ram, I saw a billy goat
Out of the west he flew
Across the whole country...never touching the ground
And the goat had a huge horn too

"The goat was enraged and it charged the ram
And the ram's two horns were *shattered*
The ram had no chance as the goat stomped him down
Nothing he did even mattered

"The goat became great, but at the peak of his power
His horn was broken off
And four horns took its place...pointing east and west
And pointing south and north

"Then a little horn came out from one of them
And as the little horn grew
It reached the south...the east...and the holy land
But *still*...it wasn't through

"It became so strong...it attacked Heaven's army
Throwing some of it down
Down to the earth...and embarrassing it
By trampling it on the ground

"It even dared to challenge the Prince of the Host
As daily worship...it cast out
And given over to it...as judgment for rebellion
Were sacrifice...and the devout

"I saw two angels talking and one asked the other
'How long for this to pass?'
'Twenty three hundred days and nights,' he replied
'Til the temple is restored at last'"

THE INTERPRETATION

"As I watched I saw a man and I heard a voice
Saying, 'Gabriel, tell the meaning to the man'
I fell prostrate in terror as he walked over to me
And then the angel began

"'The vision you saw concerns the time of the end'
Then he told me *everything*
'The two-horned ram is Media and Persia
And the goat...is the Grecian king

"'The goat's large horn is the first king of the empire
The horn is broken off...and then
Four horns replace it, which are four small kingdoms
But *they* will be replaced *again*

"'When transgressors are as evil as they can become
And the end of the four kingdoms is near
A new one becomes strong but not by *his* power
The one who can't be trusted...will appear

"'All will be astounded by the devastation he causes
And he will be a master of intrigue
Mighty leaders and holy people...he will destroy
Everything he does will succeed

"'He will even take a stand against the Prince of princes
Yet there will come an hour
When this arrogant one will be destroyed
But *not*...by *human* power

"'The dream of twenty-three hundred days and nights
That was given to you is true
But none of this will happen until the distant future
And should be sealed up by you'

"I was overcome and sick for days before I rose
And did the normal work of my hand
But *still* I was troubled by the visions I saw
For I did not understand"

THE PRAYER OF DANIEL

Now in the first year of the reign of Darius
Daniel prayed a special prayer
For God told Jeremiah the prophet about Jerusalem
And the desolation there

Daniel went before the Lord in sackcloth and ashes
He fasted and he prayed
That even though Israel...had sinned against God
Perhaps His anger might fade

Daniel did not ask because of their righteousness
But because of God's mercy so great
So he begged for the people and for the city
That God would change their fate

And while Daniel was still praying...Gabriel appeared
And told him why he had come
To bring him an answer and understanding
For Daniel was favored by the One

Gabriel said, "Seventy weeks are set for the people
And the city to put an end to their sin
To end their rebellion and atone for their guilt
And unceasing righteousness to begin

"And for them to confirm the prophetic vision
And anoint the Most Holy Place
Seven weeks and sixty-two...will pass from rebuilding
'Til they see the Anointed One's face

"The city will be rebuilt with streets and a trench
In times of trouble it will come
But after the sixty-two weeks have passed
Cut off is the Anointed One

"And the people of the ruler who is to come
Will destroy the city and Holy Place
The end will come like a flood...and there will be war
Among the human race

"The Lord has said that much will be destroyed
And the ruler...a treaty...will bring
For seven years with many, but halfway through
He'll end sacrifice and offering

"He'll set up the abomination that causes desolation
In the Holy Place...and then
There it will remain...until the wrath of the Lord
Is poured out...upon him"

DANIEL'S VISION BY THE TIGRIS RIVER

In the third year of the reign of Cyrus of Persia
Daniel received *another* revelation
It came to him in a dream and he understood it
It was of war among the nations

Daniel wrote that he had been in mourning
In mourning for three weeks time
During that time he put no lotion on his body
And consumed no meat or wine

And as he stood on the bank of the Tigris River
Daniel looked up and saw
A man dressed in linen with a belt of gold
The *finest* gold without flaw

The man's face appeared to be as lightning
His body like a precious gem
His eyes were flaming like torches
As Daniel looked at him

His arms and legs glowed like burnished bronze
Then Daniel heard him speak
His voice was the sound of a multitude of people
Daniel felt himself grow weak

The men with Daniel did not see the man
And yet in terror they fled
Leaving Daniel alone on his hands and knees
With lowered eyes and head

The man touched Daniel and Daniel trembled
And wondered what next he would do
He said, "Daniel, you are highly esteemed by God
Consider *carefully* what I say to *you*

"Stand up, for I have been sent to you," he said
Daniel trembled while standing there
"Since the day you humbled yourself before God
He has heard your prayer"

The man had come in response to Daniel's prayers
But was delayed for twenty-one days
The prince of Persia had stopped him 'til Michael came
Then Michael cleared the way

He said he came to tell him what will happen
To his people in a time yet to come
Then he gave strength to Daniel...so he could hear
The message from the One

He said, "Three more kings will rule over Persia
Then a fourth becomes richer than them
With the power of his wealth...he wars against Greece
But a mightier king appears then

"He will rule with great power and do as he pleases
Then his empire will be no more
When it seems that *everything* is under his *control*
His empire will split into four

"Then the king of the South will become very strong
Then one of his generals even stronger
The daughter of the South king will marry the North king
But her power will be no longer

"For a time will come when she'll be handed over
Along with her attendants and her child
And handed over with *her*...will also be the one
Who supported her...for a while

"Then one from her family will rise to take her place
He will attack the Northern king
He will plunder their gods, their gold and their silver
Which back to Egypt...he will bring

"For some years they will leave each other alone
But then the king of the North
Will gather together all of his armies
And they will travel forth

"They will invade the realm of the king of the South
But then they will retreat
The Northern king's sons will prepare a great army
And like a *flood*...they will sweep

"Then the king of the South will march with *his* army
'Til the army of the North they meet
In a rage...the king of the South will do battle
The Northern king...he will defeat

"He will carry off prisoners and slaughter thousands
And with pride, the king will swell
Years later the *North* king...will raise a *huge* army
And they will be armored well

"In those times the Southern king will be strong
Yet rise against him...many will
Violent men of your people will rebel...and fail
The vision...they will fulfill

"The Northern king will come and take a fortified city
Southern forces, unable to resist
Then he will set himself up...in the glorious land
And all the land will be under his fist

"He will make an agreement with the Southern king
And give his daughter's hand
In order that *she* should destroy from within
The kingdom of the Southern land

"But his plan will not succeed and he will turn
To the islands and the coast
He will plunder them...but a prince will rise up
And put to an end...his boast

"He'll turn back to the fortresses of *his* own land
But he will stumble and be no more
And to continue the royal splendor...his successor
Will tax the people...more than before

"Then in a time of security, a contemptible person
By flattery will rise
Before him, a huge army will be swept away
With a covenant prince...by surprise

"With hypocritical conduct he will form an alliance
And then...before very long
He will work deceitfully and with just a few people
He will rise...and become strong

"He will then invade the richest provinces
Just when they feel secure
And distribute their plunder among his followers
But his plans will not endure

"He will gather a large and powerful army
And overwhelm the king of the South
Two kings will sit at a table…with evil intentions
With lies flowing from each mouth

"The king of the North will go home with great riches
But as he passes on his way
He will move against the holy covenant
Doing much damage that day

"At the appointed time…he will again invade the South
This time with a different end
For ships from the West will come and oppose him
And he will turn back again

"Again he will be enraged at the holy covenant
And show favor to those who forsake it
His forces shall rise up against the holy temple
And they will desecrate it

"They will eliminate the daily sacrifice and then
As part of their desecration
They will set up in the temple…the abomination
That causes desolation

"And those who have violated the covenant
He will flatter and corrupt
But the ones who know God will stand firm and resist
And the evil one…they will disrupt

"Those who are wise will teach many people
And make them understand
For a time they will fall by the sword or be burned
Or be captured in the land

"And when they fall...they'll receive a little help
Many will *pretend* to be their friend
Some of the wise stumble, so they can be refined
And purified...until the time of the end

"And *this* king will do whatever he pleases
Himself...he will magnify
He will exalt himself above...all other gods
And blaspheme the One Most High

"But he will give honor to a god of fortresses
Unknown to his fathers before
With gold and silver, precious stones and gifts
This god...he will adore

"He will go out and attack the mightiest empires
Aided by a foreign god's hand
He will honor his followers and make them rulers
And reward them with distributed land

The Time of the End

"At the time of the end...the king of the South
Will attack the king of the North
But with a whirlwind of chariots, calvary and ships
The king of the North...will come forth

"He will invade one country after another
Sweeping through like a flood
And when he reaches the Holy Land, he will cause
Tens of thousands to shed their blood

"Many countries will fall but Edom and Moab
And the leader of Ammon will escape
He will invade and conquer Ethiopia and Libya
The treasures of Egypt he will take

"But he will get reports from the East and the North
And him...they will alarm
And he will become furious and he will set out
To annihilate and do great harm

"He will set up his royal tents between Mount Zion
And the Mediterranean Sea
But he'll come to his end...and no one will help him
His reign...will no longer be

"The Archangel Michael, who protects your people
At that time will step in
And on the earth...will be a time of trouble
As there has never been

"But many will be saved from this distress
If written in the book...is their name
Multitudes of the dead will wake up at that time
To eternal life...or eternal shame

"The wise will shine like the brightness of the heavens
And those who teach others what is right
And lead many to righteousness will shine forever
Like the stars that shine in the night

"But you Daniel...seal up this prophecy as secret
Until the end time...and not before
When many people will be going here and there
To increase knowledge, more and more

Then Daniel looked and saw two more people
By the river...one on each side
"How long will it be until the end of these wonders?"
One of the people cried

The man dressed in linen raised his hands toward Heaven
And by the Eternal One he swore
"For a time, two times and half a time," he said
Which is three and a half years...no more

"Everything will have happened when the suffering
Of God's holy people comes to an end"
Daniel asked, "What will be the outcome, Lord?"
For he did not comprehend

"Go your way Daniel, for it is a secret," he replied,
"And until the end...it will be sealed
The wicked will not understand the meaning
To the wise...it will be revealed

"In those days many will be made clean and refined
Because of the trials in the land
But the wicked will continue to be wicked
And they will not understand

"And from the time that the daily sacrifices
Shall be taken away
And the abomination that causes desolation is set up
Will be twelve hundred ninety days

"And O how blessed and prosperous are those
Who wait in patient ways
Who stand firm and unwavering until the end
Of the thirteen hundred thirty-five days

Then he finally said, "Daniel...as for you
Go on your way...until the end
You will rest and you will rise at the end of days
And receive your inheritance then"

Joel

THE LOCUSTS

Hear me O elders, who live in the land
Joel spoke to a nation bereft
What the locust swarm missed, the young ones ate
And there is nothing left

Wake up you drunkards and weep and wail
Now a nation has invaded my land
It has teeth of a lion and fangs of a lioness
It is strong and its number is grand

The vines, the fields and the fig trees are destroyed
Bark stripped and thrown away
Now mourn like a woman in sackcloth
On her husband's funeral day

Offerings are cut off from the house of the Lord
Those who minister now mourn
The harvest is destroyed, the trees dried up
The farmers are forlorn

A CALL TO REPENT

O priests and ministers, spend the night in sackcloth
For the offerings are withheld
Call the people of the land to the house of the Lord
Prayer and fasting should be compelled

Listen…for the day of the Lord is near
The day destruction will come
Has not our food disappeared before our eyes?
Joy and gladness from the House of the One?

In parched ground the seeds are shriveling and dying
No crop of grain to be found
Without pastures the livestock moan in hunger
As they all wander around

The wilderness pastures are consumed by fire
Flames have burned up the trees
The streams have dried up and even wild animals
Cry out to you, their pleas

The Day of the Lord Is Coming

Blow the trumpet in Zion and sound the alarm
On my holy hill, for all in the land
They should all tremble for the day of the Lord
Is coming and is close at hand

It is a day of darkness and gloom that is coming
A day of blackness and cloud
Like the dawn that spreads across the mountains
Comes a massive crowd

A large and mighty army such as never was before
Nor ever will be again
With flame where they've been and devouring fire
Going out ahead of them

In front of them the land is like the garden of Eden
Behind them, a desert waste
They appear as horses with a sound of chariots
No one and nothing escapes

At the sight of them the nations are in anguish
And every face turns pale
They charge as an army of warriors
The city walls they scale

Marching in line without swerving from their course
Without jostling one another
Marching straight ahead...plunging through defenses
Not breaking rank with each other

The mighty army rushes upon the city
They run along the walls
Like thieves, they climb into the houses
Through the windows, down the halls

The sun and the moon have been darkened
The earth shakes before the horde
The sky trembles and the stars no longer shine
And leading the army...is the Lord

His forces are a multitude that cannot be counted
And they follow His command
The day of the Lord is great and dreadful
Against *Him*...who can stand?

"Return to me while there's time," says the Lord,
"With all your *heart*...return to me
Come with fasting and weeping and mourning
Tear your heart, not your clothes," says He

Return to the Lord your God for He is merciful
Compassionate and abounding in love
Slow to anger...who knows...He may give you a reprieve
And not punishment from above

And perhaps instead of a punishment upon you
A blessing He may pour
Perhaps you'll be able to make an offering
To the Lord your God, as before

Blow the trumpet in Zion and declare a holy fast
Gather the people in one accord
Have the priests stand and weep between the entry and the altar
Praying, "Spare your people O Lord

"Do not make your people an object of scorn
Don't let them be a joke for the nations
Why should the unbelieving foreigners be able to say,
'Has the God of Israel left this generation?'"

THE LORD ANSWERS

Then with concern for His land and His people
His people will hear from *Him*
"I am sending you grain, new wine and oil,"
The Lord will answer them

"Enough so that you will be fully satisfied"
And He will say, "Never again
Will I make you an object of scorn to the nations"
And He will drive out the armies then

"The armies of the North will be sent," says the Lord,
"To a barren land…driven by me
And it's front and rear columns will be sent
Into the Eastern and Western sea"

Fear not my people, be glad and rejoice
The Lord has done great things
And do not be afraid O wild animals
Because green pastures, He brings

Rejoice in the Lord O people of Zion
For He is giving to you
Autumn rains of righteousness
Spring and fall rains too

The trees and the vines will bear fruit again
The threshing floor full of grain to toil
The presses will again overflow with new wine
And abundant olive oil

"I will repay you for the years the locusts have eaten
The large locust and the young
The other locusts and the locust swarm," says the Lord,
"My great army that I sent among"

"You will have plenty to eat until you are full
And you will praise the Lord's name
You will know I am in Israel and I am the Lord
You will never again be shamed"

The Day of the Lord

"After that I will pour out my Spirit on *all* people
And your old men will dream dreams
You sons and your daughters will prophesy
And young men have vision scenes

"And even on my servants... both men and women
I will pour out my Spirit in those days
I will show wonders in the heavens and on the earth
The sun will no longer shine its rays

"For the sun will be turned to darkness
And to blood the moon will turn
On earth will be blood and columns of smoke
Due to the fires that burn

"Before the great and terrible day of the Lord
This is how it will be
All who call on the name of the Lord will be saved
For there will be deliverance," says He

"At the time of those events and when I restore
Judah and Jerusalem's prosperity
I will gather the nations to the Valley of Jehoshaphat
And they will be gathered before me

"I'll judge them for what they did to my people Israel
For they scattered them among the nations
They divided my land and traded boys for prostitutes
And they sold the girls for libations

"What do you have against me... O Tyre and Sidon
And all you Philistia regions?
Are you paying me back for something I've done?
For you came up with your *legions*

"You took my silver, my gold and my finest treasures
And brought them to your temples that day
You sold the people of Judah and Jerusalem to the Greeks
To send them far away

"Now I will move them from where you sold them
What you did, I will do to you
I will sell your offspring to the people of Judah
And they will sell them to the Arabians too

"I, the Lord have spoken," so says the Lord
"Now go to the nations and proclaim
Tell them to go and prepare themselves for war
And come from every side and name

"Let the nations come to the Valley of Jehoshaphat
For there I will sit," says the Lord
"I will judge all the nations on every side," He declares
He will punish and reward

"Swing the sickle for the harvest is ripe," says the Lord,
"Come and trample the grape
For the winepress is full and the vats overflow
So great is their evil and hate"

Multitudes of people in the valley of decision
For the day of the Lord is near
The sun and the moon will be darkened
When the day of the Lord is here

In that day the stars will no longer shine
From Zion the Lord will roar
And from Jerusalem He will *thunder*
And then...as never before

The earth and the sky will tremble
But the Lord shall also be
A refuge and a stronghold for His people Israel
This everyone will see

"You will know that I, the Lord your God
Dwell in Zion then
Jerusalem will be holy and foreigners will *never*
Invade Jerusalem again

"In that day the mountains will drip with new wine
And milk will flow on the hills
A fountain will pour from the temple of the Lord
The streams of Judah will be filled

"Because of violence done to the people of Judah
Egypt will be a desolate land
And Edom will also be a desert waste
For the blood shed by their hand

"But Judah will be inhabited forever
Their sins I will forgive
Jerusalem will thrive through generations"
In Zion...the Lord God lives!

Jonah

Jonah Flees from the Lord

"Go to the great city of Nineveh," said the Lord
Speaking to Jonah one day
"And preach against it…for it is wicked!" He said
But Jonah ran away

Jonah fled to Joppa where he boarded a ship
And he paid the proper fare
For he figured if he went as far as Tarshish
The Lord would not bother him there

But of course, the Lord was watching him
As Jonah tried to flee
And the Lord sent down a violent storm
A great wind upon the sea

The ship was tossed…back and forth
The sailors were terrified
They all began to scream and pray
And to their gods they cried

They began to throw the cargo into the sea
So they could lighten the boat
They would try to do whatever they could
To be able to keep it afloat

Now meanwhile, Jonah had gone below
Where he was laying down
But while Jonah lay in a deep, deep sleep
The others were fearing they'd drown

Then the captain went down below to Jonah
"How can you sleep!?" he said
"Get up! Call your God! Maybe He will help us!
If not…we will surely be dead!"

Meanwhile on deck, the sailors were talking
They said... "A lot we will cast
Then we will know who *caused* of all this"
For they *knew* it was someone's past

When the lot fell on Jonah, the sailors asked him,
"Who's responsible for the trouble here?
Who are you? Where'd you come from? What do you do?"
The sailors were in great fear!

"I'm a Hebrew, I worship the Lord God of Heaven
Who *made* the sea and the land"
Terrified, they asked, "Then what have you done?"
For they saw the strength of God's hand

They knew that Jonah was running from the Lord
For Jonah had told them so
"What should we do to you to calm down the sea?"
Everyone wanted to know

"Pick me up and throw me into the sea," said Jonah
Telling the sailors what to do
"For I know it is my fault that this great storm
Has come upon all of you"

But the men tried instead, to row back to land
The sea grew wilder than before
And as the moments went by and things got worse
They knew they couldn't make shore

So they cried out to God, "Please do not kill us
For taking the life of this man!"
And then they threw Jonah... into the sea
And the sea... became calm again

When the water became still, they were terrified
Because of the power they saw
Now they *knew* for sure who the *real* God was
And they fell to their knees on the floor

Jonah's Prayer

Then the Lord sent a great fish to swallow Jonah
And inside its belly he stayed
Jonah was in there three days and three nights
And from inside...he prayed

Then the Lord commanded the whale to vomit
Spitting Jonah onto the shore
Then the word of the Lord came *again* to Jonah
As He spoke to him...once more

"Go to the City of Nineveh and tell them," He said,
"The message I give to you"
And this time Jonah obeyed the Lord
And did what He told him to

Now Nineveh was a very important city
And when Jonah arrived at last
He said the city would be destroyed in forty days
So the people began to fast

And when Jonah's news reached Nineveh's king
The king told the people *that day,*
"Both man and beast put on sackcloth and fast
And call on God and pray!"

"If everyone stops the violence," said the king,
"And gives up their evil ways
Perhaps the Lord will turn from His anger
And we *won't* die in forty days!"

When God saw that the people were repenting
As He looked at them from above
He had compassion and did not destroy the city
He responded instead...in love

Zephaniah

A message from the Lord came to a prophet
During the reign of Josiah
It was a warning of coming destruction
Given to Zephaniah

"I will sweep away all from the face of the earth,"
Declared the Almighty Lord
"The men and the animals, the birds and the fish"
He told how His wrath would be poured

"I will stretch out my hand against Judah," He said,
"And those living in Jerusalem"
Then the Lord continued to reveal the prophecy
For all who would listen to Him

"I will cut off from this place every remnant of Baal"
Zephaniah listened engrossed
"The names of the pagans and the priests who bow down
To worship the starry host

"Those who bow down and swear by the Lord
And swear by Molech too
Those who sought after the Lord before
Yet now . . . no longer do

"Be silent before the Sovereign Lord," He said,
"For the day of the Lord is near
He prepared a sacrifice and He has made holy
Those He invited here

"On the Day of the Lord's Sacrifice, I will punish
The leaders and the king's sons
And those who are wearing foreign clothing
And also the other ones

"The ones who are quick to enter their temples
Avoiding the threshold with their feet
The ones who are filling the temples of their gods
With violence and deceit

"On that day a cry will go up from the Fish Gate
And from the New Quarter, a wail
A loud crash will be heard from the hills
And the marketplace will fail

"I will search with lamps through Jerusalem
In every neighborhood
And punish the complacent who say that the Lord
Does *nothing*...bad or good

"Their wealth will be plundered, their houses destroyed
And the new houses they design
They won't live in and though they plant vineyards
They will not drink the wine"

The Great Day of the Lord

"The great day of the Lord is coming quickly
The great day of the Lord is near
Listen! For even the strong men and warriors
Will cry out in bitter tears

"That day will be a day of wrath and distress
A day of trouble and ruin
A day of clouds and blackness
A day of darkness and gloom

"A day of battle cry and trumpet on fortified cities
I will bring distress on the horde
The people will walk as though they were blind
For they sinned against the Lord

"Their blood will pour out on the ground as dust
Like filth their entrails will flow
On the day of the Lord's wrath they won't be saved
By their silver or their gold

"And all of the earth will be consumed," He said,
"As the fire of His jealousy unfurls
For the Lord will make a sudden end of all
Of all...who live in the world"

Now gather together, you shameful nation
Before that time will begin
Act now...before the fierce anger of the Lord
Is released by Him

All of you who are humble, seek the Lord
And follow His laws and way
Seek righteousness and maybe He'll protect you
From His anger on that terrible day

PROPHECY AGAINST PHILISTIA, MOAB, AMMON, CUSH, AND ASSYRIA

"Gaza will be abandoned, Ashkelon in ruin
And Ashdod will be empty
Ekron and Kerethite and Canaan destroyed
Woe to those living by the sea"

In the evening the remnant of Judah will recline
In the houses of Ashkelon
And the Lord their God will care for them
And restore their fortunes that were gone

"I heard the insults of Moab and the Ammonites
Who threatened my people's land
And taunted my people, so as sure as I live
They will feel my hand

"Moab will become like Sodom," said the Lord,
"As Gomorrah, the Ammonites will be
A wasteland forever...a place of salt pits
It will be a place of weeds

"The remnant of my people will plunder them
And *they* will inherit their land"
Zephaniah continued to reveal the prophecy
Describing what was planned

The Lord will destroy all the gods of the land
When He releases His might
And all of the nations will *worship* the Lord
He'll be *awesome* in their sight

A word of prophecy also came against Cush
To Zephaniah from the Lord
"You too, O Cushites," the Lord declared,
"You *too* will be slain by my sword"

"He will stretch out His hand," said Zephaniah
Describing what God will do
Nineveh will be desolate and dry as a desert
He will destroy Assyria too

In Nineveh flocks and herds will lie down
The desert and screech owls too
Will roost on her columns with rubble in doorways
And their calls will echo through

This carefree city that lived in safety
Who said, "There is *none* like *me*"
Will be a lair for beasts...and all who pass
Will *scoff* at her when they see

The Future of Jerusalem

Woe to the city of oppressors, said Zephaniah
Rebellious and defiled!
Obeying no one...and accepting no correction
Her officials and rulers beguile

Her prophets are arrogant and treacherous men
The sanctuary, her priests profane
The Lord *within* her is *righteous* and does not *fail*
Yet the unrighteous know no shame

"I have cut off nations and destroyed their strongholds
Left their streets deserted too
Their cities are destroyed with no one left," says the Lord,
"And no one passing through"

"I said, 'Surely you will fear me and accept instruction,'
And my warnings you would heed!
So I would not need to destroy your homes
But you continued your evil deeds

"Therefore, wait for me," declares the Lord,
"For the day that I will stand
I have decided to gather the nations of the world
And pour out the wrath of my hand

"The earth will be consumed by the fire of my zeal,"
Declares the Almighty Lord,
"Then I will purify their lips so the people may call me
United...and in one accord

"From beyond the Cush rivers, my scattered people
Will bring offerings to me
And on that day you will feel no shame
Because of all your deeds

"For I will remove from the city," says the Lord,
"Those who rejoice in their pride
Never again will you be haughty on my holy hill
Yet the meek and humble will reside

"Those who trust in the name of the Lord," He continued,
"The remnant of Israel will do no wrong
They will eat and sleep and will not be afraid!"
Daughter of Zion...rejoice in song!

The Lord has taken away your punishment
He has turned back your enemy
Now the Lord, the King of Israel, is *with* you
Never again in fear will you be

On that day they will say to Jerusalem,
"O Zion, do not fear
For the Lord your God, who is mighty to save
Is living with you here!

"He will take great delight in you," they will say,
"And will calm you with His love
And He will rejoice over you with singing
The mighty Lord from above

"I will remove the sorrows of the appointed feasts
They're a burden and a reproach to you
At that time I will deal severely," says the Lord,
"With those who oppressed you too"

"I will gather those who have been scattered
I will save the weak and the lame
I will give them praise and honor in every land
Where they have been put to shame

"At that time I will gather you and bring you home
I will give you honor and praise
Among all the nations...when I restore your fortunes,"
Declares the Ancient of Days

Zechariah

God spoke through the prophet Zechariah
And told the people what to do
Angry with their forefathers, He said, "Return to me
And I will return to you"

For their forefathers had paid no attention
To the warnings of the prophets before
And because they did not turn from their evil ways
They were punished by the Lord

THE VISION OF THE HORSES

During the night, Zechariah had a vision
He saw a man sitting on a red horse
Behind him three *more*…red, white and brown
Zechariah questioned, of course

"What are these my Lord?" I asked an angel
For I did not understand
The rider said, "These are the ones the Lord sent
To go throughout the land

"We've gone throughout the world," they told the angel,
"And found it at rest and peace"
The angel asked the Lord when He would have mercy
And when His anger would cease

For seventy years He had *withheld* His mercy
From Judah and Jerusalem
Then the Lord spoke comforting words to the angel
As I listened to *both* of them

The angel said God is *jealous* for Jerusalem and Zion
But angered at nations feeling secure
He'll return to Jerusalem and His house will be rebuilt
And also the whole city, for sure

His towns will once more overflow with prosperity
And He will comfort Zion again
And the Lord will choose Jerusalem, said the angel
As I listened I looked up then

I saw four horns and I saw four craftsmen
"What are these?" I said
"These are the horns that scattered Judah," he said,
"So no one could raise his head

"But the craftsmen have come to terrify them
And throw down the horns of the nations
Who rose against Judah and scattered its people"
I pondered this explanation

Then I looked and saw a man with a measuring line
"Where are you going?" I asked
"To measure the width and length of Jerusalem,"
He said, describing his task

Then another angel told the first one to *tell* the man
It will have no boundaries at all
Jerusalem will be too full of people and animals
To even have a *wall*

"*I* myself will be a wall of *fire* around it
And I will be its glory within
Flee from the land of the North!" says the Lord
Referring to where they had been

"For I've scattered you to the four winds of Heaven
Now return from where you have gone
Come escape O Zion…you who are living
In the daughter of Babylon!"

"For this is what the Lord God says," said the angel,
"After honor…He has sent *me*
Against all of the nations that plundered *you*"
Then he said…why this will be

"Whoever touches *you*, touches the apple of His eye
Against *them*, I will raise my hand
Their slaves will plunder them…then you will know
The Lord sent *me* to the land"

"Daughter of Zion, shout and be glad," says the Lord,
"For I'm coming and will live among *you*
Many nations will be joined with the Lord in that day
And will become my people too

"The Lord will have Judah as His share in the holy land
And will *again* choose Jerusalem
He has roused Himself from His holy dwelling
So be *still*…in *front* of Him"

Then I saw the high priest Joshua, in filthy clothes
Standing with the angel of the Lord
And on the right side of Joshua, *Satan* was standing
Accusations…from his mouth, poured

"The Lord rebuke you Satan!" said the Lord
And the angel spoke out then
He ordered the filthy clothes be taken off Joshua
And clean garments *put* on him

The angel told Joshua, "I have taken away your sin
And will place rich garments on you"
Then the angel of the Lord spoke of God's promise
And told Joshua what to do

"If you walk in my ways and keep my requirements,"
The angel spoke the words of the Lord,
"You'll govern my house and have charge of my courts"
Describing God's reward

"I will give you a place among these standing here"
Then the angel went on to say
He'll place a stone with seven eyes and He will remove
The sin of this land in one day

Then the angel showed me a gold lampstand with a bowl
With an olive tree on each side
I asked the angel, "What are these, my lord?"
And the angel…he replied

"This is the word of the Lord to Zerubbabel," he said
"'Not by might or by power
But by my Spirit' says the Almighty Lord"
Referring to the task of the hour

"Not even a mighty mountain will block the way
For it will become level ground
Zerubbabel started and will complete the temple
With the people cheering around

"The seven eyes are the eyes of the Lord," he said,
"That range throughout the world
The two olive trees are the two anointed
To serve the Lord of all"

Then I looked up and saw a flying scroll
Thirty feet long and fifteen feet wide
"Everyone who swears falsely will be banished"
Was written on one side

"Every thief will be banished" was written on the other
The angel said it will enter their homes
It will *remain* in their houses and *destroy* them
Both the timbers and the stones

THE WOMAN IN THE BASKET

Then I looked up and saw a measuring basket
"What is this basket?" I said
"It is filled with everyone's sins," said the angel
Lifting its cover of lead

I looked inside and there sat a woman
"This is evil," the angel said
As he pushed her back down in the basket
And placed the cover over her head

I looked up and saw two women standing
With wings blowing in the breeze
They lifted the basket between Heaven and earth
And flew away with ease

"Where are they taking the basket?" I asked
As I looked in the angel's face
"They're building a house for it in Babylonia," he said
"When ready…it will be set in its place"

Four Chariots

Then I looked up and saw four chariots coming
From between bronze mountains they came
Each chariot was pulled by a team of mighty horses
No two teams were the same

The first team was red, the second team black
The third team of horses, white
The fourth team was dappled shades of gray
I watched them in their flight

"These are the four spirits of Heaven" said the angel
As I watched, the vision unfurled
"They come forth from standing in the presence," he said
"Of the Lord of the entire world

"The one with black horses is going to the north
The one with white, to the west
The one with dappled horses goes to the south
The northern one gave my spirit rest"

A Crown for Joshua

"Take silver and gold from the exiles of Babylon,"
Was the word of the Lord to Zechariah
"Make a crown for the head of the high priest Joshua
And go to the house of Josiah"

"He will build the temple of the Lord," He said
"And be clothed in majesty
He will rule on his throne and He'll be a priest
And harmony will be

"They will come to help build the temple of the Lord
They will come from far away
You will know the Lord sent me and this will happen
If the Lord, you strictly obey"

Justice and Mercy

In the fourth year of Darius, the word of the Lord
Came to Zechariah one day
After the people of Bethel had asked the priests
And also the prophets to pray

"Should I mourn and fast in the fifth month," they asked,
"As for so many years I have done?"
But the answer from the Lord through Zechariah
Was expected... by none

"Whenever you fasted in the fifth and seventh months
Was it really just for me?
And when you *feasted*... was it not for *yourselves*?"
He tried to make them see

"My message today is the same as it was
When I spoke through the prophets before
When Jerusalem and its towns were resting and prosperous"
And then He told them more

"Administer *true* justice and show *compassion*
Show mercy and do not oppress
The widow, the fatherless, the alien and the poor"
Their behavior He addressed

"And in your hearts don't think evil of each other
But they refused to pay attention
They turned their backs and stopped up their ears," He said
They were stubborn in their dissension

"They made their hearts as hard as flint," He said,
"And would not listen to the law
Or the words that the Lord had sent by His Spirit
Through the prophets before

"So the Lord Almighty was very angry
When I called, they did not listen," He said,
"So when *they* called out to me... *I* would not listen
I scattered them to the nations instead"

The Lord's Promise to Bless Jerusalem

Again the word of the Lord came to Zechariah
"I am very jealous for Zion," He said,
"I am burning with jealousy for her," says the Lord
And He told what lay ahead

"I will return to Zion and dwell in Jerusalem
Which will be called the City of Truth
The Mountain of the Lord will be called the Holy Mountain"
Then He spoke of *those*... no longer in youth

"Men and women of old age will again sit in the streets
Children will fill the streets at play
It may seem *impossible* to the people at that time,"
The Lord went on to say

"But is it impossible for *me*?... I *will* save my people
From the countries of the east and west
I will bring them back to live in Jerusalem," He said
And told how they would be blessed

Judgment on Israel's Enemies

The word of the Lord is against the land of Hadrach
And upon Damascus it will rest
The eyes of men and all Israel are upon the Lord
The Spirit did attest

And upon Hamath too, which borders on it
And upon Tyre and Sidon
Though Tyre is a stronghold with much silver and gold
Her possessions will be gone

And the Lord will destroy her power on the sea
She will be consumed by fire
Ashkelon will see it and be gripped by fear
As they witness Almighty God's ire

Gaza will twist in agony and will lose her king
Ekron's hope will have died
Foreigners will come and occupy Ashdod
I will cut off the Philistines' pride

Those who are left will belong to our God
Leaders of Judah they will be
Ekron will be like the Jebusites then
My house will be defended by me

The Coming of Zion's King

Rejoice O Daughters of Zion and Jerusalem
For your king is coming to you
He is gentle and righteous and rides on a donkey
And He's bringing salvation too

I will remove the chariots from Israel
The war horses from Jerusalem
And the weapons of battle will be broken
With peace proclaimed by Him

He will speak and peace will come to all nations
He will rule from sea to sea
From the River Euphrates to the ends of the earth
Is where His dominion will be

As for *you*…because of my covenant with *you*
My covenant…which is blood-sealed
I will free your prisoners from the waterless pit
The Spirit of God revealed

Return to your fortress, O prisoners of hope
And I will restore to you double
I promise this day, that I will repay
Double for all of your trouble

Judah will be my bow…and Israel my arrow
Jerusalem will be my sword
And I will use it against the sons of Greece
Says the Spirit of the Lord

Then the Lord will appear above the people
His arrow will flash like lightning
And the Sovereign Lord will sound the trumpet
And then…like a whirlwind frightening

From the southern desert, He will come forth
His people He will shield
They will hurl great stones and defeat their enemies
On the battlefield

THE LORD WILL CARE FOR JUDAH

Ask the Lord for storm clouds in the springtime
It is *He* who gives the rain
The idols are deceitful and give visions that lie
They give comfort in *vain*

So the people wander like sheep without a shepherd
Punishment on their leaders He will pour
For the Lord God Almighty will care for His flock
And make them as a proud horse of war

From Judah will come the cornerstone and tent peg
From Judah will come the battle bow
And also from Judah will come every ruler
The Lord God makes it so

Together they will be as mighty men
For the Almighty Lord is with them
They will gather together and then they will fight
And overthrow the horsemen

"I will call them and I will gather them in
They will be as numerous as before
Though I scatter them, they will *remember* me
They will survive and more

"I will bring them back from Egypt and Assyria
To Gilead and Lebanon
There won't be enough room for them when they return
From the places they have gone

"They will pass through the sea of trouble
The surging sea, I will subdue
I will dry up the Nile and bring down Assyria
Egypt's reign will be through"

The Good and Evil Shepherds

I pastured the flock that was marked for slaughter
The oppressed...especially
I took two staffs and named them Favor and Union
And the flock was pastured by me

I got rid of the three shepherds in one month
And the flock detested me
I grew weary and said, "I will not be your shepherd
Let the perishing be"

Then I broke my staff called Favor
The covenant I revoked
The afflicted who watched me knew that it was
The word of the Lord that spoke

I said, "If you think it best...give me my pay"
And thirty silver pieces they paid
I threw them into the Temple...to the potter
And on the floor they laid

Then I broke my *second* staff...called Union
The Israel and Judah *brotherhood*
"I will raise up a shepherd over the land," said the Lord,
"Who will not treat them as he *should*

"One who will not care for the lost or the injured
Who will not seek out the young sheep
But instead will eat the flesh of the choicest ones
Tearing off their feet

"Woe to the worthless shepherd," says the Lord,
"The one who deserts the flock
May the sword strike his arm and his right eye!
His arm withered...and his eye blocked"

JERUSALEM'S ENEMIES WILL BE DESTROYED

Here is the word of the Lord concerning Israel
The Lord, who by His *own* hand
Created the heavens and the foundations of earth
And who forms the spirit of man

"I will make Jerusalem an intoxicating drink
"Which sets the surrounding nations reeling
Judah will be besieged, as well as Jerusalem
All of the nations dealing

"And on that day, when all the *nations* of the earth
All are gathered against her
I will make Jerusalem an immovable rock"
The nations will be deterred

"All who try to move it will injure themselves
And I will strike on that day
Every horse with panic, every rider with madness
As they all try their way

"I will keep a watchful eye over the house of Judah
But the horses of the nations I will blind
'The people are strong because the Lord is their God'
The leaders of Judah will opine

"On that day I will make the leaders of Judah like a torch
That sets a woodpile aflame
They will consume right and left, the surrounding people
But Jerusalem intact...will remain

"The Lord will save the houses of Judah first
So Jerusalem's honor won't be greater
On that day I will destroy the attackers of Jerusalem,"
So says...the Almighty Creator

Mourning for the One They Pierced

"I will pour on David's House and Jerusalem's people
A spirit of grace and supplication
And they will look on me...the one they pierced,"
Says the Lord of every nation

"And they will mourn for Him as for an only child
Grieving bitterly as for a firstborn son
On that day the weeping in Jerusalem will be great,"
Declares the Holy One

"And the land will mourn, each clan by itself
David's house, Nathan's and Levi's
And all of the rest of the clans will mourn
By themselves and apart from their wives

"And on that day, a fountain will be opened
To cleanse them from their sin
To the House of David and to those who live
In the city of Jerusalem

"On that day I will banish the names of the idols
And they will be remembered no more
I'll remove the prophets and the spirit of impurity,"
Declares the Almighty Lord

The Shepherd Is Struck, the Sheep Are Scattered

"Wake up my sword, against my shepherd
And the man who is close to me!
Strike the shepherd and the sheep will be scattered,"
Declares the Lord Almighty

"I will turn against the little ones in the whole land
Two-thirds will be struck and expire
One-third will be left and those I will take
And refine them in the fire

"I will refine them like silver and test them like gold
And they will call on my name
I will answer them and say... 'They are my people'
'The Lord is our God,' they'll proclaim"

THE DAY OF THE LORD

The day of the Lord is coming when your possessions
Will be divided in front of you
I will gather all the nations against Jerusalem to battle
And the city will be captured too

The houses will be ransacked and the women raped
Half the people into exile will go
But the rest of the people won't be taken from the city
The Lord declares it so

Then the *Lord* will go and fight against the nations
As He fights in the battle day
He will stand upon the Mount of Olives
And the mountain will split away

Half will move to the north and half to the south
In between, a great valley will be
The valley will extend all the way to Azal
And through it... you will flee

Then the Lord God will come with His holy ones
On that day there will be no light
With no cold or frost... it will be unique
Without daytime or night

On that day living water will flow from Jerusalem
Half going to the eastern sea
The other half will go to the western sea
Summer and winter, this will be

And the Lord will be the King over the earth
His name...the only name
From Geba to Rimmon, will become like the Arabah
But Jerusalem...raised up...will remain

From the Benjamin Gate to the First Gate
To the Corner Gate for sure
It will be inhabited...never again destroyed
Jerusalem will be secure

The Lord will strike the nations that fought Jerusalem
A plague will strike their place
Their flesh will rot while they stand on their feet
Their eyes will rot out in their face

Their tongues will also rot in their mouths
And the Lord will strike them with fright
Each man will seize the hand of another
And each other...they will fight

Much gold and silver and clothing will be gathered
From the surrounding nations' resources
And the plague will also strike their camels
Their donkeys, mules and horses

Then *all* of the survivors of *all* of the nations
That attacked Jerusalem
Will come up each year...before the Lord
To bow and worship Him

And also to celebrate the Feast of Tabernacles
And if any nations do *not*
The Lord Almighty will hold back the rain
From their nation and their crop

If the people of Egypt and other nations don't go
To bow and worship Him
Then the Lord Almighty will *also* send
A plague on *all* of them

And on that day... "Holy to the Lord"
Will be written on the horses' bells
The temple cooking pots will be as sacred bowls
The word of the Lord foretells

Every pot in Jerusalem and Judah will be holy
All who come... will use them in accord
And there will no longer... be any merchants found
In the temple of the Almighty Lord

Malachi

The word of the Lord came to the people of Israel
Through the prophet Malachi
For their relationship was not as it should be
With the Almighty Lord on High

The people had strayed in their worship
Not properly honoring the Lord
So He warned the Israelites through Malachi
Their behavior would *not* be ignored

He admonished them for bringing sacrifices
Of animals that were *blind*
Animals that were crippled, diseased or stolen
The *blemished* ones they could find

"Try offering them to your governor," said the Lord,
"Would *he* be pleased with you?
Would *he* accept you?" asked the Lord
This is *unacceptable* to do

"Cursed is the cheat who vows a fine ram
But then sacrifices a mutation
For I am a great King and My Name," says the Lord,
"Shall be feared among the nations"

God also reprimanded the priests through Malachi
For their teachings had caused many to sin
They had turned and not followed the laws He made
And broke Levi's covenant with Him

Then Malachi said the Lord *also* ignores their offerings
Though they flood the altar with tears
Because He is acting as a *witness* between *them*
And the wife of their *younger years*

"It's because you've broken faith with her," he said,
"The wife of your marriage covenant
"Has not the Lord God made you one?" he asked,
"Godly offspring was His *intent*

"So guard your spirit…and stay faithful to the wife
Who you married when you were young
For the Lord hates divorce and the violent man
Who *to* his wife does *wrong*"

THE DAY OF JUDGMENT

"You have wearied the Lord with your words,"
The people heard Malachi say,
"By saying all who do evil are good in His eyes
And that He is *pleased* with their ways"

"Look, I will send my messenger," says the Lord,
"Who will prepare the way for me
Then the Lord you are seeking will come to His temple
He will come *suddenly*

"The messenger of the covenant," He continued,
"The one you desire will come
But who will be able to endure it when He *does*?
Who can *stand* and *face* the One?"

"For He will be like the blazing fire of a refiner
Or like a launderer's strong soap
Then men will come and bring offerings
In righteousness and hope

"He will sit like a refiner and purifier of silver
And refine the Levites like gold
Then Jerusalem and Judah's offerings will please Him
As in the days of old

"Then I will come near to you for judgment," says the Lord,
"And I will be quick to testify
Against the sorcerers and the adulterers
And those whose testimony is a lie

"Against those who cheat laborers of their wages
Or oppress widows' and orphans' plea
Against those who deprive the aliens of justice
For *they*…do not fear *me*"

ROBBING GOD

"I am the Lord, I do not change," says the Lord,
"So I have not destroyed you
You have turned from my decrees, now return to me
And I will return to you too

"Will a man rob God?" asked the Lord
"And yet you *do rob Me*!
But you ask, 'How is it that we rob you Lord?'
In tithes and offerings, you see

"Your whole nation is under a curse," He continued,
"Robbing *Me* is the reason why
Bring me the whole tithe and test me in this,"
Says the Lord Most High

"And see if I will not open the floodgates of Heaven
And pour so much blessing upon you
That you will not have room enough to store it"
He promised what He would do

"Your crops and your vines will bear much fruit
I will rebuke the devourer by my hand
Then all of the nations will call you blessed
Yours will *be* a delightful land

"You have used harsh words against me," said the Lord
"'To serve God is useless,' you said
'What did we gain by keeping His decrees?' you ask
'Walking before Him with bowed head?

"'For now those who are arrogant, we call blessed
Evildoers prosper, *certainly*
And even those people who *challenge* God
Even *they* go free'"

Then those who feared the Lord spoke to each other
And the Lord was listening to them
A scroll of remembrance was written in His presence
Regarding those who *honored* Him

"They will be mine," says the Lord Almighty
"They will be my special treasure
As a man gives compassion to his son who serves him
Compassion I will measure

"I will spare them and you will see the distinction,"
The Lord said through Malachi,
"Between those who serve God and those who do not,"
Promised the Lord Most High

THE DAY OF THE LORD

"Look, the day is coming, burning as a furnace," He said,
"When all the wicked and the proud
Shall burn up until nothing is left of them
Neither root nor branch allowed

"But for those of you who revere my name
The sun of righteousness will rise then
With healing in its wings…and you will go forth
As calves released from a pen

"Then you will trample down the evil ones
They'll be ashes under your feet
On the day when I do these things," said the Lord
His message nearly complete

"Remember the law I gave to my servant Moses
The *decrees* I gave him to record
Look…I am sending you Elijah the prophet
Before the great and fearful day of the Lord

"He'll turn fathers' and children's hearts to each other"
Cold hearts he will reverse
"Otherwise I will come," warned the Lord,
"And strike the earth with a curse"

Part 2

The New Testament

The Life of Jesus

GABRIEL VISITS ZECHARIAH

During Herod's reign, there was a priest named Zechariah
Elizabeth was his wife
And although they were well along in years
They never had children in their life

Now Zechariah was in the temple
Burning incense one day
While all of the regular worshipers
Were gathered outside to pray

Suddenly an angel appeared by the altar!
Zechariah was *gripped* with fear!
But the angel said, "Do not be afraid, Zechariah"
He had a message for him to hear

"Your prayer has been heard in Heaven,"
The angel continued on
"Elizabeth will have a son who will be a joy to you
And you shall name him John"

"Many will rejoice at his birth," he continued
"He'll be great in the eyes of the Lord
He'll be filled with the Holy Spirit from birth
Many Israelites' faith will be restored"

Zechariah listened and then he asked,
"How can I be sure of this?
For I am aged and my wife is well along in years"
Could he really *now* get his wish?

The angel responded firmly…"I am Gabriel!
I was *sent* here to speak to you!
I stand in the presence of God!" he continued
"At the right time these words will come true

"But because you did not believe my words
You will be silent…unable to speak"
Zechariah wouldn't talk until the baby was born
Not a word…until that very week

Meanwhile, the people were still waiting outside
Zechariah was in the temple a long time
Unable to speak…he told them what happened
By using his hands to sign

Soon it came to pass that Elizabeth was pregnant
And she exclaimed with glee,
"The Lord showed favor and took away my disgrace!
The Lord has done *this*…for *me*"

Gabriel Visits Mary

In the sixth month, God sent the angel Gabriel
To Nazareth, a town in Galilee
With a very special message for Mary
The young woman he went to see

"Greetings, you who are highly favored!
The Lord is with you," said he
But Mary was greatly troubled by his words
And what this greeting might be

Then Gabriel said gently…"Fear not, Mary
For with God…you have found favor
You will be with child…and give birth to a son"
And he told her about the Savior

"You shall name the baby Jesus," he said
As Gabriel continued then,
"And God will give Him the throne of David
And His kingdom will never end"

"But I am a virgin," Mary replied
"How can this be done?"
"The Holy Spirit will come upon you," he said,
"And the baby will be God's own Son"

Then he told her that her relative Elizabeth
Was having a baby too
"For nothing is impossible with God," he said
Though she was barren, as everyone knew

"I am the Lord's servant" Mary replied
"May it be as you have said"
Then the angel Gabriel left her
As Mary bowed her head

Mary Visits Elizabeth

Soon after, Mary traveled to a town in Judea
To visit Elizabeth there
"Blessed are you among women!" said Elizabeth
"And blessed is the child you will bear!"

For when Elizabeth had heard Mary's greeting
When Mary first entered the room
Elizabeth was *filled* with the Holy Spirit
And her baby *jumped* in her womb

"But why am *I* so favored," Elizabeth asked,
"That my Lord's *mother* should come to *me*?
Blessed is *she* who has *believed*," she continued,
"That what the Lord has said…shall *be*!"

"My soul does praise the Lord," said Mary
"And My spirit rejoices," said she
"Now all generations shall call me blessed
God has done *great things* for me"

The Birth of John the Baptist

The time came for Elizabeth to have her baby
And she gave birth to a baby boy
Everyone knew that God had given her favor
And everyone shared her joy

They wanted to give the name Zechariah
To Elizabeth's new baby son
But Elizabeth spoke up...and she said, "No!
He shall be called John"

"But there is no one among your relatives
Who has *that* name," they said
Then Zechariah asked for a writing tablet
So *his* decision could be read

Then, to the astonishment of everyone
He wrote..."His name is John"
Immediately Zechariah began to speak!
Praising God...on and on

Then Zechariah was filled with the Holy Spirit
And began to *prophesy*
He spoke about the coming of the Savior
And John who would *serve* the Most High

JOSEPH IS TOLD

When Mary told her fiancé Joseph, she was pregnant
He didn't want her to be in disgrace
So he figured he would marry and quietly divorce her
So Mary would not lose face

But an angel in a dream...said, "Do not be afraid
To take Mary as your wife
For the baby is from the Holy Spirit"
His words changed Joseph's life

"Mary will give birth to a Son," said the angel
"You will name Him Jesus," he said,
"For He will save His people from their sins"
Then Joseph awoke in his bed

All of this happened to fulfill the prophecy,
"A virgin will give birth to a Son
They'll call Him Emmanuel"...which means "God with us"
Speaking of the Holy One

Then Joseph took Mary home as his wife
As the angel instructed be done
But Joseph didn't have any union with her
Until *after* the birth of her Son

THE BIRTH OF JESUS

Now several months later, Caesar Augustus
Issued a decree
A census would be taken of the Roman empire
So a tally he could see

Every person had to go to their family's town
For the Romans to register them
So Joseph and Mary traveled from Nazareth
To the town of Bethlehem

When they arrived they tried to find a room
But alas...they were unable
And the only place for them to stay
Was in a lowly stable

Mary gave birth to her baby in the stable
And laid him in a manger
While angels were gathered all around
To keep them safe from danger

That same night, there were shepherds
Living in a field quite near
They were guarding their sheep when *suddenly*
An angel did appear!

The glory of the Lord shone round him!
Lighting up the night!
The shepherds were astounded by what they saw!
And they were *filled* with fright!

But the angel told them, "Do not be afraid
I bring you good news of great *joy*
For *all* of the people...a Savior has been born!"
And he told of the baby boy

"You will find the baby wrapped in cloth
This will be a *sign* to you
You'll find him lying in a manger," he said
Telling them what to do

Then suddenly a great number of angels appeared!
Praising God and singing with zest
"Glory to God in the highest...and peace to men
On whom His favor rests"

Then the angels left them and went into Heaven
And the shepherds said, "Let us go"
So they went to Bethlehem to see the baby
Of whom they had been told

They went with haste and found the baby
Like the angel said they would
They glorified God...then traveled through the land
Telling everyone they could

And as the shepherds told the news of what happened
Those who heard the story unfurl
Were *amazed* at what they were hearing
About the Savior...of the world

JESUS IS PRESENTED IN THE TEMPLE

On the eighth day the baby was circumcised
According to God's Law
And Mary and Joseph named him Jesus
As Gabriel had told them before

God's Law *also* said that every firstborn son
Shall be dedicated to the Lord above
With the sacrifice of a young lamb and a pigeon
Or *two* pigeons...or a pigeon and a dove

So *again*, according to the Law of Moses
After the time of their purification
Joseph and Mary brought Jesus to the Temple
To present Him for consecration

Now the Spirit of God had led a man named Simeon
To the temple that very day
He was a righteous man and he was devout
And was *often* in the temple to pray

The Holy Spirit had previously revealed to him
That before his death, he would see
The *Savior* who was sent from Heaven above
And *who* the Messiah would be

There was also a prophetess named Anna
Who would *always* fast and pray
Anna was old and *never* left the temple
So she *too* was there that day

And when Simeon and Anna each saw Jesus
They *knew* that the baby boy
Was the Redeemer of Israel...the Messiah
And *both* were filled with joy

The Visit of the Wise Men

Now Wise Men traveled from the East
And to Jerusalem they came
Where they questioned the people about the baby
But they did not know His name

"Where is the One," they asked the people,
"Who's been born king of the Jews?"
But the people became upset and disturbed
When the Wise Men brought this news

"We saw His star in the east and we followed it
We came too worship him," they said
But when King Herod heard of their search
He was filled with dread

So he gathered the chief priests and teachers
To ask *them* about this One
For he had *heard* of a coming Messiah
And was disturbed about God's Son

"Where will the Savior be born?" asked Herod
"In Bethlehem," they said,
"For this is what the prophet has written"
And to him…the Scriptures…they read

"And you, O Bethlehem, in the land of Judah
By no means…the least are *you*
For from you will come a leader who will shepherd
My people Israel too"

Then Herod had a meeting with the Wise Men
And sent them on to *Bethlehem*
"Find *me* the child so I can worship Him *too*," he said
But Herod was *lying* to them

When the Wise Men continued to follow the star
They found Mary and Jesus with her
They bowed and worshiped and gave Him gifts
Of frankincense, gold and myrrh

The angels, the star, the shepherds, the Wise Men
Mary watched it all from the start
And she treasured up *all* of these things
And *pondered* them in her heart

THE WISE MEN LEAVE BETHLEHEM

One night the Wise Men were warned in a dream
To *not* go back to Herod that day
So when they left to return to their country
They went back…by a different way

Herod became *furious* when he realized
What the Wise Men had done
He gave orders to *kill*…all the boys in Bethlehem
Under two years old…every one

But an angel appeared to Joseph in a dream
And told him to leave the land
"Take the child and His mother and escape to Egypt"
And he told him of Herod's plan

When Herod finally died...again an angel came
To Joseph, in a dream, and said,
"Get up, take Mary and the child to Israel
For those who tried to kill Him are dead"

So Joseph took Mary and Jesus to Nazareth
As directed in his dream
Which fulfilled what was said through the prophets:
"He'll be called a Nazarene"

And during the years they lived in Nazareth
Jesus grew and He became strong
He was filled with wisdom and the grace of God
Was upon Him all along

The Boy Jesus in the Temple in Jerusalem

Now each year the family went to Jerusalem
To attend the Passover Feast
It was the custom for all of the people to do this
From the greatest to the least

And every year when the feast was over
Everyone would head for home
But when Jesus was twelve, He stayed behind
In Jerusalem...all alone

Mary and Joseph thought He was with them
As they traveled on for a day
But then they couldn't find Him in their group
And they had gone a long way

So they went back to Jerusalem to search for Him
They looked for Him everywhere
After three days of searching, they went to the temple
And found Jesus *sitting* there

He was sitting among the temple teachers
Asking questions and listening to *them*
They were *amazed* at His understanding and answers
For they *also* listened to *Him*

When Mary and Joseph saw Him they exclaimed
"Son!...We've been *searching* for you!"
"Didn't you know I'd be in my Father's house?" He asked
They didn't understand what He had to do

Then Jesus went home with Mary and Joseph
And He was *obedient* to them
He continued to grow in wisdom and stature
And in favor with God and men

JOHN THE BAPTIST PREPARES THE WAY

Many years later...John the Baptist
Was preaching in the Desert of Judea
"Repent," he said, to all who would listen,
"For the kingdom of Heaven is near"

His clothes were made of camel's hair
Round his waist was a leather belt
And when he spoke...his words were strong
His righteousness...could be *felt*

The people asked him, "Are you the Messiah?"
"I am not the Christ," said John
"Are you Elijah?...Are you the Prophet?"
Their questions went on and on

"After me there will come," John explained to them,
"One more powerful than I
The strings of His sandals...I am not worthy
To kneel down...and untie

"I baptize you with water for repentance
But He who is coming is higher
He will baptize you," John exclaimed,
"With the Holy Spirit and fire!"

The Baptism of Jesus

Now one day Jesus went to the Jordan River
So *He* could be baptized too
But John resisted...and said to Jesus,
"*I* need to be baptized by *you*"

Jesus responded, "Let it be so now
It is proper to do this," He said
So John lowered Jesus, under the water
'Til water flowed over His head

And as Jesus came up from the water
The Heavens opened above
And the Spirit of God descended
Upon Him...like a dove

Then a voice came from Heaven, saying,
"This is my Son...whom I love
With Him I am well pleased," said the voice
Coming from the sky above

Jesus was filled with the Holy Spirit
Then the Spirit led Him away
And the Spirit led Jesus into the desert
Where He would fast and pray

The Temptation of Jesus

After Jesus had fasted for forty days
The devil came and said,
"If you are *truly* the Son of God
Tell these stones to turn to bread"

"It is written, man does not live on bread alone,"
Jesus said as He stared in his face
"But on every word from the mouth of God"
He put the devil in his place

They went to the top of the holy city temple
Far above the ground
"If you are the Son of God," said the devil,
"Then go . . . and throw yourself down

"For it is written He'll command His angels," he taunted
As Jesus stood there alone
"And they will lift you *up* . . . so you will not *strike*
Your foot upon a stone"

But Jesus said to him, "It is *also* written,"
Answering the devil then,
"Do not put the Lord your God to the test"
Defeating the devil *again*

Then the devil took Him to a very high mountain
So the kingdoms of the world He would see
"All of this I will give to you," offered the devil,
"If you will bow down and worship *me*"

"Away from me Satan! For it is written,"
Jesus quoted scripture again,
"Worship the Lord your God and serve *Him only*"
And the devil left Him then

Three times the devil had tempted Jesus
To get Him to bow down
But Jesus rebuked him . . . and when the devil left
Ministering angels . . . came around

JESUS BEGINS HIS MINISTRY

Now Jesus traveled to Galilee
Where He would begin to teach
At that time He was around thirty years old
When He began to preach

And one day as He was walking
By the Sea of Galilee
He saw two brothers . . . Simon and Andrew
And told them, "Follow me"

When Simon and Andrew heard His words
They dropped their nets right then
They were ready to follow...and Jesus said,
"I will make you fishers of *men*"

Then two other fishermen, James and John
Two sons of Zebedee
Dropped *their* nets when Jesus called
And followed immediately

At one point Jesus turned to Simon
And said He was changing his name
He named him Cephas, which is Peter
And his life...would never be the same

The next day as Jesus was walking
Another man...He did see
The man was Philip, who came from Bethsaida
And Jesus said..."Follow me"

Then Philip found Nathanael and told him
"We have found the *One*
Written about by Moses and the prophets
Jesus of Nazareth...Joseph's son!"

"Can anything good come from Nazareth?" said Nathanael
And Philip said, "Come and see"
And when Jesus said Nathanael was a true Israelite
He responded..."How do you know *me*?"

"I saw you when you were under the fig tree," said Jesus,
"Before Philip *called* to you"
"Rabbi, you are the Son of God!" said Nathaniel
For in his heart...he knew

"You believe because I told you," said Jesus,
"That I saw you under the tree
But greater things than that," He continued,
"*Greater* things you will see

"I tell you the truth…you will see Heaven open,"
Jesus told him then,
"And the angels of God ascending and descending
Upon the Son of Man"

JESUS CHANGES WATER INTO WINE

Now Jesus was attending a wedding in Cana
And as the reception wore on
Mary, His mother, came and told Him
That all of the wine was gone

"Dear woman, my time has not yet come," He said
"What would you have me to do?"
Mary turned to the servants and said to them,
"Do whatever He tells you to"

Six stone jars were standing nearby
For ceremonial water
Each jar would hold up to thirty gallons
Jesus saw them and gave an order

"Fill the jars with water," He told the servants
They filled them to the brim
"Now draw some out for the master of the feast"
So they brought a cup to him

The master didn't know where it came from
As he tasted the water turned wine
And he marveled when he tasted it
For *this* was truly *fine*

He called the bridegroom and exclaimed to him,
"This is better than the *rest*!
Everyone else serves the finest wine *first*
But you *waited* to serve the best!"

This miracle showed the glory of Jesus
At Cana in Galilee
And His disciples put their faith in Him
When *this*…they were able to see

Jesus Teaches Nicodemus

Now, there was a man of the Pharisees
Nicodemus was his name
He was a member of the ruling council
And by night...to Jesus...he came

"Rabbi, we know you are a teacher from God,"
He said in the light so dim,
"For no one could perform the miracles you do
If God were not with *him*"

Then Jesus responded..."I tell you the truth
No one can see the kingdom of God
Unless he is born again," He concluded
But this answer was very odd

"How can a man be born...when he is old?"
Nicodemus mused
"Can he enter again the womb of his mother?"
He was clearly confused

"Flesh gives birth to flesh...the Spirit gives birth to spirit,"
Jesus answered him
"You should not be surprised at my saying
You must be born again

"For God so loved the world," He continued,
"That He gave His only begotten Son
That whoever believes in Him shall not perish
But have eternal life"...said the One

"For God did *not* send His Son," He said,
"Into the world to condemn"
Nicodemus listened as Jesus explained
"But to *save* the world *through* Him"

"And whoever believes in Him is not judged
But whoever does not," He went on
"Is *already* judged for *not* believing in the name
Of God's *only* begotten Son

"Light has come into the world," said Jesus,
"But men love darkness instead
And those who do evil...won't *come* into the light"
Nicodemus pondered what He said

JOHN THE BAPTIST TESTIFIES

One day as Jesus and John were both baptizing
Some people questioned John
He explained why the people were going to Jesus
As John's disciples looked on

"I am not the Christ...but I am sent ahead of Him"
He said this for his purpose was planned
"The bride belongs to the bridegroom," he said
Trying to make them understand

"A friend who attends the bridegroom waits"
Elevating Jesus was his choice
"He listens for him and is joyful when he hears
The sound of the bridegroom's voice

"That joy is mine...and is now complete"
With conviction John did stress
"Now *He* must become greater," he said,
"And *I* must become less"

THE WOMAN AT THE WELL

Now as Jesus was traveling through Samaria
He rested by Jacob's well
A Samaritan woman who had come to draw water
Would be *amazed*...at things He would tell

When He asked her to give Him a drink, she replied,
"I am a Samaritan and you are a Jew
How can you ask me for a drink?" she asked
For this was something a Jew would not do

"If you knew the gift of God," Jesus replied,
"And who it is that asks you for a drink
You would have asked *Him*...and He would give *living* water"
The woman didn't know *what* to think

"But Sir...you have nothing to draw with
And the well is deep," she stated
"Where can you *get* this living water?" she asked
"Are you greater than our father Jacob?"

"Whoever drinks *this* water," Jesus answered,
"Will become thirsty again
Whoever drinks the water *I* give...will *never* thirst"
Continuing, He said then:

"The water I give...will become in him a spring
Welling up to eternal life"
"Give *me* this water so *I* won't get thirsty," she cried
He had cut to her spirit like a knife

"Go call your husband and come back," He said
"I have no husband," she replied
"You are right when you say you have no husband," said Jesus
He would have known if she had lied

"You've had five husbands and the man you *now* have
You are not married to"
"Sir, I can see that you are a prophet," she said
For her life...He already knew

Then He spoke to her about worship and the Father
"I know that Messiah is coming," said she,
"And when *He* comes, He will explain *everything* to us"
Jesus said, "I who speak to you...am *He*"

Then the woman left her jar and hurried off
To tell the people of the town
"Come see the man who told me all I've ever done"
And the people *all* came around

When the Samaritan people came to see Jesus
They asked Him if He would stay
He stayed for two days...and many became believers
And then...He went on His way

The people told the woman, "We no longer believe
Just because of what *you* said
We *know* that this man is the Savior of the world"
For they believed what they *saw*...instead

JESUS HEALS A BOY IN CAPERNAUM

Now there was a royal official whose son lay sick
Near death...in Capernaum
Hearing Jesus was in Cana, he went to see Him
To ask if He would come

"Sir, please come down," the official begged,
"Before my child dies"
"Unless you see miracles, you won't believe," said Jesus
But He took mercy on his cries

He said, "You may go...your son will live"
The man took Him at His word
And on his way home...his servants met him
And told him what had occurred

His son was healed...then he asked his servants,
"What time did he get up from his bed?"
"Yesterday, at the seventh hour," they responded
Which was the same time Jesus had said

JOHN IS IMPRISONED

Meanwhile, John the Baptist was put into prison
Because of Herod's wife
She was angry at John...for he spoke of her sin
And *that* would cost John...his life

Jesus Is Rejected in Nazareth

At one point...Jesus returned to Nazareth
The town where He was raised
On the Sabbath He was speaking in the synagogue
And the people were amazed

He read from the scroll of the prophet Isaiah
Isaiah 61...1 and 2
And every eye in the Temple was on Jesus
When His scripture reading was through

Then He rolled up the scroll and handed it back
Looked at the people and said,
"Today this scripture is fulfilled in your hearing"
Referring to what He had read

They marveled at the words that came from His lips
They were eager to listen and learn
But soon their attitude began to change
And on Jesus...they would turn

"Isn't this the son of Joseph?" they asked
Then Jesus said to them
"You want me to do great things in my hometown
As I did in Capernaum"

He said, "No prophet is accepted in his hometown"
Then He spoke of a story they would know
"God did not send Elijah to a widow in Israel
It was to *Zarephath,* he had to go

"And in Israel at the time of Elisha," He said,
"Leprosy was had by many
Yet Elisha healed Naaman the Syrian
And in Israel...he didn't heal any"

When Jesus said this, the people became *furious*
And they took Him to the top of a hill
To throw Him off a cliff...but He walked through the crowd
And the people...just stood still

A GREAT CATCH OF FISH

Now one day by the Lake of Gennesaret
As Jesus stood by the shore
The people were *crowding* around to hear Him
So He stepped into a *boat* He saw

Then Jesus asked Simon, the fisherman
To take the boat out a bit
Then He taught the people...from the boat
Where He was able to sit

When Jesus finished speaking, He told Simon
To take the boat out to the deep
And let down the nets...for a catch
He knew what they would reap

Simon said, "Master, we've worked hard all night
And haven't caught a thing
But because *you* say so...I will let down the nets"
Not knowing *what* this would bring

When they let down the nets...they became so full
That they began to break
So they signaled their partners in the other boat
To join them on the lake

When the others came out, they filled *both* boats
So full they began to sink
The fishermen were so astonished
They didn't know *what* to think

"Go away from me Lord!...I'm a sinful man!"
Simon cried out then
But Jesus told him..."Do not be afraid
From now on...*you* will catch *men*"

Jesus Preaches in the Synagogues

After this, Jesus went to Capernaum again
And in the synagogue He taught
"This man teaches with such authority!"
Was everybody's thought

A man with an unclean spirit was in the temple
"Let us alone!" the spirit cried out
"Jesus!...What do you want with us?"
The spirit continued to shout

"Have you come to destroy us? We *know* who you are!"
Then Jesus began to speak
He said, "Be quiet!...Come out of him!"
And the spirit...fled with a shriek!

The people were amazed when it happened
"What *is* this that we see?
Even unclean spirits obey Him!" they said
And it spread through Galilee

Jesus Heals Many

One night at the house of Simon and Andrew
Simon's mother-in-law had a fever
Jesus took her by the hand, and she stood up
And the illness did immediately leave her

Many people were brought to Jesus that night
Who were sick or demon possessed
And while many crowded at the door to watch
Jesus healed the rest

The next morning, He rose before daylight
And went out by Himself to pray
Then He went throughout Galilee teaching and healing
And casting out demons on the way

JESUS HEALS THE LEPER

Now one day a leper came to Jesus
And begged Him on his knees
"If you are willing," he said "you can make me clean"
Jesus was moved by his pleas

He reached out His hand…and touched the man
And said, "I am willing…be clean"
The man was cured and Jesus sent him to the priest
In order for the man to be seen

"See that you don't tell this to anyone," said Jesus
As He sent the man away
"Offer sacrifice…and show yourself to the priest"
And so the man went that day

But the man went out and spread the news
Then Jesus couldn't enter a town
So He stayed outside…in lonely places
But the people *still* came around

JESUS HEALS A PARALYTIC

Now when Jesus was in a house in Capernaum
The people heard He was there
And so many gathered, that there was no room
Neither inside nor outside…anywhere

And while He was preaching, some men arrived
They were bringing a cripple to Him
But because the house was so very crowded
They could not get him in

So the men made an opening in the roof
And lowered the man on his mat
And because of the faith Jesus saw in these *men*
He forgave the man's sins for *that*

But the Pharisees and teachers were thinking,
"Who forgives sins but God *alone*?"
Jesus heard their thoughts and to show His authority
Said, "Take up your mat and go home"

Immediately the man stood up and praised God
Took his mat and went on his way
Then the *people* praised God, saying in awe,
"We've seen remarkable things today!"

The Calling of Levi

One day as Jesus taught a crowd by a lake
Levi...a tax man...He did see
Who immediately got up and followed Him
When Jesus said, "Follow me"

Then Levi held a banquet in honor of Jesus
The most unusual of dinners
For Hebrews would *never* eat and drink
With tax collectors and sinners

"Why does He eat with tax collectors and sinners?"
He heard the Pharisees complain
"It is not the healthy who need a doctor, but the sick,"
Jesus tried to explain

Then they remarked that His disciples weren't *fasting*
Jesus looked at them at last
"The time will come when the bridegroom is taken
In *those* days...they will fast"

Healing at the Pool of Bethesda

One day at the pool of Bethesda in Jerusalem
Jesus saw a man who was lame
He said, "Pick up your mat and walk"...and he *did*
But the man didn't know Jesus' name

Later, the man was confronted by the Pharisees
As he was walking on his way
"The law forbids you to carry your mat," they said
For this was the *Sabbath* day

He replied that the man who had made him well
Said to pick up his mat and go
They asked him who it was that had *healed* him
But he really didn't know

Jesus saw the man later and said, "Stop sinning
Or something *worse* may happen to you"
Now the man *knew* who it was who had healed him
And he told the Pharisees too

Then the Pharisees came and confronted Jesus
But He turned to them and said
That the *Father* gave Him authority to do these things
And to even raise the dead

He also told them that the Father judges no one
But has entrusted judgment to the Son
So all may honor the Son as they honor the Father
For the Father has *sent* the One

One day He'll call everyone to come from the grave
Those who've done good…to live
Those who've done evil will be condemned
The Son will condemn or forgive

Later as He walked through a field with His disciples
They were hungry and picked some grain
The Pharisees said it was unlawful on the Sabbath
Again Jesus tried to explain

"The Sabbath was made for man," He began
"Not man for the Sabbath," He stated
"And the Son of Man is Lord…even of the Sabbath"
Now *Jesus*…the Pharisees *hated*

On another Sabbath, as Jesus was teaching
There was a man with a shriveled hand
The Pharisees watched to see if He would heal him
To accuse Him...was their plan

"Is it lawful to heal on the Sabbath?" they asked
"If any of you has a sheep," He replied
"And it falls into a pit, will you not lift it out?"
Using a parable...He tried

"How much more valuable is a man than a sheep?
Therefore, it is *lawful* to do good"
Then He took the man with the shriveled hand
And in front of all, He stood

"Stretch out your hand"...the hand was healed
Everyone was still
But the Pharisees were furious and began to plot
How Jesus...they might kill

News of His miracles spread through the land
People gathered from far and near
To be saved from afflictions and evil spirits
And for His *messages*...to hear

Jesus Appoints Twelve Apostles

One day He went alone to a mountainside
And spent the night in prayer
When morning came...He called His disciples
And waited 'til all were there

Then He chose twelve men...and made them apostles
And as He called each name
James...John...Philip...Bartholomew
Their lives would forever change

Simon...who was called the zealot
Judas...son of James
James...the son of Alphaeus
Jesus called their names

Peter...Andrew...Matthew...Thomas
And Judas Iscariot...who later
Became well known through the generations
For *he*...became the traitor

After that, Jesus came down with His men
And stood on a level place
A large crowd gathered to hear and be healed
Everyone seeking His face

The Sermon on the Mount

Jesus saw the crowd and He healed the people
Then He went up the mountain and sat down
His disciples went with Him...and He began teaching
While the people all gathered around

"Blessed are those who are poor in spirit
For theirs is the kingdom of God," He said
"And blessed are those who mourn and weep
For they will be comforted

"Blessed are the meek for they'll inherit the earth"
The crowd was large yet stilled
"Blessed are those who hunger for righteousness
For they...shall be filled"

"Blessed are the merciful...they will find mercy
Blessed are the pure in heart
For they will see God," Jesus continued
The crowd enthralled from the start

"Blessed are the peacemakers for they will be called
The sons of God," said the Lord
"Blessed are the righteous, persecuted for my name
Rejoice...for great is your reward

"But woe to you rich...you've received your comfort
Woe to those of you well fed
For you will go hungry...And woe to you who laugh
You will mourn and weep instead

"Woe to you when all men speak well of you
For it was also in this way
That your fathers treated the false prophets"
And much more He had to say

Then Jesus continued and told the believers,
"You are the salt of the earth
But if salt should lose its saltiness
Then it has lost its worth

"You are the light of the world," He said,
And Jesus told them then
To put their light on a stand...like a lamp
And to let it *shine* before men

"Do not think I came to abolish the Law or Prophets
I came...for them to *fulfill*"
Then He spoke of the sixth commandment by saying,
"You heard it said, 'Thou shalt not kill'

"But he who is *angry* at his brother without cause
Will be subject to judgment as well
And if anyone says, 'You fool!'...they will *also*
Be in danger of the fire of hell

"And if at the altar, you remember a conflict
Leave the altar for a while
Offer your gift later...but first go to your brother
So you can reconcile

"Settle matters quickly with your adversary
Who is taking you to court"
He tried to make them understand that a *trial*
Should be the last resort

"I tell you that if anyone looks lustfully at a woman
He has committed adultery in his heart
And if your eye or your hand should cause you to sin
It is better to *lose* that part

"He who divorces his wife, except for fornication
Makes her become an adulteress
And whoever *marries* her *also* commits adultery,"
Jesus went on to stress

Then Jesus told the people not to swear at all
Not by earth or Heaven...God's throne
Or by anything else...for it *all* belongs to God
And *nothing* is really their own

He said, "Instead of living by what had been said,
'Eye for eye and tooth for tooth,'
Do unto others as you would have them do to you"
He was teaching them new truth

"Do not love your *neighbor*...and hate your enemies
But love your enemies as well
Pray for them, be merciful and your reward will be great
When in Heaven, you dwell

"When you give to the needy...do not announce it
The way the hypocrites do
They've received their reward from men and will *not*
Receive one in Heaven too

"Don't pray like the hypocrites, in temples and on corners
Where they can be seen by men
Pray in your room...in secret to your Father
And *He* will reward you then

"And when you pray...do not babble like the pagans
Who think they will be heard
The Father *knows* what you need, *before* you ask
Not because of many words"

Then Jesus told them specifically
The words that they should say
Honoring the Father and forgiving others
He taught them how to pray

"Our Father who art in Heaven," He said
"Hallowed be your name
Your kingdom come, your will be done"
Jesus went on to proclaim

"On the earth as it is in Heaven" He said
"And give us our bread each day
And forgive us our sins as we forgive others"
Jesus continued to pray

"Lead us not into temptation but deliver us from evil,"
Jesus finished His prayer
Then He spoke to them about fasting
And told the people there

"When you fast...do not look somber," He said
"Like the hypocrites do
Do it in secret...so only the Father knows
And the *Father*...will *reward* you

"Store up treasures in Heaven...not on earth"
He tried to make them see
"For wherever you store your treasures," He said,
"There also your heart will be"

"For no one can serve two masters,"
Jesus did observe
"He'll be devoted to one and despise the other
Both God and money...you cannot serve

"The eye is the lamp of the body...and if sound
Your body will be full of light
But if *unsound*...your body will be full of *darkness*
As deep as the darkness of night

"Do not worry about your life," He continued
"What you will eat or drink
The birds of the air do not sow or reap"
His words made people think

"And yet your Heavenly Father feeds them," He said
"Are you not more valuable than they?
Who can add a single hour to his life by worrying?"
And then He went on to say

"And why do you worry about clothing?
See the lilies of the field how they grow?
Not even Solomon was dressed like these," He said
Speaking of the seeds *God* sows

He told them God dresses the fields with beauty
In a way they could relate
"So will He not much more clothe *you*?" He asked
"O you of little faith?

"So don't worry and say, 'What will we eat or wear?'
For your Heavenly Father already knew
Seek *first* His *kingdom* and His *righteousness*
And all these *things* will be *given* to you

"Do not *judge*…and you will not *be* judged"
He was teaching them how to live
"Do not *condemn* and you will not *be* condemned
You will be forgiven…if you forgive

"Give and it will be given to you," He continued
Telling them what to do
"For with the measure you use," Jesus went on,
"It will be measured to you

"Why do you look at the speck of sawdust
In your brother's eye?
And pay no attention to the plank in your own?"
He made *them* wonder why

"First take the plank from your own eye," He said,
"And *then* you will see clear
To remove the speck from your *brother's* eye"
His words…held *every* ear

"Do not give to dogs what is sacred," He went on,
"Or throw your pearls to swine
They may trample on them and *turn* on you
And tear you to pieces in time"

Then Jesus said, "Ask…and it will be given to you
Seek…and you will find
Knock…and the door will be opened to you"
His promise for all mankind

"Which of you, who are evil…if his son asks for bread
Will give to him a stone?
How much more will your Father in Heaven give?"
He said things no one had known

Then He told them, "Enter through the narrow gate
For wide the gate and broad the road
That leads to destruction," Jesus continued,
"And many go through it"…He forebode

"Beware of false prophets in sheep's clothing
They are ferocious wolves at their root
A tree will either produce good fruit or bad
You will *know* them by their fruit

"For the good man brings forth good things
From the good stored up in his heart
But the evil man's heart contains evil
And *that*…*he* will impart

"From the overflow of the heart, the mouth will speak
Whatever it may be
And not everyone will enter the kingdom of Heaven
Who says, 'Lord, Lord,' to me

"Only he who does the will of my Father in Heaven
Will enter on that day
Many will come who *think* they will enter
But I will send them away

"They'll say, 'Didn't we perform miracles and prophesy
And drive out demons in your name?'
And I will say, 'Away from me, you evildoers
I never knew you!'" He exclaimed

"And why do you call me Lord, Lord," Jesus asked,
"And yet...do not *do* what I say?"
Then He spoke about wise and foolish builders
In a parable way

"The man who comes to me and hears my words
And then applies them to his life
Is like a wise man who built his house on a rock
And then was faced with strife

"For when the rain came down...and the water rose
And the house was beaten by the storm
It did not fall...for it had its foundation
Upon the *rock* all along

"But the man who doesn't apply my words to his life
Is like a house built with sand at its feet
And when the storm came...the house collapsed
Its destruction...was complete"

When He finished speaking, the crowd was amazed
For in all they heard Jesus say
He spoke with *authority*...unlike their teachers
Who had *never* spoken that way

JESUS HEALS THE CENTURION'S SERVANT

After Jesus had finished speaking to the people
He entered Capernaum
Where a centurion's servant lay ill, near death
Then Jesus heard about him

For the soldier sent Jewish elders to Jesus
To plead for Him to come
"This man loves our nation and built our synagogue,"
They said of the centurion

Then the soldier sent *another* messenger to Jesus
After the *elders'* appeal
"I don't deserve to have you under my roof," he said,
"But say the word and my servant will be healed"

Jesus was amazed at the centurion's faith
After the message He received
"Go," replied Jesus... "It will be done
Just as you believed"

Jesus Raises the Widow's Son

One day as Jesus entered the town of Nain
A funeral procession had begun
A widow was crying... for in the coffin
Was the widow's only son

When Jesus saw her... His heart went out to her
And He said to her, "Do not cry"
As He touched the coffin... everyone wondered
In a moment... they would know why

"Young man... I say to you, get up!" He said
The crowd just stood and gawked
But then in awe... they all praised God
When the man sat up and talked

Jesus and John the Baptist

Now John was in prison so he couldn't go to Jesus
So he sent two disciples instead
"Are you the one who was to come... or should we expect
Someone else?" they said

"Go back and report to John," Jesus answered,
"What *you* have seen and heard
The blind receive sight... the lame can walk"
For they *saw* these things had occurred

As they listened carefully, Jesus continued
He said, "The lepers are cured
The deaf can hear...and the dead are raised
The good news is preached to the poor"

When the messengers left, Jesus spoke to the crowd
He called John "a prophet and more"
"Of those born of woman...there is no one greater"
No one had heard this before

"Yet the one who is least in the kingdom of God
Is greater than John," He said then
"Heaven has been forcefully advancing until now
And laying hold of it are forceful men

"If you're willing to accept it, he *is* the Elijah
Who *was* to come," He went on
"For all of the Prophets and the Law," He said
"Had prophesied...until John"

Anointing By a Sinful Woman

Now a woman went to a house where Jesus was dining
All stared as she approached the Master
The woman was carrying expensive perfume
In a jar made of alabaster

She was a sinful woman and she knew the risk
So she first had to conquer her fears
Then she walked up to Jesus and knelt at His feet
And *wet* His feet...with her tears

She wiped them with her hair...and then she kissed them
Then the alabaster jar she broke
She poured out the perfume and anointed His feet
Watching this...no one spoke

Now the man who owned the house was a Pharisee
He had invited Jesus to the dinner
He thought..."If this man were a prophet He would *know*
That this woman...is a sinner"

But Jesus said, "Simon, I have something to tell you"
For his thoughts...Jesus had read
Then He spoke of two men who borrowed from a lender
"One borrowed fifty denarii," He said

"While the other man borrowed *five hundred* denarii,"
Jesus told His host
"Neither could pay...and the man cancelled both debts
Now *which* man will love him the most?"

"The one who had the bigger debt cancelled," said the host
"You have judged correctly," Jesus said
But because of what Jesus said next to the Pharisee
In shame he would hang his head

"Do you see this woman?" Jesus asked
As the woman He regarded
"When I entered, you gave me no water for my feet"
Jesus' reproach had started

"But she wet my feet with her tears," He said,
"And wiped them...with her hair
You did not give me a kiss," He continued
As every person stared

"But she has been kissing my feet since I entered"
His reprimand nearly complete
"You did not put oil on my head," said Jesus,
"But she poured perfume on my feet

"Therefore I tell you, her many sins are forgiven
For she has loved much," He said
"But he who was *forgiven* little... *loves* little"
Immediately whispering spread

"Who is this who even forgives sins?" cried the guests
As their indignation increased
Jesus paid no attention but said to the woman
"Your faith has saved you...go in peace"

A House Divided

As Jesus traveled, many people were healed
Everywhere he'd been
With Him were His disciples and some women
Including Mary Magdalene

Now she had been cured of seven evil spirits
For the demons, Jesus did bind
One day a demon-possessed man was brought
Who was also mute and blind

Jesus healed the man and cast out the demon
Now the man could speak and see
"Is this not the son of David?" the people exclaimed
But not the Pharisees

"He casts out devils through Beelzebub," they said
Jesus heard their reprimand
"A city or a house divided," He responded,
"Against itself...cannot stand

"If Satan casts out Satan," He continued,
"Against *himself*...he is *divided*
How then shall his kingdom stand?" He asked
But no answer, they provided

"He who is not with me is against me," He said
"He who does not gather with me, scatters"
Then Jesus spoke to them about the unforgivable sin
Information that gravely matters

"I say to you that all manner of sin and blasphemy
Shall be forgiven men
But blasphemy against the Holy Spirit," He said,
"Shall *not* be forgiven them

"Everyone shall give account on the day of judgment
Of each idle word spoken by them
For by your words you will be justified," He said
"By your words...you will be condemned"

Then the people asked Jesus to give them a sign
So to them, He could prove His worth
Instead...He said as Jonah was three days in the whale
So shall the Son be...in the heart of the earth

Fear God, Not Man

"Do not be afraid of those who kill the body," said Jesus,
"And after that, can do no more
Fear Him who has the power to throw you into hell"
No one had taught like this before

"And whoever acknowledges me before men
I will acknowledge before my Father," He said
"But he who disowns me before men...will be disowned"
He warned of what lay ahead

"And when you are brought before rulers and authorities
Do not worry about what you will say
For the Holy Spirit will give you the words at that time"
In everything...He showed them the way

And as Jesus went on traveling and teaching
All throughout the land
He continued using parables to teach the people
So they could easily understand

The Parable of the Sower

Jesus said Heaven is like a farmer sowing seed
Some fell along the path as he sowed
But the birds came down and they ate those seeds
Before they had a chance to grow

Some of the seeds had fallen on *stony* places
Where there was not much soil
They had no roots...and so they were scorched
When the sun began to broil

Some other seeds had fallen among the thorns
Which sprung up and *choked* the seeds
But *some* seeds had fallen onto *good* ground
Away from thorns and weeds

"Those seeds brought forth fruit," He told them
"What does this mean?" they exclaimed
"The seed is the word of God," He replied
And with patience... He explained

"The seeds along the path are the people who hear
But the devil takes the word from their heart
The seeds in the thorns are those who hear and are *joyful*
But are choked before they start"

"For they cared for the riches and pleasures of this life
So their faith has never grown
The good ground are good hearts... who will bring forth fruit
They keep with patience... what is sown"

THE PARABLE OF THE WEEDS

Jesus said Heaven is like a man who sowed good seed
But then, while the man was asleep
And enemy sowed weeds and when the crop sprang up
There were weeds among the wheat

When his servants asked if they should pull the weeds
The farmer told them, "No
For while pulling the weeds, you might pull the wheat
So together they must grow

"When it is harvest time, I will tell the reapers
To bundle up the weeds," He went on
"And throw them in the fire and *then* gather the wheat
And put it in my barn"

Later... when Jesus was alone with His disciples
They said they didn't understand
He explained that the one who sows the good seed
Is the Son of Man

The good seed are the children of the kingdom
And the world... is the field
The weeds are the children of the wicked one
And then more... He revealed

The enemy who sowed the bad seeds is the devil
The harvest... is the world's end
Then He said that the reapers are the angels
Which the Son of Man shall send

They'll gather the evil ones and throw them in the fire
They'll weep and gnash their teeth... every one
Then the righteous will go to the Kingdom of Heaven
Where they will shine... like the sun

PARABLE OF THE LAMP ON A STAND

Jesus said no one lights a lamp and puts it under a bowl
Or puts it under a bed
In order for those coming in... to see the light
He puts it on a stand instead

"For nothing is secret that will not be disclosed,"
The people heard Jesus say
"Whoever has will be given more... and he who has *not*
What *he* has, will be taken away"

THE PARABLE OF THE MUSTARD SEED

Jesus said that Heaven is like a mustard seed
Which a farmer plants in his field
And though it is the smallest of all of the seeds
The largest plant it will yield

It will continue to grow and become a tree
And then the birds of the air
Will sit on its branches and build their nests
And make their homes in there

THE PARABLE OF THE NET OF FISH

Jesus also said that Heaven is like a fishing net
Which was cast into the sea
When full, they kept the good and discarded the bad
Whatever they might be

Then He told the people it will also be that way
At time of the end of the world
The angels will separate the good from the evil
Into the furnace...the evil will be hurled

JESUS CALMS THE STORM

When Jesus finished teaching, He got into a boat
On the evening of that same day
He had been surrounded by a large crowd of people
And wanted to get away

He told His disciples to cross over the water
And then He went to lay down
But before long they were waking Him and shouting,
"Master...we're going to drown!"

For while He was sleeping in the stern of the boat
A furious squall rose up
And though some of the disciples were fishermen
All were terror-struck

Then Jesus stood and commanded the storm
"Quiet!...Be still!" He said
Immediately the wind and the waves died down
Then Jesus turned His head

He said to His men..."Do you still have no faith?
Why are you afraid?"
But they were terrified and asked, "Who is this?
Even the wind and waves obey!"

The Demon-Possessed Gerasene

After this happened, they sailed to Gerasene
And when they pulled ashore
Out of the tombs came a man with an evil spirit
Who no one could restrain anymore

He lived in the tombs and the people chained him
On his hands and on his feet
But he had broken the chains and when he saw Jesus
He ran out to Him... to meet

The man fell on his knees in front of the Lord
And the spirit said with a shout,
"Son of the Most High God, what do you want?"
And Jesus told the demon, "Come out!"

Jesus asked the demon, "What is your name?"
"My name is Legion," he replied
"For we are many," the demon continued
Referring to other demons inside

The demon begged Jesus not to send them away
He begged Him again and again
Then the demon saw a herd of pigs on a hill
And he turned to Jesus then

"Send us to the pigs!... Let us to go into *them!*"
The demon Legion cried
Jesus sent them to the pigs... and they ran into the lake
And two thousand pigs... all died

The pig herders went and told the whole town
Who came back to see what they'd find
They all saw the man who had been possessed
Dressed... and *in* his right *mind*

The people were afraid and asked Jesus to leave
But the man who had been crazed
Went *all* around the country telling *everyone*
And the people were amazed

A Sick Woman and a Dead Child

Later, when Jesus had again crossed the lake
A large crowd gathered around
And a synagogue ruler named Jairus came
And fell at Jesus' feet on the ground

He pleaded with Jesus, "My daughter is dying
Please touch her so she will live"
Then Jesus left and went with the man
For He was always willing to give

A large crowd followed and pressed around Jesus
And a woman was there in the crowd
The woman had been subject to bleeding for years
But to stop Him...would she be allowed?

She came up behind Him and she touched His cloak
Because the woman believed
"If I just touch His clothes, then I will be *healed*"
Right then...her affliction was relieved

But as soon as she did it...Jesus knew
That power had gone out from Him
"Who touched my clothes?" He asked the people
And the disciples answered then

"You see the people pressing against you," they said
"And yet you ask...'Who touched me?'"
But Jesus ignored what His men were saying
And kept looking around to see

Then the woman who knew what happened to her
Came and fell at His feet
Trembling with fear she told Jesus the truth
Not knowing what fate she would meet

"Daughter...your faith has healed you"
Jesus looked down and said
The woman was afraid that she would be punished
But He gave her mercy instead

While Jesus spoke, men came from Jairus' house
And said, "Your daughter is dead
Why bother the teacher anymore?" they asked
But Jesus ignored what they said

"Do not fear," He told Jairus..."Just believe"
And so they traveled on
But He didn't allow the people to follow
Only Peter, James and John

At Jairus' house, people were crying and wailing
Jesus asked, "Why this *commotion*?
The child is not dead...she is *asleep*"
But this *changed* their emotion

They began to laugh for they *knew* she was dead
Then Jesus took her hand
He said, "Little girl...I say to you...get up!"
And immediately...she did stand

She began to walk and the people were amazed
That the girl was on her feet
Then Jesus told them not to tell anyone
And to give her something to eat

Two Blind Men Healed

After Jesus healed the child, He left Jairus' house
Followed by two blind men
They were calling, "Have mercy on us, Son of David!"
Wanting a *healing* from Him

"Do you believe I am able to do this?" He asked
"Yes, Lord," they replied
"According to your faith...let it be done," He said
As Jesus touched their eyes

Immediately, the two men were able to see
But Jesus instructed them
To not tell anyone...but the men went out
And spread the news of Him

JESUS REJECTED AGAIN IN NAZARETH

After Jesus left...He again went to Nazareth
And on the Sabbath, as before
He taught in the synagogue and many who listened
Were again...in awe

"Where did He get these things?" the people asked
"What is the wisdom of this one?
"He even does miracles!...Isn't this the carpenter?
Isn't this Mary's son?

"Brother to Joseph, James, Judas and Simon?"
To them...it made no sense
"Aren't His sisters here with us?" they asked
And at Jesus...they took offense

"Only in his own town is a prophet without honor," He said
And while elsewhere He was praised
He could only heal a *few* of the afflicted in Nazareth
At their lack of faith...He was amazed

JESUS SENDS OUT THE TWELVE DISCIPLES

Now as Jesus traveled throughout Galilee
Through towns and villages teaching
He felt compassion for the crowds and healed many
Of the people He was reaching

He told His disciples, "The harvest is plentiful
But the laborers are few"
He gave them authority to heal and cast out demons
And sent them out...two by two

He told them to tell the lost sheep of Israel
That the kingdom of Heaven is near
Heal the sick, raise the dead, drive out demons
His instructions were very clear

He told them to take no possessions with them
But to find a worthy person in each town
And to stay at his house as long as they are there
As they traveled all around

"If a home is worthy, let your peace be on it"
He said of the people they would meet,
"If people don't welcome you or listen to your words
Then shake the dust from your feet"

He warned them that people would betray them
And they would be put under arrest
"All men will hate you because of me," He said
When about Him...they attest

THE BEHEADING OF JOHN THE BAPTIST

Herod had married his brother's wife, Herodias
And John the Baptist spoke of his sin
When John did *that*...Herod put him in prison
But didn't *know* what to *do* with him

Now Herod's wife Herodias...hated John
And wanted to have him killed
But John was a holy man and Herod wouldn't kill him
Just because Herodias willed

Now Herodias had a beautiful daughter
Salome was her name
And Herodias waited for her opportunity
One day...it finally came

Herod had a birthday and held a grand banquet
He invited many to attend
Including high officials and military commanders
And Galilee's leading men

At one point, as they were all celebrating
Salome entered the hall
And to entertain Herod for his birthday
She danced in the sight of all

And by the time the music ended
Herod was entranced
He offered Salome anything she wanted
In gratitude for her dance

"Ask for *anything* and I'll give it to you," he said
She could have whatever she desired
But Herod would come to regret his offer
When he heard...what she required

For Salome went to her mother, Herodias
"What shall I ask?" she said
Herodias seized her opportunity and replied,
"Ask for John the Baptist's head"

Salome stood before Herod...the hall grew quiet
As the guests all ceased their chatter
"My wish," she said..."is that you give me the head
Of John the Baptist...on a platter"

Herod immediately regretted the oath he had made
In front of everyone
But because of his oath...and all of the witnesses
This...would *have* to be done

So Herod sent an executioner to the jail
With orders to bring John's head
The man returned with John's head on a platter
John the Baptist...was dead

JESUS FEEDS FIVE THOUSAND

When the disciples returned they reported to Jesus
And then they climbed into a boat
For so many people were coming and going
They needed a place more remote

So they headed for a place where they could rest
Upon the opposite shore
But people saw them from the towns and ran ahead
Gathering more and more

When Jesus saw the crowd, He didn't get upset
He felt compassion instead
For they were like sheep without a shepherd
That had wandered on ahead

So He welcomed them and He healed the sick
And then He began to teach
He spoke to them of the Kingdom of God
It was nearing the Passover feast

As Jesus was teaching…it became late in the day
Yet the crowd still sat at His feet
His disciples asked Him to send the people away
So the people could buy something to eat

Jesus looked at the crowd and responded,
"Give them something to *eat*," He said
But all they could find was a boy with two fish
And five small loaves of bread

Jesus told His disciples to have all of the people
Sit in large groups on the grass
He looked to Heaven and gave thanks for the food
And gave it to His disciples to pass

There were about five thousand men in the crowd
Yet all ate and had their fill
When the disciples gathered the remaining food
There were twelve full baskets still

Now all of the people saw what had happened
And marveled at what Jesus had done
In awe they exclaimed, "This is surely the Prophet!
The Prophet who is to come!"

JESUS WALKS ON WATER

Then Jesus told His disciples to go ahead in the boat
And He sent the crowd away
When everyone was gone…He went up a mountain
To be by Himself to pray

By the time He came down from the mountain
The boat was in the midst of the sea
And the wind and the waves were battering it
To a dangerous degree

Now Jesus came walking out to the boat
During the fourth watch of the night
When the disciples saw Him walking on the water
They were filled with fright

Their eyes grew wide as they peered through the darkness
"It's a ghost!" they cried in fear
But Jesus replied..."Take courage!...It is I"
And He continued to draw near

"Lord, if it's you, tell me to come to you on the water,"
Peter said with a shout
Jesus said, "Come"...and as they looked at each other
Peter...climbed out

Now Peter was walking on the water toward Jesus
But when he looked at the wind and the sea
He became afraid...and began to sink
He cried out, "*Lord...save* me!"

Jesus reached out His hand and caught him
So Peter wouldn't drown
"O you of little faith, why did you doubt?" He asked
And once in the boat...the wind died down

Then the men in the boat began to worship Him
"Truly you're the Son of God!" they said
When they landed at Gennesaret...people *saw* Him
And the news He was there, quickly spread

People came from all over, bringing their sick
And to Jesus, they appealed
To allow them to touch the edge of His cloak
And all who touched it were healed

But the Pharisees complained to Jesus about His disciples,
"They don't wash their hands when they eat bread"
Jesus told the Pharisees that they were hypocrites
And quoting Isaiah, He said:

"These people honor me with their lips
But their hearts are *far* from me
They worship me in vain, teaching rules of men"
He tried to make them see

"You lay aside the Commandments of God," He said,
"And hold to traditions of men
Attending to *little* things…like washing pots and cups"
But the Pharisees were *offended* then

"What goes *into* the mouth just goes into the belly,"
Jesus told them then
"What comes *out* of a man…comes from the *heart*
And *that* defiles a man"

After this, He and His disciples continued to travel
Going from town to town
Jesus told the people about the Kingdom of God
And healed them as He traveled around

Jesus Feeds Four Thousand

Around four thousand men were gathered together
And Jesus called His men
"These people have been with me for three days," He said,
"And I have compassion for them"

"They have nothing to eat and if I send them home now
They'll collapse along the way"
"But where can we get enough bread to feed them?"
His disciples began to say

"How many loaves do you have?" asked Jesus
"We only have seven," they said
Then Jesus told the crowd to sit down on ground
And then He took the bread

He gave thanks, broke it and gave it to His disciples
Who passed the bread around
The people all ate and when they gathered the pieces
Seven full baskets they found

Peter Confesses Jesus as the Christ

At one point, when they were on the coast
Of Caesarea Philippi
Jesus asked His disciples an interesting question,
"Who do people say…am I?"

"Some say you are John the Baptist," they replied,
"And some say you are Elijah"
The disciples continued to offer possibilities
"Others say you are Jeremiah"

"But who do *you* say that I am?" asked Jesus
Each pondered this in his head
"You are the *Christ*…the Son of the Living God,"
Simon Peter said

Jesus said, "Blessed are you Simon, son of Jonah,"
Turning from the other eleven,
"For flesh and blood have not revealed this to you
But my Father…who is in Heaven

"You are Peter the rock…and upon this rock,"
Jesus went on to commit,
"I will build my church…and the gates of hell
Will not *prevail* against it"

He said He would give Peter the keys to the kingdom
And Peter could bind and loose as well
But He told the disciples not to say He was the Christ
And *no* man…should they tell

JESUS FORETELLS HIS CRUCIFIXION

Now Jesus began to tell His disciples
That to Jerusalem He must go
And suffer many things under the elders and priests
For He wanted them to know

He said He would be killed...and raised in three days
But Peter said, "Be it *far* from *true!*"
He took Jesus aside and he said, "*Never* Lord!
This shall *never* happen to you!"

But when Jesus responded...He startled Peter
"Get behind me, Satan!" He said
"You don't have in mind the things of God, but of men"
For Peter didn't know what lay ahead

THE TRANSFIGURATION

Six days later, Jesus took Peter, James and John
Up on a mountain so high
And as they watched, Jesus was transfigured
Right before their eyes

His face began to shine...bright like the sun
His clothing was white as light
Then Moses and Elijah appeared and *spoke* with Him
The disciples were in awe at the sight

Then a bright cloud came and enveloped the three
And a voice...came from the cloud
"This is my beloved Son, in whom I am well pleased
Listen to Him!"...said the voice clear and loud

When the disciples heard the voice they were terrified
And fell face down on the ground
Jesus touched them saying, "Get up...do not fear"
And the disciples looked around

Moses and Elijah were no longer there
Jesus looked at them and said,
"Tell no one what you have seen until the Son of Man
Has risen from the dead"

Then the disciples asked Jesus, "Why do the scribes say
That first Elijah must come?"
Jesus said it was *true*...and Elijah *did* come already
But no one *recognized* the *one*

"And as Elijah suffered under these people," He said,
"Likewise shall the Son of Man do"
Jesus was speaking of John the Baptist
And now the disciples knew

Jesus Heals a Boy with an Evil Spirit

Now when they came back to the other disciples
They saw them surrounded by a crowd
The teachers of the Law were arguing with them
Animated and loud

Jesus asked them what they were arguing about
And He was answered by a man
Who knelt and said, "Lord have mercy on my son"
Then his story he began

He said his son was possessed by an evil spirit
That seizes him and throws him to the ground
He said he thought the disciples could *free* his son
And so, he brought him around

But when the disciples tried to drive out the spirit
They were not able to
Then Jesus said ,"O unbelieving generation
How long shall I put up with you?"

Then He said to them..."Bring the boy to me"
So they brought the son of the man
But when the evil spirit in the boy saw *Jesus*
A violent *convulsion* began

"How long has he been like this?" asked Jesus
The father said, "Since he was a child
It often throws him into fire or water to *kill* him!"
The behavior of the boy was wild

"I command you," said Jesus, "Come out of him!
And never *enter* him again!"
The demon immediately came out of the boy
And the disciples asked Jesus then

"Why could *we* not cast out the demon?" they asked
"Because of your *unbelief*," He declared
"With faith as small as a mustard seed…you can tell a *mountain*
To move from here to there"

Later He told His disciples that He would be killed
But *first*…He would be betrayed
Then He'd rise in three days…but they didn't understand
And didn't ask…for they were afraid

WHO IS THE GREATEST?

When they came to Capernaum Jesus asked His disciples,
"What were you arguing about on the way?"
But they were disputing which of them was the greatest
So no one wanted to say

Then Jesus said to them, "If anyone wants to be first
He must be the last…and servant of all"
Then He called a little child and had him stand among them
In the center of the hall

He told his disciples that unless they change
And become as little children
They would never enter the kingdom of Heaven
And Jesus told them then:

"Whoever welcomes one of these little children
In my name…welcomes *me*
And whoever welcomes *me*…doesn't welcome *me*
But the one who *sent* me," said He

"And if anyone causes one of these little ones to sin
These children who believe in me
It would be better for him to have a stone 'round his neck
And to be cast into the sea"

Works Done in the Name of Jesus

"We saw a man driving out demons," said John
"He was doing it in your name
We told him to stop because he's not one of *us*"
Then Jesus began to explain

"No one who does a miracle in my name," He said,
"Can say anything *bad* about me
Whoever is not against us is *for* us," said Jesus
And His disciples began to see

"I tell you the truth," Jesus told His men,
"Anyone who gives to *you*
A cup of water in my name…because you are *mine*
Won't lose the reward he is due"

Rebuke and Discipline of the Brethren

"If a brother sins against you, go show him," said Jesus,
"Between only the *two* of you
If he will not listen, then come back with others
Come back with one or two

"If he refuses to listen, then tell it to the church
And if he will not listen to *them*
Then treat him as you would a tax collector
Treat him as a pagan

"What you bind on earth will be bound in Heaven,"
Jesus went on to say
"What you loose on earth will be loosed in Heaven"
He taught His men the way

"And if two of you agree about anything you ask
It will be done by my Father in Heaven
For wherever two or three are gathered in my name
I am there...in the midst of them"

The Unmerciful Servant

One day Peter came to Jesus and asked Him,
"How many times shall I forgive my brother?
Up to seven times?" he ventured a guess
As they looked at one another

Jesus responded, "I say to you *not* seven times
But seventy times seven"
Then He told a parable to all who were listening
About the kingdom of Heaven

He said Heaven is like a king who had a servant
Who owed him ten thousand *talent*
His family would be *sold* if he could not pay
And away they would be sent

The servant cried, "Lord, have *patience* with me"
As he fell down and begged the king
As the king's heart softened...the servant continued,
"I will pay back *everything*"

The king canceled the debt, for he was so moved
By his servant's desperate plea
But when the servant left he found a *fellow* servant
Who owed *him*...a hundred *denarii*

He grabbed the other servant by the throat
Began to choke him and demanded,
"Pay back what you owe me!"...and unlike the king
He treated him heavy handed

His fellow servant fell on his knees and begged
"Please be patient with me!" he said
"I will pay you back"...but the first servant refused
And had him thrown in prison instead

When the other servants saw what had happened
They went and told the king
Who said to the servant, "You *wicked* servant
I forgave you *everything*!

"Shouldn't *you* have had mercy on your *fellow* servant
As *I* had compassion on *you*?"
And he turned him over to the jailers for torture
Then Jesus *explained* the parable too

"This is how my Heavenly Father," He said,
"Is going to treat each of *you*
Unless you *forgive* your brother... from your *heart*"
He made it clear what everyone must do

The Woman Caught in Adultery

One day as Jesus taught in the temple courts
The teachers and the Pharisees
Tried to trap Him by bringing Him a *woman*
Who was caught in adultery

They asked Him what they should *do* with her
For according to Moses' *Law*
She should be *stoned*... But instead of *answering*
He bent down and began to draw

They continued to ask... Jesus stood up and spoke
"Let him who is *without* sin
Be the first one to cast a stone at her," He said
And then He bent down again

All eyes were upon Him as Jesus bent down
And with a finger of His hand
Jesus began... with deliberate measure
Writing in the sand

Everyone was watching Him as He wrote
And by the time that He was done
They had each dropped their stones and walked away
One... by one

The woman crouched waiting…for the onslaught of rock
Not knowing what Jesus had drawn
"Woman…has no one condemned you?" He asked
She looked…but the crowd was gone

"No one, Sir," the woman replied
Jesus looked at her and then
He said, "Neither do I condemn you…now go
And *leave* your life of sin"

THE GOOD SHEPHERD

"I am the gate for the sheep," said Jesus
After healing a man born blind
"He who enters through me will be saved
And pasture he will find

"The thief comes to steal and kill and destroy"
He tried to make them see
"But *I* have come that they may have *life*
And have it *abundantly*

"I am the *Good* Shepherd," Jesus continued,
"Who lays down His life for His sheep
When the wolf comes, the hired hand *abandons* them
For they are not his to keep

"Then the wolf attacks the flock and scatters it
And the hired hand runs away
For the man cares *nothing* for the sheep"
Then Jesus went on to say:

"I am the *Good* Shepherd, I *know* my sheep
And *my* sheep…know *me*
As the Father knows me and I know the Father
And I lay down my *life* for the sheep

"No one *takes* it from me," Jesus continued
"I lay it down of my own accord
I have authority to lay it down…and to take it up again"
The people heard the words of the Lord

JESUS HEALS TEN LEPERS

As Jesus was traveling through Samaria and Galilee
On His way to Jerusalem
Ten lepers called, "Jesus!...Have mercy on us!"
And Jesus took pity on them

"Go and show yourselves to the priests," He said
And so they went to be seen
And as they walked...they were amazed
For they were all made clean

When a Samaritan saw that he had been healed
He went back to Jesus again
Kneeling before Him, he began praising God
But Jesus said, "Were there not ten?

"Where are the other nine?" Jesus asked the man
"Was no one else found to return
Except for this foreigner to give praise to God?"
Jesus asked with concern

Then Jesus looked lovingly...down at the leper
Who listened and heard Him say,
"Your faith has made you whole
Arise and go your way"

THE SEVENTY-TWO DISCIPLES

Now Jesus had once again sent out disciples
Their number was seventy-two
He was very specific in all His instructions
As to what they were to do

And when the disciples returned to Him
They excitedly exclaimed
"Lord!" they said, "even the *demons*
Submit to us in *your name!*"

Jesus told them He saw Satan fall like lightning
And that He gave them *authority*
To trample snakes and scorpions and to overcome
All the power of the enemy

But He told them that they should not be rejoicing
Because spirits *submit* to them
But to rejoice for their names are written in Heaven
And they *know*...they are not condemned

The Good Samaritan

"What must I do," a lawyer stood and asked Jesus,
"To inherit eternal life?" he said
"What is written in the Law?" Jesus asked the man
But the man knew only what he read

"Love the Lord your God with all your heart," he said,
"And all of your soul and strength
And all of your mind...and your neighbor as yourself"
He knew the *Law*...in its whole length

Then Jesus said, "You have answered correctly
Do this and you shall live"
But the lawyer said, "But who *is* my neighbor?"
He wanted *Jesus*...more to give

"A man went from Jerusalem to Jericho," said Jesus
"And he fell among thieves," He said,
"Who stripped him of his clothes and beat him
And left the man for dead

"A priest going down the road *saw* the man
But passed by on the other side
Then a Levite saw the man and did the same
And no aid did *he* provide

"But then a Samaritan traveling on the road
Saw him and didn't pass by
For when he saw the man he felt compassion
And wouldn't leave him there to die

"The Samaritan treated the injured man's wounds
And then he bandaged him
Then he put the man upon his *own* donkey
And took him to an inn

"He took care of the man, while at the inn
And before he left the next day
He paid the *innkeeper* to care for him and told him,
'When I return this way

"'I will reimburse you for any expense you may have'"
Then Jesus asked the questioning man,
"Which of these men...was a *neighbor* to the man
Who fell into the robbers' hands?"

The lawyer replied, "The one who had mercy"
His answer was no surprise
Jesus nodded as He looked at the lawyer and said,
"Now go...and do likewise"

MARY AND MARTHA

Jesus and His disciples stopped in Bethany
On their way to Jerusalem
Where there lived a woman named Martha
Who opened her house to them

Now Martha was distracted by all the preparations
And as Jesus took a seat
Martha was working while her sister Mary
Just sat at Jesus' feet

Martha said, "Lord, don't you care that my sister
Has left all the work to me?
Tell her to help me!" Martha cried
And Jesus answered her plea

"Martha, Martha...you worry about *many* things"
Her busyness He would deter
"Only *one* thing is needed...Mary chose what is better
And it will *not* be *taken* from her"

Jesus Affirms His Own Deity

Now at the time of the Feast of Dedication
Jesus was in Jerusalem
And one day He was walking in the temple
In the Colonnade of Solomon

"How long will you keep us in suspense?"
Some people asked of Him
"If you are the Christ, then tell us plainly"
And Jesus looked at them

"I *did* tell you," He said, "but you do not believe"
For the people did not see
"The miracles that I do in my Father's name
They testify for me

"But you do not believe, for you are not my sheep
My voice...my sheep *do* hear
I know them and they follow me," said Jesus
Making it very clear

"I give them eternal life...and they will never perish"
His explanation nearly done
"No one can snatch them from my Father's hand
I and the Father are one"

The Parable of the Place of Honor

Jesus went to the house of a prominent Pharisee
Where He was invited to eat
And He noticed how the guests were trying
To sit in an honor seat

"When someone invites you to a wedding," He said,
"Do not sit in the honor place
For the host may move you for someone *higher*
Shaming you in that case

"Take the lowest place and then when the host arrives
He may come and *say* to you,
'Move to a better place'...and in front of the guests
You will be honored too

"For everyone who exalts himself will be humbled,"
Jesus gently said,
"And he who humbles himself will be exalted"
He referred to times ahead

PARABLE OF THE LOST SHEEP

Tax collectors and sinners gathered around Jesus
So they could listen to Him
While Pharisees murmured, "This one receives *sinners*
And He even *eats* with them!"

But Jesus heard them and told them a parable
As usual, they had tried to malign
"If one of you has a hundred sheep and loses one," He said,
"Does he *not* leave the ninety-nine

"To search for the lost one until he finds it?" He asked
To this...they would certainly agree
"When he finds it, he puts it on his shoulders and goes home
And tells his friends...'Rejoice with me'

"Likewise," He said, "there is more rejoicing in Heaven
Over one sinner who repents
Than over ninety-nine righteous...who do not need to"
His parable made perfect sense

THE PRODIGAL SON

Jesus told a story about a man who had two sons
The youngest asked the father one day
To give him his inheritance and the father did
Soon after...the son went away

In a distant land, he wasted his wealth on wild living
And soon....he was in need
So he went to work for a farmer who sent him out
To the pigs in his field to feed

No one gave him anything and the man was so hungry
He was ready to eat the *pigs'* food
Finally, he came to his senses and realized
This lifestyle he must conclude

"How many of my father's servants," he thought,
"Have bread enough to eat and to spare?
And I'm starving to *death*...I'll go to my father
And speak to him when I am there

"I'll say, 'Father, I've sinned against Heaven and you
I'm not worthy to be called your son
Please make me one of your hired servants'"
His repentance had *already begun*

So the man got up and started back to his father
And when he was still a distance away
His father saw him and felt compassion in his heart
For the one who had gone astray

He ran out to meet him and threw his arms 'round him
And then he kissed his son
The son said he wasn't worthy and he was a sinner
For the things that he had done

But the father told his servants to dress him in the finest
And to put a ring on his hand
And to kill the fatted calf and prepare a feast
And so...the celebration began

Meanwhile, the older son had been in the field
But now, as he came near
He heard music and saw dancing, so he asked a servant,
"What is happening here?"

"Your brother has come home!" the servant replied
But the son began to frown
"And your father has killed the fatted calf," he said,
"For he is back, safe and sound!"

But the son became angry and would not go in
Then his father came outside
He pleaded with his son...who then responded
And to his father he cried:

"All these years I've been serving you
And *never* have I disobeyed
Yet you never even gave me a *goat* to celebrate!"
He continued his tirade

"But as soon as this *other* son of yours comes home
Who *squandered* your property
You kill the fatted calf for him!" he exclaimed
Most incredulously

"Son, you're *always* with me...and all I *have* is yours,"
The father told him then
"But it is *right* to celebrate...for your brother was *dead*
And he is *alive* again"

As the older brother contemplated these words
So strong and so profound
His father gently concluded by saying,
"He was lost...and now is found"

THE RICH MAN AND THE BEGGAR

Jesus told of a rich man who was dressed in fine linen
His table was always a feast
But by his gate lay a beggar named Lazarus
A man of the very least

He was covered with sores and he longed for food
From the rich man's table...whatever fell
Yet when he *died*...angels carried him to Abraham
While the rich man...went to hell

In torment, the rich man looked up and saw Abraham
With Lazarus by his side
"Father Abraham!" he called "Have pity on me!"
And continuing...the rich man cried

"Send Lazarus to dip his finger in water
To cool my tongue," he said,
"Because I am in agony in this fire"
But Abraham spoke of the lives they'd led

Then Abraham pointed to a great gulf between them
Impassable by them or others
"Then I beg you, send Lazarus to my father's house
For I have five more brothers!

"Let Lazarus warn them, so *they* will not come
To this place...of torment"
Abraham said, "Let them hear Moses and the Prophets"
But the man *knew*...they wouldn't repent

"But if someone who is *dead* goes to see them
They will repent," the man said
"If they don't hear Moses or the Prophets," said Abraham,
"They won't believe if one rises from the dead"

The Pharisee and the Tax Collector

There were some men who looked down upon others
But were proud of their own righteousness
Jesus spoke to them and told them a parable
For their pride...He would address

He said a Pharisee and a tax collector went to the temple
In order that they could pray
As the Pharisee stood...he prayed about himself
And he had much to say

"God, I thank you that I am not like other men," he said
He wasn't praying to atone,
"Like robbers, adulterers or this tax collector
I fast...and give a tenth of all I own"

Meanwhile, standing far off with eyes lowered
The tax collector confessed
"God have mercy on me...I'm a sinner," he said
As he beat upon his breast

Jesus said *this* man was the one justified before God
As the Pharisee's pride, He assaulted
"For he who exalts himself will be humbled," He said,
"He who humbles himself...will be exalted"

THE LABORERS IN THE VINEYARD

Jesus said Heaven is like an owner of a vineyard
Who went out early one day
He hired men to work for him...and all agreed
On one silver piece as pay

A little while later, the man went out again
The hour was now around nine
He hired *more* laborers and sent *them* out too
To also tend to his vines

He went out again at noon and mid-afternoon
And hired yet more men
And near the end of the day...he went out once more
And found laborers, yet again

"Why do you stand here idle?" he asked them
"Because no one has hired us," they grieved
He sent them to his vineyard and for payment he said,
"Whatever is right...you will receive"

When evening came, he called his steward
For the work of the day was done
"Call the laborers in and pay them," he said
"Start with the last...to the very first one"

Each of the laborers received one silver piece
Even those hired...near the end of the day
The first ones hired...thought *they* would get more
But they *all* received the same pay

The first ones complained to the landowner
And began to put up a fuss
"These last men only worked one hour," they said,
"And you made them equal to *us*!"

But the landowner responded to one of them saying,
"Friend, I did you no wrong
Did you not agree with me...on *one* silver piece?
Take what is yours...and move along

"Can I not do what I want with my own money?
I gave to the last the same as to you
Are you jealous because I'm generous?" he asked
"Is it unlawful for me to do?"

Then Jesus concluded the parable by saying,
"And so the last shall be first
And the first shall be last"...showing how in Heaven
Rewards will be disbursed

The Death of Lazarus

Jesus received a message from Mary and Martha
That their brother Lazarus was ill
They asked that He return to Bethany immediately
But that was not His will

He stayed where He was for two more days
Then He said, "Let us now go back"
But His disciples tried to discourage Him from going
Because of a prior attack

"But Rabbi," they said, "the people tried to stone you
And you want us to go back *there*?"
Then Jesus told them that Lazarus had died
Of this...they were not aware

As they neared Bethany, Martha came to meet them
"Lord, if you had only been *here*
My brother would not have died," she said
For the Lord...she did revere

"But even now I know God will give you what you ask,"
Martha told Him then
Jesus looked at her with compassion and replied,
"Your brother will rise again"

"I know he will rise again in the resurrection," she said,
"The resurrection on the last day"
Then Jesus said, "*I* am the resurrection and the life"
And then He went on to say

"He who believes in *me*...shall live though he dies
Do you believe?" said the One
"Yes Lord, I believe you're the Christ," she answered,
"The Son of God...who was to come"

Then Martha told Mary, "The teacher is here
And He is asking for *you*"
As Mary quickly went to see Jesus, people followed
They thought she was going to the tomb

When Mary reached the place where Jesus was
She fell at His feet and cried
"My Lord, if you had been here," she sobbed,
"My brother would not have died"

When Jesus saw Mary and the other mourners weeping
Compassion, through His heart swept
He asked where they laid him...they said, "Come and see"
And at that moment...Jesus wept

"Look how much He loved him," some people said
As many others were crying
"Could not *He* who opens the eyes of the blind
Have kept this man from dying?"

Then Jesus stepped up to the tomb of Lazarus
Where he had been for four days
He said, "Take away the stone"...But Martha responded
"Lord by *this* time...he decays"

"Did I not say if you believed that you would see
The glory of God?" Jesus said
So they obeyed His command and moved the stone
Then Jesus raised His head

He thanked His Father for having heard His prayer
Even though He knew
The Father always hears Him, but He said it for the people
So they would hear it too

Then looking at the tomb, Jesus commanded
With a voice that showed no doubt
"Lazarus...come forth!" He said
And Lazarus...came out

His hands, feet and head were wrapped in linen
Then Jesus turned and said,
"Take off the grave clothes and let him go"
For Lazarus was no longer dead

THE COUNCIL PLOTS TO KILL JESUS

After *that*, many people put their faith in Jesus
For they saw it...every one
But some of them left and went to the Pharisees
And told them what Jesus had done

Then the chief priests and Pharisees had a meeting
Saying, "What are we to do?"
They were worried for if Jesus came into power
What would happen...no one knew

They said if they did nothing and all men followed Him
That would be *extremely* bad
For the Romans would come and take from *everyone*
Everything they had

Then a man named Caiaphas stood up to speak
He was the high priest of the year
"You know nothing at all," Caiaphas began
His demeanor...very austere

"You do not realize that it is better for *you*,"
Referring to the things they cherish,
"That *one man die* for the *people*," he continued,
"Rather than the whole nation *perish*"

Now Caiaphas had not said this on his own
As high priest...he had *prophesied*
That for the good of all of the Jewish nation
Jesus Christ...would die

From that day on, the priests and the Pharisees
Began to plan His death
They ordered anyone who knew His location to report it
So they could arrange His arrest

THE RICH YOUNG RULER

A rich young man wanted to gain eternal life
He asked Jesus, "What must I do?"
Jesus told him to obey the Ten Commandments
But this, he already knew

"Teacher...I have kept these since I was a boy," he said
Jesus looked at him, loved him and said,
"Go sell whatever you have and give to the poor"
But the man began to feel dread

"And you will have treasure in Heaven," He continued
"Then come and follow me"
But the man went away sad...for he had great wealth
And a great sacrifice this would be

Then Jesus said, "How hard it is for the rich
To enter the kingdom of God!"
His disciples were *astounded* at what He said
Why would it be so hard?

Then Jesus elaborated and told them it is easier
For a camel to go through the eye
The eye of a needle...than for a rich man to enter
The kingdom of Heaven when he dies

The disciples all asked, "Who then can be saved?"
Feeling confusion and dread
Jesus answered, "With man this is impossible
But all is possible with *God,*" He said

Then Peter said, "We have left *everything* to follow you
What shall *we* have therefore?"
Jesus said they would sit on thrones with Him in Heaven
And then He told them more

Those who leave loved ones for Him will gain eternal life
And a hundred times as much as the past
But He also said that many who are last will be first
And many who are first will be last

JESUS AGAIN PREPARES THE DISCIPLES

As they continued on their journey to Jerusalem
Jesus told His disciples again
That He would be handed over to the Gentiles
And what would happen then

They will mock Him, insult Him and spit on Him
He said as He looked in their eyes
They will flog Him and kill Him but on the third day
He told them...He will rise

But the disciples did not understand what He meant
For the meaning was *hidden* from them
Then James and John, the sons of Zebedee
Asked a *favor* of Him

"Let one of us sit at your right hand," they said,
"And the other at your left in your glory"
But Jesus said they didn't know what they were asking
For they didn't know the whole story

He asked them if they could drink the cup He drinks
Or the same baptism, receive
They said, "Yes," and Jesus agreed that they would
Though He knew, they were naive

"But to sit at my right or left…is not for *me* to grant"
He said as the two men stared
"Those places belong to those," He continued,
"For whom they have been prepared"

When the other disciples heard what had happened
They were indignant with the brothers
But then Jesus gathered them all together
So He could speak to the others

He pointed out that although the people in power
Lord it over men
That is definitely not the way it is
When it comes to them

Instead, with them, if any one of them
Wants to become great
They must become as servants to each other
If *Him*…they would emulate

For even Jesus Himself did not come to earth
In order to be served
But to serve and to give His life as a ransom
For *many*…to preserve

JESUS AND ZACCHAEUS

Zacchaeus was a wealthy tax collector in Jericho
In stature he was not a tall man
So he couldn't see Jesus because of the crowd
And so…ahead he ran

Then Zacchaeus climbed up a sycamore tree
For Jesus was coming that way
And he figured he would be able to *see* Him
So in the tree…he would stay

But Jesus said, "Zacchaeus…come down at once"
As He looked at him overhead
"I must stay at your house today," He continued
Zacchaeus was surprised at what He said

He climbed down immediately and welcomed Jesus
But the people began to grumble
"Look... He is going to be the guest of a sinner"
And Zacchaeus heard their mumble

"Behold Lord," he said... as everyone watched,
"Half my goods I will give to the poor
And if I have cheated anyone out of anything," he said,
"I will pay back the amount... times four"

Then Jesus said to the people who were watching
Salvation came to that house that day
He said that Zacchaeus was *also* a son of Abraham
And that *now*... he saw the way

"For the Son of Man came to seek," said Jesus,
"And to save... what was lost"
The people all listened and pondered this
Though no one understood the cost

The Blind Beggar Bartimaeus

As Jesus approached Jericho, He passed a blind beggar
Named Bartimaeus... by the roadside
He called out when he heard the noise of the crowd
"What is going on?" he cried

"Jesus of Nazareth is passing by," they said
Again Bartimaeus called out
"Jesus... Son of David... have mercy on me!"
But they tried to quiet his shout

Some people rebuked him and told him to be still
But he would not let it be
Instead, Bartimaeus shouted all the more,
"Son of David... have mercy on me!"

Then Jesus said, "Call him," and the people told him,
"Get up! He is calling *you!*"
And when he made his way to Jesus... Jesus asked
"What do you want me to do?"

"Lord...I want to see," Bartimaeus replied
Jesus considered him and said,
"Receive your sight...your faith has healed you"
Then He turned and walked ahead

Immediately the blind man was able to see
And began to follow behind
He was praising God and the people did too
For Bartimaeus...was no longer blind

JESUS IS ANOINTED AT BETHANY

Six days before the Passover, Jesus was in Bethany
The guest of a man who was known
As Simon the Leper...And in honor of Jesus
Simon held a dinner in his home

The disciples, Lazarus, Mary and Martha
Were all in attendance there
And Mary poured a pint of pure nard on Jesus' feet
Then wiped them with her hair

The house was filled with the beautiful fragrance
Of this very expensive perfume
But one of the disciples of Jesus *objected*
The one who would *betray* Him soon

"Why wasn't this perfume sold," said Judas,
"And the money given to the poor?
It was worth a year's wages!" he scolded
But his motive was devious for sure

For he did not say this out of concern for the poor
But for a reason he did not reveal
He was keeper of the money bag and from its contents
Judas himself would steal

Jesus rebuked him saying, "Leave her alone"
And then He went on to say,
"It was intended that she should save this perfume
For my burial day

"You'll always have the poor but not always have me," He said
So Mary, they would not deter
"Wherever the gospel is preached in the world," He said,
"This will be told...in memory of her"

The Triumphal Entry into Jerusalem

As Jesus and His disciples traveled to Jerusalem
They came to the town of Bethpage
Jesus sent two disciples ahead to get a donkey
A donkey of a tender age

He told them where to find it...and to bring it back
And then He said to them,
"If any man asks you why are you doing this
Say, 'The Lord has *need* of him'"

So the two disciples followed Jesus' instructions
And they went on ahead
They found the donkey...and the owner inquired
Just as Jesus said

So they told the owner, "The Lord has *need* of him"
And the owner let them go
They put cloaks on the donkey and Jesus sat upon it
Why this was important...they didn't know

It was after Jesus was glorified, the disciples realized
What they hadn't understood at the time
For this had been plainly prophesied in Scripture
In Zechariah...9:9

Meanwhile, a great crowd had come for the Passover
And they heard Jesus was on His way
They went out to meet Him, spreading cloaks and palms
With raised voices, He heard them say:

"Hosanna! Hosanna!...Blessed be the King
Who comes in the name of the Lord!
Peace in Heaven and glory in the highest!" they shouted
The people in one accord

But He *also* heard, "Master!...Rebuke your disciples!"
Which some of the *Pharisees* said
Jesus answered, "I tell you...if they keep quiet
The *stones* will cry out instead"

Now when Jesus approached Jerusalem
He saw the city...and He wept
For Jesus foresaw its destruction
And this was hard to accept

Then Jesus spoke to the *city* and said,
"If you had only known
On *this* day...what would bring you peace"
There was heartache in His tone

"But now it is hidden from your eyes," He continued,
"But the day will come around
When your enemies will surround you on every side
And dash you to the ground

"They will not leave one stone upon another
Because *now* you didn't *recognize*
The time of God's coming to you," He said
As tears rose in His eyes

When they entered Jerusalem, the city was stirred
"Who is this?" the people said
"This is Jesus, the *prophet*!" some answered
The excitement continued to spread

But the Pharisees were saying to each other,
"*This* is getting us *nowhere*!
Look how the whole world has gone *after* Him!"
For them...a disturbing affair

Jesus Drives the Merchants from the Temple

Now it was almost time for the Passover
When they traveled to Jerusalem
And when they arrived at the temple courts
They found there...many men

But some were not there to worship the Lord
They were there to *sell*
They bargained for doves, cattle and sheep
Some exchanged *money* as well

And when Jesus saw them…He became angry
And began to drive them out
He overturned tables and scattered animals
Chasing the men with a shout

"How *dare* you turn my Father's house," He said,
"Into a marketplace!"
His anger was righteous and justified
Their behavior was a disgrace

As He cleared the Temple, He continued to shout
For He had no patience for these
"It is written, 'My house will be a house of *prayer*'
But *you've* made it a den of *thieves*!"

Then the people demanded a miraculous *sign*
To *prove* His authority
But Jesus *spoke* to those who were asking
Instead of doing what they wanted to see

"Destroy this temple and I'll raise it in three days"
But they didn't understand what He said
For the temple *He* referred to…was His *body*
Which He would raise from the dead

The Fig Tree

Jesus and His men went back to Bethany that night
And when they arose the next day
They started walking again to Jerusalem
But stopped along the way

For Jesus saw a fig tree…and He was hungry
He thought it had fruit at first
But when He reached it, there were only leaves
And the fig tree…Jesus cursed

"May no one *ever*...eat fruit from you again,"
His disciples heard Him say
And they saw the fig tree withered from the roots
When next they passed that way

The disciples were amazed and expressed their surprise
About the withered tree
Jesus said that with *faith*...*they* could tell a mountain
To throw itself into the sea

And if their hearts had no doubt...it would be done
And if they *truly* believed
Then when they prayed...*whatever* they asked for
Would *also* be received

JESUS SPEAKS ABOUT THE PURPOSE OF HIS DEATH

Jesus said to His disciples, "The hour has come
For the Son of Man to be glorified
If a grain of wheat falls, it remains a single seed
But produces *many*...once it has died

"The man who loves his life in this world will lose it
He who hates it here will have eternity
Whoever serves me must follow me...and where I am
There also my servant will be

"Now my soul is troubled, yet what shall I say?
Father...save me from this hour?
It is *for* this hour I *came*...Father, *glorify* your name!"
Then a voice came from Heaven with power

"I *have* glorified it...and will glorify it again"
The people heard and said it was thunder
Others said that an *angel* had spoken to Jesus
As the people stood in wonder

"This voice has come for your benefit," said Jesus
"Now is a judgment of this world
Now shall the ruler of this world be cast out"
He was telling how the plan would unfurl

"But I will draw all men to myself," He said,
"When lifted from this earth am I"
He said this to show them the kind of death
That He was going to die

"We heard that Christ will stay forever," said the people,
"So what is this *you* say
'The Son of Man must be lifted'...Who is the Son of Man?"
What was Jesus trying to portray?

"For just a short time the light is with you," He replied,
"Walk while you have the light
Believe in the light so you become *sons* of the light
And are not overtaken by the night"

THE AUTHORITY OF JESUS IS QUESTIONED

As Jesus was teaching in the temple in Jerusalem
Though the people were in awe
Some *demanded*..."Who gave you this authority?"
They were priests and teachers of the Law

Jesus told them He would answer their question
If *they* would answer *one*
"Was John's baptism from Heaven or men?" He asked
But this could be answered by none

They started to discuss it among themselves
"If we say 'from Heaven,'" they began,
"Then He will ask us why we didn't *believe* him
But if we say, 'from man'

"The people will *stone* us, for they believe John a *prophet*"
So they answered, "We don't know"
"Nor will I tell you by what authority *I* do things," said Jesus
And they had to let it go

THE PARABLE OF THE TENANTS

Then Jesus told a story of a man who owned a vineyard
After planting, he leased it out
And while the tenants were working the vineyard
The landlord traveled about

When harvest time came, the landlord sent a servant
So he could collect the rent
But the tenants beat the servant and paid him nothing
And back to the landlord he went

So the landlord sent another...and then another
But the tenants beat each one
Then the landlord figured they would be *respectful*
If he sent to them...his *son*

But when the tenants saw the son approaching
Among themselves they said,
"If we kill the heir...we'll get his inheritance"
So then...the son was dead

"So when the landlord goes to the vineyard," said Jesus,
"What then will he do?
He will kill the tenants and give the vineyard to others"
Everyone knew this to be true

"Have you never read the Scripture," He continued,
"'The stone the builders rejected
Has become the cornerstone; the Lord has done this'?"
Then He told who would not be accepted

"Therefore I tell you that the kingdom of Heaven
From *you* will be taken away
And given to people who will produce its fruit"
But they didn't *like* what He had to say

The priests and the teachers knew it was *themselves*
That the parable portrayed
So they wanted to *immediately* have Jesus arrested
But of the crowd...they were afraid

THE PARABLE OF THE WEDDING BANQUET

Then Jesus said the kingdom of Heaven is like a king
Who prepared a wedding banquet for his son
He sent his servants to call for the invited guests
But the people refused to come

Then the king sent out *more* servants to the people
But they ignored the servants again
Some of them even mistreated and *killed* them
And the king became *furious* then

So he sent out his army to kill all of the murderers
And also their city to burn
Then he told his servants to go out to the streets
And before they would return

They had to invite everyone they could find
From the worst... to the best
They followed his orders and the banquet hall
Was *filled* with all of the guests

But when the king entered the wedding feast
He saw a man not properly dressed
He questioned the man... but the man couldn't say
Why he wasn't wearing his best

Then the king told his servants, "Bind him hand and foot!
Throw him into darkness outside!
They'll weep and gnash their teeth... for many are invited
But few are chosen," he cried

GOD AND CAESAR

Trying again to trap Jesus, the Pharisees asked,
"Is it right to pay taxes to Caesar or not?"
Jesus answered, "Give me a coin that I might look at it"
For He knew....it was a plot

"Whose image is this? And whose name?" He asked
As He held it for all to see
"Caesar's," the people replied as they wondered
What His next comment would be

"Give to Caesar what is Caesar's," Jesus told them
And then He went on to say,
"And to God what is God's," which amazed the Pharisees
They were silent…and went away

THE GREATEST COMMANDMENT

"Which is the greatest Commandment?" asked a scribe
Jesus answered the question in length
"Love the Lord your God with all your heart and soul
And with all of your mind and strength

"And Love your neighbor as yourself," He continued,
"*This* is the *second* one
There is *no* Commandment greater than *these*,"
Concluded God's own Son

THE SEVEN WOES

Then Jesus told His disciples and the people
To do what the Pharisees teach
"But don't do what they *do*…for they do *not*," He said,
"Practice what they preach

"They tie up heavy burdens to put on the shoulders
The shoulders of *other* men
But they are not willing to lift a finger
To help move any of them

"They do all of their works to be seen by men
They love sitting in the honorary seat
And they love to hear men calling them Rabbi
When in the market they meet

"You will *not* be called Rabbi...for you have *one* Master
And the rest of you are brothers
And you have only *one* Father...and *He* is in Heaven
Do not say '*father*'...to others

"Don't say 'teacher' for the *only* Teacher is *Christ*"
Their pride...Jesus assaulted
"Whoever exalts himself will be humbled," He said,
"Whoever humbles himself will be exalted

"Woe to you scribes and Pharisees...you hypocrites!
You shut up heaven before men
You yourselves do not enter...nor will you *allow*
Those who are *trying* to get in

"You travel over land and sea to win a convert
Then make him twice as bad as you
You give a tenth of your spices and yet neglect faith
Justice and mercy too

"You clean only the outside of the cup and the dish
Inside are self-indulgence and greed
First clean the *inside* of the cup and the dish
Then the outside will be clean indeed

"O Jerusalem, Jerusalem, you who kill the prophets
And stone those sent to you
How often I have longed to gather your children
But you were not willing to"

Signs of the End of the Age

Some disciples pointed out the beautiful buildings
As they left the temple ground
But Jesus said, "Not one stone will be left on another
Every one...will be thrown down"

Later, as they sat with Jesus on the Mount of Olives
The disciples asked, "When will this be?
What will be the signs of your coming and the end of the world?"
Jesus said, "Many will come saying, 'I am He'

"They will come in my name saying, 'I am the Christ,'
And many they will deceive
There will be wars and rumors of wars, but do not fear
These things you *must* perceive

"And though such things must happen first
The end will not come right away"
He said that nations will rise against nations
Then other signs, He went on to say

Earthquakes in various places and signs from Heaven
Famine and pestilence
He said His followers will be hated by all nations
Persecution will be intense

And when they see all these things begin to happen
It is the beginning of birth pain
Betrayed by loved ones, people will be killed
All on account of His name

But when they're arrested and brought to trial
They shouldn't worry about what to say
For He'll give words of wisdom that can't be disputed
At the right time on that day

False prophets will appear and deceive many people
With increased wickedness, love will grow cold
But he who stands firm to the end will be saved
And then much more He told

When the Gospel is preached to the entire world
Jesus' words were strong
When they see the abomination that causes desolation
Standing where it does not belong

When they see that Jerusalem is surrounded by armies
They'll know it's desolation is near
Those in Judea should flee without hesitation
His words were very clear

They will be taken as prisoners to all of the nations
By the sword...many will be killed
And Jerusalem will be trampled by the Gentiles
'Til the time of the Gentiles is fulfilled

Those days of distress will be unequaled from the beginning
And never will be equaled again
No one would survive...but for the sake of the elect
The Lord has *shortened* them

So if anyone says, "Look...there is the Christ"
Jesus told them they should not believe
For false Christs and prophets will appear and do miracles
For even the elect...to deceive

And immediately after those days of distress
Darkness will come on the sun
No light from the moon...stars fall from the sky
These things will truly come

Heavenly bodies will be shaken and seas will roar
Nations will be perplexed
Men will faint from terror and apprehension
Of what is coming next

Then all of a sudden...appearing in the sky
Will be the sign of the Son of Man
And all of the nations of the earth will mourn
He continued to reveal the plan

They will see the Son of Man with power and glory
Coming on the clouds of the sky
When these things begin...they should lift their heads
For their redemption...is drawing nigh

And with a loud trumpet call, He will send His angels
And they will gather His elect
From the ends of the heavens to the ends of the earth
But the evil ones...He will reject

Jesus said that no one knows the day or the hour
Not the angels, nor the Son
Only the Father knows when this will happen
When that time will come

And it will be as it was in the days of Noah
When the Son of Man comes that day
The people didn't know what was happening
'Til the flood came and swept them away

Therefore everyone should be alert and prepared
For at a time when they least expect
Lightning will flash and the Son of Man will come
To gather the elect

THE PARABLE OF THE TEN VIRGINS

Then Jesus told His disciples what Heaven will be like
When that time will arrive
Like ten virgins who went out to meet a bridegroom
Five were foolish...five were wise

The foolish ones brought lamps...but did not bring oil
While the wise brought extra with them
When the bridegroom was late, they all became drowsy
And fell asleep *waiting* for him

"The bridegroom is coming!...Go out and meet him!"
They were awakened by a shout
Then the foolish ones cried, "Give us some of your oil!
Our lamps are going out!"

But the wise ones said, "No...there may not be enough
For all of us and you
Go to those who sell oil and buy it for yourselves"
Which was what they had to do

The bridegroom took the wise ones into the wedding
While the foolish ones were gone
Then the door was shut...and when the others returned
They began to carry on

"Lord...Lord!...Open the door for us!"
The foolish virgins cried
But the answer was, "Truly...I do not know you"
When at last the groom replied

THE PARABLE OF THE TALENTS

Then Jesus said that Heaven would be like a man
Who was leaving on a journey
He wanted to entrust some money to his servants
And so he sent for three

He gave each an amount according to their ability
To the first...he gave five *talent*
To the second, he gave two and to the third, he gave one
Then off on his journey he went

The servant who had five put it to work and doubled it
And so did the servant with two
But the servant with the one talent hid it in the ground
So nothing...did it accrue

When the master returned, he called them together
As he had done before
The first one said, "Master, you gave me five talent
And I have earned five more!"

"Well done, good and faithful servant!" said the master
His gratitude he wanted to express
"You've been faithful with a little, now I'll give you more
Come *share* in my *happiness*"

Now the same thing happened with the second servant
But when the *third* one came
"Master," He said, "I knew that you're a *hard* man,"
The servant began to explain

"You harvest where you have not sown," he said,
"And gather where you did not seed
I was afraid and so I buried your money"
But the master was displeased

He told the servant he was wicked and lazy
And because the servant *knew*
That the master harvested...where he had not *sown*
He should have *known* what to do

He should have at *least* put the money in the *bank*
So that when the master returned
He would receive his money...plus the interest
Which the money would have earned

Then he ordered that the talent be taken from the servant
And given to the one with ten
For all who have will be given more...and have much
Jesus told them then

And from him who has not, even what he has will be taken
Jesus continued to teach
He'll be thrown into darkness where there will be weeping
And there will be gnashing of teeth

THE DAY OF JUDGMENT

Jesus said that when the Son of Man comes in His glory
And all the holy angels with Him
He shall sit upon His throne...before all of the nations
And the dividing...will begin

He will separate the people the way that a shepherd
Divides the goats from the sheep
He'll set the sheep on His right and the goats on His left
But not all...will He keep

He'll tell those on His right..."Come blessed of my Father
Inherit the kingdom prepared for you
From the beginning of the world...for I was hungry
And you gave me food

"I was thirsty and you gave me a drink," He continued
"I was a stranger and you took me in
I was naked and you clothed me, sick and you visited"
The disciples listened to Him

"I was in prison and you came to me," said Jesus
And then the righteous shall say,
"Lord, when did we see you hungry and feed you?"
Jesus continued to portray

"When did we see you a stranger and take you in?
Or naked and clothe you...when?
When did we see you sick or in prison and come to you?"
Then the King shall say to them:

"Truly I say to you, inasmuch as you have done it
To one of the least of my brothers
You have done it to me," Jesus continued
But the King shall turn to the others

He'll tell those on His left..."Be gone, you accursed
Into everlasting fire
Prepared for the devil and his angels," He said
The disciples could see His ire

"For I was hungry and thirsty and you gave me nothing
A stranger and you didn't take me in
I was naked and you did not clothe me
Or visit when I was sick or in prison"

Then those on His left will answer Him asking,
"Lord, when did we see *you*
Hungry or thirsty, a stranger or naked, sick or in prison
And *nothing* did we do?"

Then Jesus said that the King will answer them
He will look at them and say, "*Truly*
If you did not do it to the least of my brothers
Then you did not do it to me"

Then Jesus told them that all of those people
Will then be sent away
To eternal punishment...but the *righteous* will go
To eternal life that day

JUDAS PLOTS TO BETRAY JESUS

Now Jesus wanted to prepare His disciples
So with these words He tried,
"The Passover is in two days and the Son of Man
Will be betrayed and crucified"

Meanwhile, the chief priests and elders were meeting
For they wanted Jesus dead
Then one of the disciples...Judas Iscariot
Came to them and said:

"What will you give me if I hand Him over to you?"
Delighting the community
They paid thirty silver pieces...and Judas began seeking
His opportunity

THE LAST SUPPER

On the first day of the Feast of Unleavened Bread
The disciples asked Jesus to reveal
Where He wanted them to make the preparations
To partake in the Passover meal

So Jesus told Peter and John to go to the city
And before they would go too far
They would come across a certain man
Carrying water in a jar

He said to follow the man and when he enters a house
To the owner they should say,
"The teacher is asking...where is the guestroom
Where we can eat on the Passover day?"

He told them that the man would take them up
To a large room...up the stair
The room would be furnished and *ready* for them
And to make the preparations there

As they reclined at the table for the Passover meal
Jesus got up from His place
Then He took off His outer clothing
And wrapped a towel 'round His waist

The disciples wondered what He was doing
For they were preparing to eat
But He knelt on the floor with a bowl of water
And began to wash their feet

Peter said, "*Lord . . . you* would wash *my* feet?"
Holding up his hands
Jesus said, "You do not realize what I am doing
Later you will understand"

But Peter still objected . . . "No!" he said
"You shall *never* wash my feet!"
"If I *can't* wash you . . . you have no part with me," said Jesus
Looking in his eyes so deep

Then Peter responded, "Lord . . . not only my feet
But also my hands and my head!"
"He who *is* clean . . . need only wash his feet
To be clean all over," Jesus said

"And you *are* clean," He said . . . "But not *all* of you"
As He looked the other way
He said this for He knew that Judas Iscariot
Was the one who would betray

When Jesus had finished washing their feet
He asked if they understood
For He was showing His disciples by example
That they *also* should

After this and before they began to eat
Jesus told *everyone*
That He would not drink again of the fruit of the vine
Until the kingdom of God would come

Then He took...and blessed...and broke into pieces
And passed out a loaf of bread
"This is my body...which is given for you
Do this in memory of me," He said

Then He raised a cup and spoke again
His words...strong and true
"This cup is the new covenant in my blood
Which is poured out for you"

Later on Jesus said..."I tell you the truth
One of you...will betray me"
The disciples were saddened and wondered
Which one could it be?

"But woe to the man who betrays the Son of Man!" He said
"Better for him...to have not been born"
Then the disciples began to stare at each other
Each one...feeling forlorn

One by one, they each asked the question
"Lord...is it I?"
"It is the one that I will give this piece of bread to,"
Some heard Jesus reply

Then dipping the bread...He gave it to Judas
And as Judas took the bread
Jesus told him, "What you are about to do...do quickly"
But no one understood what He said

And as soon as Judas took the bread
Satan entered him
And he left the table and went into the night
To pursue his deed so grim

Once Judas had left, Jesus spoke to the others
About what lay ahead
"My children I will be with you only a little longer
Where I go, you cannot come," He said

Then He gave to them a new commandment
That they must love each other
As *He* did...for people will know His disciples
By their love for one another

Then Peter asked, "Why can't I follow you *now?*
I will lay down my *life* for your sake"
But he was not prepared for the response of Jesus
For it would be hard to take

"Will you lay down your life for me?" Jesus asked
As He looked in Peter's eyes
"This very night...you will disown me three times
Before the rooster...crows twice"

Then He said..."Do not let your hearts be troubled
Trust in God...trust also in Me
In my Father's house there are many rooms"
His words...a guarantee

"I go to prepare a place for you," He continued,
"And I will come again
I will take you...and you will be *with* me,"
Jesus promised then

"You *know* the way to where I am going," He said
Thomas asked, "How can that be?"
Jesus answered..."*I* am the way, the truth and the life
No one comes to the Father...but through *me*"

He said anyone who has seen *Him, has* seen the Father
"I am in the Father and the Father is in me"
He said those with faith in Him will do what He's been doing
And even greater things they will see

Then Jesus told them that He will ask the Father
And the Holy Spirit...the Father will send
The world won't accept Him...for it doesn't *know* Him
But on *Him...they* can depend

For they *will* know Him...and He will be in them
He will teach and He will remind
Remind them of the things that Jesus told them
This promise...for all mankind

He said the Spirit will guide them into all truth
And He will *not* speak on His own
For the Spirit will only speak what He *hears*
And will tell what is yet unknown

"Peace I leave you, my peace I give you," He said
Another promise made
"Do not let your hearts be troubled
And do not be afraid

"I am the vine and you are the branches," He said
"If you remain in me, I will remain in you
And you will bear much fruit, but apart from *me*
Nothing can you do

"Love each other as I have loved you," He continued
Speaking of a love that transcends
"Greater love has no man than this," He said,
"That he lay down his life for his friends"

Then Jesus tried to prepare His followers
For what was going to come
"If the world hates you...remember it hated me first"
And He warned them...not to succumb

"If you *belonged* to the world it would *love* you
But from the world, I have *chosen* you
No servant is greater than his master," He said
"If they persecute me...they'll persecute you too

"They'll put you out of the synagogues," He continued
And then what He said was so odd
"A time is coming when those who *kill* you
Will think they offer a *service* to God"

He said they will do these things for they do *not*
Know the Father...or know Him
Jesus warned them...so that when it happened
They'd remember His warning so grim

Then He said, "In a little while you will not see me
Then in a little while you will see me again
You will weep and mourn and the world will rejoice
But your grief will become joy," He said then

Then He told them, "My Father will give you
Whatever you ask for in my name
Ask and you will receive and your joy will be full,"
Jesus did proclaim

Then Jesus prayed to the Father for Himself
And then He prayed for His men
Then Jesus prayed for all of the believers
That God's love and He be in them

THE GARDEN OF GETHSEMANE

After praying Jesus and His men left the city
And went to Gethsemane
Then He left some disciples and walked on with Peter
And the two sons of Zebedee

He said He was overwhelmed with sorrow unto death
"Stay here and keep watch," He said
Then He walked a little farther and fell on His knees
And Jesus bowed His head

In anguish He prayed, "Abba, Father if you are willing
Please take this cup from me
Yet not my will...but yours be done"
Jesus presented His plea

An angel from Heaven came to strengthen Him
Then His prayer was so profound
That His sweat became...great drops of blood
Falling to the ground

When He rose from prayer and returned to the disciples
He found they were all asleep
"Could you not keep watch for one hour?" He asked
But one hour they could not keep

"Watch and pray so you'll not fall into temptation," He said
"The spirit is willing...but the body is weak"
Then again He went to pray...but when He returned
Again...they were asleep

Then Jesus left the disciples one more time
To pray the very same prayer
When He returned He said, "Are you still sleeping?
Look...the hour is here

"The Son of Man is betrayed into the hands of sinners!
Rise...let us go!
Here comes my betrayer"...but His men were confused
What was happening...they didn't know

As Jesus was speaking, Judas Iscariot arrived
And a mob was following him
The people carried clubs and swords and torches
Searching in the light so dim

But before they had left to go to Gethsemane
Judas had told them *this*
That he would walk up to Jesus when he saw Him
And signal them...with a kiss

So Judas went to Jesus and kissed Him on His cheek
And said to Him..."Greetings Rabbi"
"You betray the Son of Man with a *kiss*?" Jesus asked
But Judas had no reply

The guards seized Jesus and arrested Him
Then Peter...who was standing near
Drew his sword...and struck the high priest's servant
Cutting off his ear

But Jesus told Peter to put away his weapon
For all who draw the sword
Will die by the sword...then He healed the servant
And then He turned to the horde

"Am I leading a rebellion that you come with swords
And with clubs to capture me?"
And while Jesus was still speaking...one by one
His disciples began to flee

"Every day I was with you, teaching in the temple
And you never laid a hand on me"
But it happened this way to fulfill how the prophets
Had said...it was going to be

JESUS IS BROUGHT TO TRIAL

The guards brought Jesus to Annas and then Caiaphas
Where the Sanhedrin had gathered together
Peter followed at a distance...and then sat outside
By a fire in the chilly weather

The priests and Sanhedrin wanted to put Jesus to death
So they looked for false *evidence*
And though many false witnesses testified
They could find no serious offense

The high priest asked Jesus, "Will you not answer?"
As He stood in front of the court
The room grew silent as they waited for a response
But Jesus...made no retort

"Are you the Christ? The Son of God?" he demanded
And Jesus answered finally,
"Yes...It is true what you say...And I tell you all
In the days to come you will see

"The Son of Man sitting at the right hand of God
Coming on the clouds of Heaven," He said
"Blasphemy!" shouted the high priest as he tore his clothes
Desperately wanting Jesus dead

"Do we need any further witnesses?" he demanded
"You've *heard* Him!...What do you think?"
Then the people shouted, "He deserves to die!"
And then...they crossed the brink

The crowd closed in and they spat in His face
Striking Him with their fists
Then the guards pulled Jesus out of there
With ropes tied round His wrists

They blindfolded Him and they mocked Him
And then *they* beat Him too
As they hit Him they taunted..."*Prophesy* to us!
Tell us which one of us *struck* you!"

Meanwhile, a servant girl saw Peter by the fire
She peered at him closely and then
She said, "You were also with Jesus of Nazareth"
But Peter denied it was him

"I do not know what you are talking about," he said
And he went out to the gate
But another woman recognized him and called out
With accusation and hate:

"This man is one of them!"...And the people stared
Peter was gripped with fear
"I do not know the man!" he protested again
And later...*others* came near

"Surely you're one of them!...You're a Galilean!"
But Peter again denied
Then the rooster crowed...and he recalled Jesus' words
And Peter...bitterly cried

By early morning the Sanhedrin reached a decision
And their decision would apply
The chief priests and the elders of the people
Condemned Jesus of Nazareth...to die

When Judas Iscariot heard Jesus was condemned
He was overcome with regret
He went back to the temple to return the money
And Judas...was clearly upset

"I have sinned," he cried, "I've betrayed innocent blood"
But the people didn't care
The chief priests responded..."What's that to us?
That is *your* affair"

Then Judas threw the silver coins into the temple
Turned and walked away
And consumed with guilt for what he had done
He hanged himself that day

The coins couldn't be put back into the treasury
So they bought a potter's field
Which was *exactly* what Jeremiah the prophet
Had previously revealed

The Sanhedrin had authority to hand down judgments
But executions...they couldn't carry out
So they brought Jesus to Pontius Pilate, the Roman governor
For *he* could bring it about

But to avoid ceremonial uncleanliness at the palace
The Pharisees would not enter in
They knew Pilate would not execute for *blasphemy*
So a tale...they would have to spin

When Pilate came outside to meet them, he asked
"What charges do you bring?"
"Subversion...and He opposes paying taxes to Caesar
And He claims to be Christ...a King!

"If He wasn't a *criminal* we wouldn't have brought Him
And turned Him over to *you*"
Pilate told *them* to judge Him...but they responded,
"But we cannot execute!"

So Pilate went inside and he questioned Jesus,
"Are you the king of the Jews?"
Jesus looked at Pilate and finally responded,
"What you have said is true"

Then He said that His kingdom is not of this world
That He came to testify to what is true
Pilate asked, "What is truth?"...not waiting for an answer
For his questioning was through

Pilate then went outside and he told the crowd,
"I find no basis for a charge"
But the crowd insisted on his involvement
His duties...he had to discharge

Then Pilate heard that Jesus was from Galilee
Which was *Herod's* jurisdiction
So Pilate had the soldiers take Jesus to Herod
To avoid involvement...in His conviction

Now Herod was *pleased* when they brought him Jesus
Who he'd wanted to see all along
He had heard about the many miracles Jesus had done
And wanted to see Him perform

But with no response from Jesus, Herod grew impatient
His interrogation became intense
But Jesus just stood there...and He remained silent
Putting up no defense

The chief priests and teachers of the Law stood shouting
Hurling accusations and then
Herod and his soldiers made fun of Him and laughed
And sent Him back...to *Pilate* again

Then once again Pilate stood before the people
And for release...he made another bid
For not only had *he* found no basis for charges
Now also...*neither* had Herod

And while Pilate was sitting in the judgment seat
He received a message from his wife
"Have nothing to do with that righteous man," it said
Trying to spare Jesus' life

"For I have suffered much today," her message read,
"Because of *Him*...in a dream"
Now Pilate had *more* reason to release Him
And not punish Him in the extreme

Since it was custom during the feast to release a prisoner
Who was chosen by the crowd
He asked if they wanted Jesus...or Barabbas, a murderer
They responded...by shouting out loud

"Give us Barabbas!...Give us Barabbas!"
But what Pilate didn't know
Was the priests and the elders had persuaded the crowd
In the way they wanted it to go

"Then what shall I do with Jesus?" he asked
The mob shouted, "Crucify Him!"
"But why?" Pilate asked, "What crime has He done?"
But the atmosphere was grim

The crowd grew louder, "Crucify Him!"
They continued to shout
Pilate could see...they were not giving up
Of that...there was no doubt

"You can see He's done *nothing* to deserve *execution*,"
Pilate said in exasperated breath,
"So I will *punish* Him...and then I will *release* Him"
But the people still called for His death

Then Pilate's soldiers took Jesus outside to a place
And bound Him to a post
They would use the whips to do the flogging
That would tear at Him the most

There were many strips of leather connected
To the handle of each whip
And there were jagged pieces of metal and bone
At the end of every strip

Bound to the post with a soldier on each side
There was nowhere for Jesus to go
Taking turns with their whips...the soldiers struck
His body receiving each blow

Again and again, the soldiers whipped Him
And each time the whips came down
They tore at His flesh...with agonizing blows
And His blood...seeped into the ground

They beat Him the length of His body
Causing pain He had never known
By the time they were done...His skin was stripped
Exposing...muscle and bone

Then the soldiers put a scarlet robe on Him
And a crown of thorns on His head
They *pressed* the thorns down...into His skull
From more wounds now...He bled

They put a staff in His hand and knelt in front of Him
"Hail king of the Jews!" they said
They spat on Him and took the staff and struck Him
Again and again on His head

And then...as if *all* they had already done
Was not *enough*...of a disgrace
They took handfulls of the hair of Jesus' beard
And ripped them...from His face

Then once again Pilate went out to the people
And *again* he said to them,
"I'm bringing Him out to you...and I find no basis
For any charge against Him"

Then he brought Jesus out, in front of the people
And Pilate said... "Here is the man"
He was beaten beyond recognition... and the people gasped
Yet once again... they began

"Crucify Him!... Crucify Him!" the people shouted
"*You* crucify Him!" was Pilate's reply
Then they shouted, "He claims to be the Son of God!
According to the Law, He must die!"

On hearing this, Pilate became even *more* afraid
And took Him back inside
"Where did you come from?" he demanded of Jesus
"You still won't speak?" he cried

"Don't you know I have the power to crucify or free you?"
Then Jesus finally answered him
"You would have no power over me," He said,
"If from above... it were not given

"So the one who handed me over to you
Is guilty of a *greater* sin"
After that... though Pilate still tried to release Him
This conflict... he would not win

For the people shouted, "You're no friend of Caesar
If you would let this man go!
Anyone claiming to be a king is against Caesar!"
Their anger continued to grow

Then Pilate brought Jesus outside yet again
And then he said to the crowd,
"Here is your king... Shall I crucify your king?"
But the crowd became *more* loud

"We have no other king but Caesar!" they yelled
Then Pilate understood
He was getting nowhere... and for all he had said
It had done no good

It was apparent that a riot was imminent
So he decided to give the order
But first he turned to a servant and told him
To bring him a bowl of water

Then Pilate washed his hands in front of the crowd
"I am innocent of His blood," he said
The people shouted back, "Let His blood be on us!
And on our children's head!"

THE CRUCIFIXION

Pilate's men put a cross on the shoulders of Jesus
And led Him down the road
Weakened by the beating and loss of blood, He stumbled
Under the heavy load

So the soldiers made *Simon* carry the cross
A man who was passing by
And as they walked...many people jeered
Many women...moaned and cried

Then Jesus turned and said to the women,
"Do not weep for me
Weep for yourselves and your children"
And He told them what was to be

"One day people will call to the mountains and hills
'Fall and cover us!' they will cry
For if they do these things now, when the tree is green
What will they do...when it is dry?"

At the third hour they came to the Place of the Skull
Golgotha, its Aramaic name
The soldiers offered Jesus wine mixed with gall
Which was used to block out pain

But after He tasted it, He refused the drink
So next they laid Him down
Upon the crossbar of the cross
Laying on the ground

They took seven-inch nails, a half-inch around
And placed one on each wrist
And with deliberate aim, the soldiers brought down
The hammers in their fists

Again and again they pounded the nails
And each time the hammers came down
A shot of pain went through His body
And His mother cringed at the sound

Then they nailed His feet to the cross as well
And they made a sign that read,
"Jesus of Nazareth, the King of the Jews"
And nailed it above His head

When they raised the cross up, He felt searing pain
As His body pulled on the nails
Beneath Him some people were uttering insults
While others...cries and wails

And in the midst of His suffering, not thinking of Himself
He raised His eyes and said,
"Father forgive them, for they know not what they do"
Praying for the people instead

Then the soldiers cast lots to divide His clothes
The people still calling out,
"If you're the Son of God, come down from the cross!"
They continued to jeer and shout

"You were going to destroy the temple," they yelled,
"And rebuild it in three days!"
"He saved others," they shouted, shaking their fists,
"But Himself He cannot save!"

Meanwhile, two criminals were being crucified
On His left and on His right
"If you're the *Christ*...save yourself and *us*!" said one
But the other was contrite

He rebuked him and said, "We deserve our punishment
But this man's done nothing wrong
Lord, remember me, when you enter your kingdom"
Knowing He would be there before long

"Truly I tell you, today you will be with me in Paradise,"
Jesus looked at him and declared
Upon hearing these words, the man realized
From damnation...he was spared

Near the cross stood Mary, the mother of Jesus
And as He looked at her from above
He also saw her sister and Mary Magdalene
And the disciple that He loved

He said to His mother, "Dear woman...here is your son"
So she wouldn't be alone
Then He told the disciple, "Here is your mother"
So he would take her into his home

From the sixth to the ninth hour, darkness came over
Now it was harder to see
In a loud voice, Jesus cried out..."My God...my God
Why have you forsaken me?"

As the hours on the cross took their toll on His body
The pain grew worse and worse
With little strength left...and dehydrated
Jesus said..."I thirst"

A jar of wine vinegar stood nearby
So they soaked a sponge in it
They put it on a stalk of the hyssop plant
And held it up to His lip

Then Jesus strained...to take a final breath
And as those who loved Him cried
He breathed His last...and said..."It is finished"
And He gave up His spirit...and died

At that very moment, the earth began to shake
Tombs opened and rocks were split
And the curtain which hung in the temple
From top to bottom was slit

The people at Golgotha were terrified
Including the centurion squad
And in fear and awe...one of them exclaimed,
"Surely He *was*...the Son of God!"

The Burial and Resurrection

Now since it was the day before the Sabbath
The people wanted the bodies taken down
They went and asked Pilate to have the *legs* broken
So they could be lowered to the ground

The soldiers broke the legs of the two criminals
Who next to Jesus had died
But when they came to Jesus...He was already dead
So instead...they put a spear in His side

When the soldiers did this...no one realized
At the time when Jesus was killed
That these things happened in just that way
So prophecy would be fulfilled

Now Joseph of Arimathea was a member of the council
And for himself, he had a new tomb
He asked permission from Pilate and then with Nicodemus
He brought Jesus to His burial room

They wrapped Him in linen with aloe and myrrh
As was customarily done
Then they rolled a big stone in front of the entrance
And laid to rest...the Son

The next day, the chief priests and Pharisees
Went to Pilate and said
That Jesus had told them that after three days
He would rise again from the dead

Then they asked that the tomb be made secure
Until the third day had passed
Or His disciples might steal His body and say He rose
That deception would be worse than the last

So Pilate told the men to take a guard
And make the tomb secure
With the guards and sealed stone the body was safe
Now they could be sure

But on the third morning, the soldiers experienced
A terror they had never known
As the ground shook, an angel appeared as lightning
And rolled away the stone

He sat on the stone in clothes white as snow
The guards still frozen in fear
Then Mary Magdalene and two others arrived
And the angel said, "He is not here

"He has risen...just as He told you
Come and see the place where He lay
Then go quickly and tell His disciples"
So they looked...then hurried away

Trembling and confused, the women fled
But then...along the way
Jesus appeared..."Greetings," He said
"Do not be afraid"

Then He told them to tell His disciples
To go to Galilee
The women told the disciples what had happened
And Peter and John ran out to see

In the tomb they found the burial linens folded
That were wrapped round His body and head
But Jesus was gone...He was not there
For He had risen...from the dead

The Road to Emmaus

Now that same day, two of the disciples
Were walking to a town
Called Emmaus...about a seven-mile walk
When Jesus came around

He began to walk down the road with them
But they did not recognize
For He didn't want them to know who He was
So He kept it from their eyes

He asked them what they were talking about
They stood with faces downcast
"You don't know the things that happened in Jerusalem?"
The one named Cleopas asked

"What things?" Jesus asked the disciples
And then the two men replied,
"About Jesus of Nazareth...a prophet of God"
Then they said He was crucified

They said He was powerful in word and deed
And they had hoped He was the *One*
The One they all waited for...Israel's Redeemer
The Messiah who was to come

They said some of their women had amazed them
They had gone to the tomb at dawn
And came back and said an angel said Jesus had risen
And indeed, His body was gone!

Then some of their companions ran to the tomb
But His body they did not see
Then Jesus told them..."How foolish you are
And how slow you are to believe"

And then...in meticulous detail
Jesus began to explain
How the prophesies since Moses, about the Messiah
Were fulfilled, in the One who was slain

And as they approached the town of Emmaus
Jesus pretended He was going on
But they wanted to spend more time with Him
Before He would be gone

"Stay with us," they said, "It is getting late
And the sun is going down"
So they sat at a table and Jesus gave thanks
Broke bread and passed it around

Immediately, the eyes of the disciples were opened
Sitting there that night
And they recognized that the stranger was *Jesus*
Then He *vanished*...from their sight

"Didn't our hearts burn within us," they exclaimed
Their excitement growing inside,
"On the road...as He opened the scriptures to us?"
To each other they cried

Immediately they got up and returned to Jerusalem
To where the others had stayed
They found the disciples hiding behind locked doors
Because they were afraid

As the two disciples told what happened in Emmaus
And explained everything they knew
Suddenly...Jesus appeared before them
And said..."May peace be *with* you"

Startled and frightened, they thought it was a ghost
But Jesus said, "Why do you fear?"
"And why do you have doubts coming up in your minds?"
Then He began to draw near

"It is I," He said...and He came even closer
And then He said..."Touch me
A ghost does not have flesh and bones
And I do...as you can see"

The disciples looked closely…yet warily at Jesus
At the holes in His hands and feet
As they stood in disbelief…amazement and joy
He said…"Do you have anything to eat?"

Then they gave Him a piece of broiled fish
Which He ate in *front* of them
And as they stared at Him in awe and wonder
He started to *speak* again

"I told you this when I was with you," He said
They began to settle and be calm
"All must be fulfilled that is written about me
In the Law, the Prophets and the Psalms"

Then He said to them again, "May peace be with you
And as the *Father* has sent *me*
I am sending *you*"…Then Jesus took a breath
And on His disciples…He breathed

"Receive the Holy Spirit," He said to them
And He said they could now forgive sin
He was in the final stages of preparing His disciples
For their ministry would soon begin

He told them to go and preach the Good News
To tell it to all creation
And to baptize the people and teach His commands
And make disciples of all nations

He said signs will accompany those who believe
They will drive out demons of hell
Speak in new tongues and lay hands on the sick
And the people will get well

"Whoever believes and is baptized will be saved," He said
"Who does not…will be condemned"
And He told them He would always be with them
Even to the end

Doubting Thomas

Now meanwhile, Thomas, one of the disciples
Wasn't there when Jesus came
And when the others told him they saw the *Lord*
Their excitement was in vain

"Unless I touch the nail marks in His hands
And put my hand into His side
I will not believe it," Thomas told them
And no proof could they provide

Eight days later, they were in the room again
And Thomas was there too
When Jesus appeared and stood among them
And said... "Peace be with *you*"

He told Thomas, "Put your finger here... see my hands
And now put your hand in my side"
Then Jesus said, "Thomas, stop doubting and believe"
"My Lord and my God!" Thomas cried

Then Jesus said to Thomas, "You have believed
Because now you have *seen* me
Blessed are those who have *not* seen," He said,
"And *yet*... who do believe"

Jesus and the Great Catch of Fish

Sometime later, some disciples were fishing
On the Sea of Tiberias
Though an uneventful night... the following morning
Was amazing and mysterious

After fishing all night and catching nothing
They would not fish anymore
But early in the morning, the disciples looked
And a man was standing on the shore

They did not realize that the man was Jesus
And then He called *out* to them,
"My friends...haven't you caught any fish?"
"No," they answered Him

"Throw the net on the right side and then you will,"
The disciples heard Him call
When they did...they were unable to pull in the net
Because of the weight of the haul

When they turned again to look at the man
John said..."It is the *Lord*!"
And when Peter heard *that*...he did not wait
He jumped right overboard

As the others rowed the boat, towing the net
Peter swam ahead
When they landed they saw that *fish* were cooking
And there was also bread

"Bring some more fish and come have breakfast,"
Jesus called out and said
This was the third time He had appeared to them
Since He had risen from the dead

Peter Is Reinstated

"Peter, do you love me more than these?" Jesus asked
When their meal was through
"Yes Lord," Peter answered Jesus
"You *know* that I love you"

"Feed my lambs," Jesus said...and then He asked,
"Do you *truly* love me?"
"Yes Lord, you *know* that I love you," he answered
And Jesus said..."Tend my *sheep*"

Then yet again...Jesus asked Peter,
"Peter...do you love me?"
But Peter was hurt, for the times Jesus asked
Now added up to three

"Lord, you know all things," said Peter
"You *know* that I love you"
"Feed my sheep," said Jesus...and then He said,
"I will tell you the truth"

Then Jesus told Peter, something of his future
That He wanted him to know,
"When you are old, someone will dress you and lead you
Where you do not want to go"

When Jesus finished speaking about Peter's death
"Follow me," He said then
John was also following and Peter asked,
"Lord...what about *him?*"

Jesus said, "If I want *him* to live until I *return*
What is that to you?"
The disciples later speculated about what He meant
But none of them really knew

There were many other things that Jesus did
But if they were *all* written down
The whole *world* might not have room enough
For all the books...of His renown

Acts

Jesus Is Taken into Heaven

Now during the forty days after Jesus had died
And had risen from the dead
He appeared to His disciples on several occasions
And on His final visit He said:

"Do not leave Jerusalem, but wait for the gift
The gift you have heard me speak of"
He was referring to the gift of the Holy Spirit
Who would soon descend from above

"For John baptized with water," He went on,
"But in a very few days
You will be baptized with the Holy Spirit,"
He said...as He met their gaze

They asked if He would now restore Israel's kingdom
Thinking *that*...was His priority
"It is not for you to know the times or dates," He said,
"That the Father set by His authority

"But you shall receive *power*," Jesus continued,
"When the Spirit comes upon you
You'll be my witnesses to the ends of the earth"
Then they would *know* what to do

When Jesus finished speaking...He was taken up
Before their very eyes
Within moments He was hidden in the clouds
But still...they stared at the skies

Suddenly...two men dressed in white appeared
They were sent to the disciples to say,
"This same Jesus, who was taken up to Heaven
Will come *back*...in the very same way"

After that, the disciples returned to Jerusalem
To the upper room, where they stayed
The mother and brothers of Jesus were there
And they all continually prayed

Since Judas Iscariot, the betrayer, was gone
The apostles were now *eleven* men
They prayed about it…and added Matthias
And so they were *twelve* again

Now forty days later, on the day of Pentecost
They were gathered in the room together
When they heard a sound…like a mighty rushing wind
Like a wind in violent weather

As they all looked around, it filled the house
Above them were tongues of flame
Which touched them and filled them with the Holy Spirit
And none…would ever be the same

They all began to speak in different languages
As the Spirit spoke through each one
And gathered outside, were Jews from all nations
The ministry…had begun

The people outside were confused and they asked,
"Are these not all Galileans…every one?
How is it that each of us hears what they say
In each of our own tongue?"

There were Parthians, Mesopotamians and Elamites
People from Mede and Judea
People from Cappadocia, Pontus and Asia
Egypt and Pamphylia

Some of them came from Libya, near Cyrene
And some had come from Rome
But no matter where each of them came from
The language they heard…was home

They asked each other, "What does this mean?"
Some said they were drunk with wine
But Peter spoke up, "These men are not drunk!
It is morning...the hour is nine!"

Then Peter told the people all that had happened
About Jesus, God's own Son
He showed how the prophesies had been fulfilled
Proving Jesus...was the One

Many people who heard, believed what he said
And asked, "What should we do?"
"Repent and be baptized," Peter answered,
"Every one of you"

About three thousand people chose to respond
And were added to the church that day
They faithfully followed the apostles' teachings
And they gathered to eat and pray

One day as Peter and John walked to the temple
They saw a beggar, who was lame
"Silver and gold I have none," said Peter,
"But rise up...in Jesus' name"

As the man looked up, Peter reached down
And took him by the hand
And as Peter lifted...the man was healed
And he was able to stand

Walking and jumping, the man *followed* them
Praising God above
For the healing had not really come from *Peter*
But from God's resounding love

And when the townspeople recognized the beggar
And saw that he was walking
They were filled with amazement and wonder
And *everyone* was talking

Then Peter addressed them... "Men of Israel!"
The people ceased their talk
"Why do you marvel... as though by *our* power
We have made this man walk?

"The God of Abraham, Isaac and Jacob
Is glorifying Jesus... His *Son*
The man who you handed over to be killed
The *holy* and *righteous* One

"You killed the Author of life," he continued,
"But God raised Him from the dead
And in the name of *Jesus*... this man was healed"
They listened to each word he said

Then Peter told the people how the prophesies
Were fulfilled by Jesus' life
The Holy Spirit and the words *convinced* them
Piercing them... like a knife

But this angered the priests of the temple
For they didn't *want* Peter and John
Telling the people about Jesus the Savior
They wanted this *Jesus*... gone

So the priests, the Sadducees and the temple guard
Arrested them that same day
But many who had seen and heard now *believed*
That Jesus... was the way

And once again... the number of believers grew
There were about five thousand then
The next day the temple priests gathered and said,
"What shall we do with these men?

"That they have performed an outstanding miracle
Is clear... to the people in Jerusalem
But to stop this from spreading *any farther*
We must *threaten* them!"

So the priests commanded Peter and John
Not to speak in Jesus' name
But Peter and John refused to obey them
For Jesus...they *would* proclaim

"Whether it is right in the sight of God," they said,
"To listen to *you*, more than *God...you* judge
For we can't *help* speaking of what we have *seen*"
Peter and John wouldn't budge

Then the priests continued to threaten them
But they had to let them go
For there was no way that they could punish them
And not have the people know

Now after Peter and John were released
They went to their friends again
And told them about the priests and elders
And all they had said to them

Then they all raised their voices together
And prayed in one accord
They asked that they be enabled to speak
With *boldness* in the name of the Lord

And as they prayed they asked the Lord
To stretch out His hand to heal
And to give them miraculous signs and wonders
His majesty...to reveal

Then the meeting room began to shake
And the Spirit descended once more
They were *all filled*...and spoke the word of God
More boldly than before

Great miracles were worked by the apostles
And even when Peter walked past
People were *healed*...not only by his touch
But by where his *shadow* was cast

THE APOSTLES ARE ARRESTED

The high priest and Sadducees became very jealous
Of the teachings about Jesus, who had risen
Consumed with anger, they arrested the apostles
And threw them into prison

But an angel came to the apostles in the prison
And opened the doors in the night
Then he told them to teach in the temple courts
Which they did...at dawn's first light

At the same time the Sanhedrin was assembling
So the apostles they could dispel
But when the officers went to get them from jail
There was no one in the cell

Then someone came and told the Sanhedrin,
"They're teaching in the temple court!"
So the captain and his temple guard went out again
After hearing this report

The temple guard brought *back* the apostles
To be questioned, yet again
"We gave you orders *not* to teach about Jesus!"
But the apostles responded then

"We must obey God, rather than men," they said
"The God who raised Jesus from the dead
That same Jesus...who you killed upon a tree"
The Sanhedrin listened with dread

"God raised Him to Heaven...as Prince and Savior
And *He* forgives men of sin!
We are *witnesses* and God gave the Holy Spirit
To those who *believe* in Him"

The Sanhedrin was furious and wanted them killed!
But Gamaliel...a Pharisee
Had the apostles removed and told the gathering
"Men of Israel, *listen* to me!

"Consider carefully," Gamaliel began,
"What you want to do to these men
For Theudas appeared and claimed to be someone
And remember what happened then?

"He had four hundred followers...but then he was *killed*
And his followers were scattered
After *him*...Judas the Galilean led a group in revolt"
And they *knew*...*his* cause was shattered

"Therefore, I advise you...leave these men alone
If human, their activity will fail
But if it *IS* from God...there is nothing you can do
And against *God*...you will rail"

The Sanhedrin was swayed by Gamaliel's speech
And they figured that before very long
The apostles would scatter...and forget about Jesus
But they were very wrong

STEPHEN, THE FIRST MARTYR

After that day...in the temple courts and houses
The apostles continued their teaching
And Stephen...a man full of God's grace and power
Did miracles and Spirit-filled preaching

But opposition arose from the synagogues
Of Alexandria and Cyrene
They argued with Stephen...but they were no match
For such wisdom...they'd never seen

And though witnesses came and falsely testified
That he spoke against the temple and the Law
Stephen's face had the appearance of an angel
Then he spoke...of their ancestors before

He spoke about Abraham and Isaac and Jacob
Joseph and Moses and Solomon
And how their forefathers had *killed* the prophets
Who foretold of the Righteous One

"And now *you* have betrayed and murdered Him
You who *received* the Law
But have not *obeyed* it," Stephen told them
Now they were angrier than before

Then Stephen, who was filled with the Holy Spirit
Looked up above their heads
"Look!...I see Heaven opened and the Son of Man
At the right hand of God!" he said

The people covered their ears and began to yell
When he told them what he saw
As they screamed, they rushed at Stephen
And dragged him out the door

The people dragged him out of the city
Then...they began to throw stones
Hitting Stephen and knocking him down
Crushing flesh and breaking bones

"Lord Jesus...receive my spirit," he prayed
Then falling on his knees he cried,
"Lord...do not hold this sin against them!"
And after he said it...he died

Meanwhile, witnesses laid down their cloaks
At the feet of a man named Saul
Who had watched the crowd kill Stephen
Approving of it all

On that very day...persecution broke out
Against the church in Jerusalem
Saul went through the city from house to house
Seizing Christians and jailing them

PHILIP

Meanwhile, the Apostle Philip preached in Samaria
Demons fled and cripples were healed
Many welcomed the Gospel of Jesus with joy
And with grateful hearts they kneeled

SAUL

As Saul went around...persecuting Christians
And speaking threats of slaughter
He got permission to seize Christians in Damascus
Every man, woman, son and daughter

But as Saul was traveling on the *road* to Damascus
There suddenly shone a great light!
It *enveloped* him...and he fell to the ground
Where he huddled...trembling in fright

Then a voice from Heaven spoke and said, "Saul!
Why do you *persecute* me?"
Cowering, Saul asked, "Who are you Lord?"
Afraid of what the answer would be

"I am Jesus...whom you are persecuting"
Saul was terrified through and through
"Now get up and go into the city," said Jesus,
"And you will be told what to do"

The men traveling with Saul were speechless
They heard sound...but saw *no one*
And as Saul stood up...he found he was blind
His conversion...had begun

The men led him by the hand into Damascus
For three days, he didn't eat or drink
Then the Lord told Ananias to go and visit him
Ananias didn't know *what* to think

"Lord, I have heard *reports* of this man," he said,
"Of how much *evil* he has done!
He has come here to arrest your followers!" he cried
Why would God want *this* one?

But the Lord said again to Ananias, "Go!
He is my chosen *instrument*"
Then He told Ananias that Saul would preach
And where he would be sent

So Ananias went to where Saul was staying
Laid hands on him and then
Said, "The Lord Jesus who appeared to you *sent* me
So that you may *see* again

"And may be filled with the Holy Spirit," he said
And as scales fell from his eyes
Saul was able to see…and he stood up
And then he was baptized

Now after some days, Saul began to preach
That Jesus was God's own Son
But everyone who heard him was astonished
For they *knew* what Saul had done

"Is this not the man who *persecuted* Christians?"
But Saul preached all the more
And after many days…some plotted to kill him
And Saul knew *exactly* what for

They watched the city gates, to ambush him
But the disciples took him by night
And lowered him over the wall in a basket
And Saul was able to take flight

Then he went and preached in Jerusalem
And with the *Grecian* Jews he debated
But they *too* wanted to kill him, so he went to Tarsus
Where Saul might not be hated

PETER AND THE CENTURION

Now a devout man in Caesarea, named Cornelius
Was a centurion in the army of Rome
And an *angel* appeared to him and told him
To have Peter brought to his home

So Cornelius sent two of his servants
And a soldier who was *also* devout
To Joppa…so they could bring back Peter
To find out what it was about

And as the men were on their journey
Around noon, the following day
Peter, who was staying with Simon the tanner
Went up on the roof to pray

Peter fell into a trance and God showed him
An amazing visual scene
"Do not call *anything* impure," said a voice,
"*Anything* that God has made clean"

As Peter contemplated the vision that he saw
The Spirit spoke about the men
"Do not be afraid to go with them," He said,
"For *I* am the One who sent them"

And when Peter saw the men, he asked them
Why they came to Joppa that day
"An angel told Cornelius to send for you," they said,
"To hear what you have to say"

Now Cornelius had gathered his family and friends
In his house for Peter to meet
And when Peter entered, Cornelius met him
And in reverence…fell at his feet

But Peter told Cornelius that he should stand up
"I am just a man myself," he said
Then as Peter told the people all about Jesus
The Holy Spirit…came down on each head

Then the people began to speak in tongues
And God, they began to praise
The believers who *came* with Peter saw it
And they were all amazed

Then Peter had them baptized with water
Now understanding God's ways
For he *now knew*…that God accepts Gentiles
And he stayed with them for several days

And when Peter arrived back in Jerusalem
The believers had already heard
That Peter had gone into a non-Jewish house
And brought to them...the Word

Then Peter told all of the believers there
Of the vision he had seen
Where the Lord had shown him...*nothing* was impure
That God Himself had made clean

JAMES IS KILLED AND PETER IS IMPRISONED

Now Herod the king, had the brother of John
James, the disciple...killed
He then seized Peter, because Herod believed
It was what the people willed

He put Peter in prison with sixteen soldiers
Placed around him as a guard
He was bound with chains...but as he slept
The church was praying hard

Suddenly an angel appeared before Peter
And a light shone down in his cell
The angel told Peter "Quickly, get up!"
And the chains on Peter fell

"Put on your clothes and sandals," said the angel,
"And your cloak and follow me!"
Peter thought that he was having a vision
That this really couldn't be

But the angel led Peter past the guards
Through the gates and into the street
The angel left and Peter went to Mary's house
Where he knew, his friends, he would meet

When Peter knocked...a servant girl, Rhoda
Heard him at the door
The believers let him in and Peter explained
All that had happened before

Then Peter left for another place
And on the very next day
When Herod sent for Peter, he was told
That Peter had gotten away

Herod had his soldiers search for Peter
And when he wasn't found by them
He had the prison guards thoroughly questioned
And then they were condemned

Barnabas and Saul Are Chosen

Now the prophets and teachers were gathered
In the church at Antioch to pray
As they worshiped, the Holy Spirit directed them
That Saul and Barnabas go away

So the people gathered around them
To lay hands on them and pray
And when they finished praying and fasting
They sent them on their way

Barnabas and Saul, who was also called Paul
Journeyed from town to town
Teaching about Jesus...and everywhere they went
The people gathered around

After they preached on the isle of Cyprus
Paul and Barnabas set sail again
And they traveled to Perga in Pamphylia
And Antioch in Pisidian

They went to the synagogue in Pisidian Antioch
On the Sabbath day
And after the reading, the rulers invited them
To say what they had to say

So Paul stood up and told the people
About Jesus...God's own Son
And that they no longer had to wait for *Messiah*
For Jesus *was* the One

Then he showed them all, how the life of Jesus
Fulfilled what the prophets had said
Which included His crucifixion and death
And God raising Him...from the dead

And as they were leaving, the people invited them
To return the following week
Which they did...and almost the whole city gathered
To hear the disciples speak

But some people were there who were *jealous*
And they tried to cause an *outburst*
But Paul and Barnabas *boldly* told them,
"We had to speak God's word to you *first*

"But since you *reject* the salvation message," they said
For the people didn't *want* to understand,
"*Now* we shall take the Word to the Gentiles
For the Lord gave us this command

"'I have set you to be a light for the nations,'"
Their mission...the saving of souls
"'That you may bring salvation to the ends of the earth'"
God had clearly set their goals

The Gentiles welcomed the Word when they heard it
Gladly receiving eternal life
But there were certain people in the region
Who continued causing strife

The city was divided in the dispute about Jesus
And there was *much* deceit
So Paul and Barnabas left the region
Shaking the dust from their feet

They went on to Iconium, Lystra and Derbe
Preaching the Good News
Many believed, repented and were saved
Both the Gentiles and the Jews

As they preached, they showed signs and wonders
And many were *healed* by them
Everywhere they went, large crowds gathered
As the Holy Spirit worked again

But there was also trouble for Paul and Barnabas
As they went from town to town
There were always some who wanted to stone them
Or beat them to the ground

Most of the time, they were able to get away
If they had been warned ahead
But a mob got Paul in Lystra and stoned him
Until they thought...that he was dead

But Paul recovered and they resumed their journey
Preaching wherever they went
When they returned to Antioch, they stayed with disciples
And spoke of where they were sent

PAUL'S SECOND JOURNEY

After some time, Paul said to Barnabas
That they should visit again
The cities where they'd been and seen the people
To see how they were doing then

But Paul and Barnabas disagreed as to others
Who should go with them that day
And their disagreement became so severe
That each went his own way

Barnabas took Mark and sailed for Cyprus
And Silas went with Paul
But Paul's journey was suddenly interrupted
His route changed...after all

They went through Syria, Cilicia and Galatia
Then Mysia and Troas too
But while in Troas, Paul had a vision
Which changed what they were to do

In his vision they were called to Macedonia
Though Paul was not told why
And they immediately left for that region
To the city of Philippi

While there, they were met by a slave girl
As they were on their way to pray
She had an evil spirit…and could tell the future
And she followed them day after day

"These men are servants of the Most High God!"
As she followed, she would shout
But after a while…Paul turned and ordered
The evil spirit to come out

The owners of the slave girl became furious
For her talent was no longer for sale
And the owners had Paul and Silas arrested
Beaten and thrown into jail

PAUL AND SILAS IN PRISON

The jailer put Paul and Silas in the inner prison
And put their feet in stocks
But at midnight…as they sang praises to God
An earthquake…opened the locks

The jailer woke up and he saw the open doors
And he thought that they had *fled*
So he drew out his sword to kill himself
For he would rather be dead

For to face the wrath of his superiors
There was no greater fear
But Paul called out, "Don't harm yourself!
For we are all *right here!*"

Calling for torches, the jailer trembled
And then he ran into the cell
"What must I do to be saved?" he cried
While on his knees he fell

"Believe in the Lord Jesus and you will be saved
You and your household too"
The jailer brought them home and cleaned their wounds
They wondered what next, he would do

The jailer set a meal before Paul and Silas
Then the apostles spoke the Word
The jailer and his house were baptized and rejoiced
At the wonderful news they heard

Next day, the officials released them and they left
Preaching wherever they went
People loved them and people hated them
No matter where they were sent

PAUL IN JERUSALEM

At one point, while preaching in Jerusalem
Some enemies tried to kill Paul
But a Roman commander came and rescued him
Not knowing what was going on at all

When the commander asked Paul who he was
And what it was that he had done
He couldn't hear a thing, because of the crowd
And the *shouting* of everyone

So he arrested Paul and brought him to the castle
Because even though unfair
He could *force* him to answer his questions
By *torturing* him there

But Paul asked the commander if it was *legal*
To torture a citizen of *Rome*
This question made the commander very afraid
For Paul's citizenship was now known

Meanwhile his enemies still plotted to kill him
But the commander was made aware
And sent hundreds of soldiers to take him from prison
And escort him out of there

They took Paul to Governor Felix in Caesarea
And for two years...prison was his home
Then Felix was replaced by Governor Festus
And Paul was sent to Rome

PAUL'S JOURNEY TO ROME

Now Paul was delivered to a centurion named Julius
And aboard a ship they set sail
But the winds were not what they needed them to be
And possibly their journey would fail

From port to port they traveled on the ship
But too much time went by
And by then...seafaring was dangerous
Winter...the reason why

When they came to a place called Fair Havens
Paul spoke up and said
That their voyage would be *disastrous*
If they continued on ahead

But the owner and captain said they should sail
And so, their departure was set
And though the harbor was unsuitable to stay in
This decision...they would regret

They hoped they could sail to Phoenix in Crete
It would be safer harbor...and where
They could better spend the winter months
...If they could only *make* it there

When a gentle south wind began to blow
It was good...so they set sail
They stayed steady along the shore of Crete
But the wind became a gale

They were unable to sail the ship *into* the wind
And so it was driven ahead
The sailors could barely secure the lifeboat
Some feared...they would be dead

They dropped the sails and dragged an anchor
In the terrible stormy weather
They even passed ropes *underneath* the ship
To try to hold it together

The next day the storm *continued* to rage
So they tried to lighten the load
They began to throw the cargo overboard
And *this*...Paul had foretold

On the third day, they threw the tackle
Over the rail and into the sea
The men became terrified and wondered
What their fate would be

For many days, the storm raged on
The situation was grave
By that time the men had lost all hope
All hope of being saved

Now day after day, the men would not eat
Then Paul stood up and said
Though they should have taken his advice *before*
They should now have *courage*...not dread

For an angel had appeared and told him not to fear
And the angel had *also* told Paul
That he would be tried before Caesar in Rome
And that God gave him the lives of all

The lives of all of the men sailing with him
And none of them would drown
However, they were going to lose the ship
And they would run aground

On the fourteenth night, they were still being driven
Across the Adriatic Sea
But the sailors sensed land, so they measured the water
To see how *deep* it would be

A hundred twenty feet was the depth of the water
Then later...ninety feet
Fearing the rocks, they dropped four anchors
To avoid the fate they could meet

Then some of the sailors let down a lifeboat
They had decided they would flee
But Paul warned the centurion and the soldiers
And the soldiers cut it loose in the sea

Then Paul told everyone that they should eat
For this was the fourteenth day
The men all watched, as Paul broke bread
And bowed his head to pray

When daylight came...they saw a beach
But they didn't recognize the land
They made for the beach, but hit a shoal
And ran aground in the sand

There were two hundred seventy-six men aboard
And they swam and floated ashore
The ship was lost...but the men were saved
As the angel had told Paul before

They all washed up on an island called Malta
Where the men would quickly find
The treatment they received from the islanders
Was unusually kind

The weather was cold and it was raining
So they built a fire in the sand
But as Paul added wood...a serpent came out
And bit into his hand

Everyone expected that Paul would die
For this was a venomous snake
But it fell from his hand, into the fire
When he gave his hand a shake

The people all watched and they waited
But he didn't die...very odd
When a long time passed and he was still well
They said that Paul was a god

Paul stayed at the estate of the chief official
Publius was his name
As it happened, the official's father was ill
So to his bedside...Paul came

He prayed as he laid his hands on the man
Then the man rose up and was fine
Paul healed *all* the sick and gave glory to God
For the healings were divine

They remained on Malta for the winter
And then they set sail for Rome
Where Paul was allowed to live by himself
With a soldier to guard him at home

For the next two years, Paul stayed in Rome
Where he continued to teach
He welcomed everyone who came to his house
They came to hear him preach

Some were persuaded by what he said
And some did not believe
Which Isaiah the prophet foretold long before
"Hearing and seeing...they'll not perceive"

Meanwhile, the other apostles followed
Wherever the Spirit led
And as they traveled throughout the land
The Good News of Jesus spread

They brought people to salvation in the Lord
Instructing them in God's ways
They guided them and they healed them
And gave Jesus all the praise

The apostles' lives were lives of service
Their deaths...were sacrifice
But they *knew*...they would spend eternity
With the Lord...in Paradise

Romans

From Paul, a servant and apostle of Christ
To the beloved of God in Rome
From God our Father and the Lord, Jesus Christ
Grace to you and shalom

First, I thank God, through Jesus Christ
For every one of you
Your faith is talked about all over the world
And I pray for all of you too

I am eager to come there and preach the gospel
For I am not ashamed
For it is the power of God for salvation
To all who believe in Jesus' name

THE WRATH OF GOD

But I tell you that Heaven is revealing
A message of God's wrath
Warning those who *know* the laws of God
But *instead* choose their own path

Though they claim to be wise, they become fools
Exchanging the truth of God for a lie
Worshiping the creation, instead of the Creator
They are choosing to defy

Men and women who commit unnatural acts
Though the truth in their hearts they know
Receive in themselves the due penalties
For the way they choose to go

They decide that keeping the knowledge of God
Is simply not worthwhile
So He gives them over to minds of depravity
Wicked, evil and vile

Full of envy, murder, deceit and malice
And every manner of strife
They invent new ways of doing evil
In the ways they lead their life

They are gossips, slanderers and God-haters
Boastful and arrogant
They disobey parents, they're ruthless and heartless
Senseless and insolent

Though they know that the righteous decree of God
Is that doing so deserves death
They continue and approve of the others doing so
Approving with every breath

But those who pass judgment on someone *else*
For doing what *they* also do
At whatever point they are judging the other
They're condemning themselves too

On the day of God's wrath, He will give to each one
According to what they have done
Glory and honor and eternal life for the good
Wrath and distress for the evil ones

Remember it is written that no one is righteous
No one... not even one
But we're justified before God through our *faith*
In Jesus Christ... His Son

All have sinned and fall short of the glory of God
And are justified by His grace
Through the redemption that is in Christ Jesus
For atonement... He took our place

And though someone might die for a good man
God showed *His* love thus
By the fact that while we were still sinners
Jesus *died*... for us

So shall we go on sinning, so grace can increase?
No!...We *died* to sins!
When we are baptized into the *death* of *Christ*
New life in *Him* begins!

LIFE IN THE SPIRIT

And for those who are in Christ Jesus
There is now no condemnation
A mind controlled by the Spirit is life and peace
A sinful mind is controlled by temptation

God works all things for the good of those who love Him
Who according to His purpose are called
And He who did not spare His own Son Jesus
But gave Him up...for us all

And if God is for us...who can be against us?
We should not worry about *those*
Those who bring *any* charge against God's people
We are the ones God *chose!*

For Jesus who was raised, is at God's right hand
And for *us*...He intercedes
Who can separate us from the love of Christ?
No one can, indeed!

Therefore, in all kinds of trouble and persecution
We are *more* than conquerors through *Him*
And neither death nor life...neither angels nor demons
Nor *whatever* might begin

Neither the present nor the future
Nor any power, depth or height
Nor anything in creation can separate us
From the love of God in Christ

GOD'S CHOSEN PEOPLE

I am feeling great sorrow and increasing anguish
Anguish in my heart
For I could wish I was cursed and cut off myself
Separate from Christ...apart

For the sake of the people of Israel
My own race...my brothers
Theirs is the adoption as the children of God
The divine glory above the others

They received the temple worship and the promises
The covenants and the Law
They have the patriarchs...and the lineage of Christ
Is from *their* ancestors before

Yet they pursued righteousness by their own *works*
Not by *faith* in Jesus' *name*
They *stumbled* over the stone...but those who trust Jesus
Will *never* be put to shame

If you confess with your mouth that Jesus is Lord
And believe God raised Him from the dead
Then you will be saved...as in Joel 2:32
That is what the scripture has said

I do not want you to be ignorant of this mystery
And in arrogance, do not behave
For when the full number of the Gentiles has come in
Then *all* of Israel will be saved

A LIVING OFFERING

So in view of God's mercy, offer your bodies
As a living offering
Holy and pleasing to God, as an act of worship
A sacrifice...you can bring

No longer conform to the pattern of this world
Be transformed by the renewing of your mind
Then the good and pleasing and perfect will of God
You will be able to find

Also, do not think about yourself more highly
Than you ought to do
Think of yourself with sober judgment in accordance
With the faith God gave to you

Just as each of us has a body with many parts
And each part has a different role
Though we are many in Christ, we form one body
Each belonging to the others...makes it whole

And in His grace, God has given us different gifts
So if God has given to *you*
The gift of prophecy, use it in proportion to your faith
For what He has given you to do

If someone's gift is to serve...let them serve
If to teach...then let them teach
If their gift is to encourage...let them encourage
Out to others, they should reach

If their gift is contributing to the needs of others
Let their giving be ample
If it is leadership, let them lead with diligence
And by setting a good example

If their gift is the gift of showing mercy
Let them do it with cheer
And regarding the love you have for others
Love must be sincere

Hate what is evil and cling to what is good
Be devoted to each other
Share with God's people who are in need
And honor one another

You must keep on praying and work very hard
Serve the Lord enthusiastically
Be joyful in our hope and patient in trouble
And practice hospitality

Bless those who persecute you and do not curse them
Rejoice with those who rejoice
Mourn with those who are in mourning
Make living in harmony your choice

Do not be conceited or be too proud
Be willing to *associate*
With people of *lower* position than *you*
Do not repay *hate* with *hate*

Never pay back evil with evil or take revenge
Be careful what you do and say
Leave room for the wrath of God, for it is written,
"Vengeance is mine... *I* will repay"

On the contrary, if your enemy is hungry
You should give him food instead
If he is thirsty give him a drink... and in doing so
You'll pile burning coals on his head

And so... do not let evil overcome you
But overcome evil with good
Submit to governing authorities for God put them there
This should be understood

Love your neighbor as yourself
For love fulfills the Law
Wake from your sleep... for salvation is closer
Than when we *first* believed... *before*

The night is nearly over
The day is almost here
Abandon dark deeds... put on the armor of light
The time is drawing near

So let us live in decency all of the time
And behave as we do in the day
Not in drunkenness or sexual immorality
Or in dissension or a jealous way

Do not judge or look down on your brother
For before God...we will all stand
And we will each give an account of ourselves
And each will be judged...by *His* hand

I believe you are full of goodness and knowledge
And are competent to teach
I have written you boldly to remind you of things
For God gave me the grace to preach

Corinthians

1 Corinthians

I appeal to you friends...in the name of our Lord
That all of you agree
So that you are united in mind and thought
For some have *come* to me

They said you are arguing about whom you *follow*
Saying you follow Paul or others
Is Christ divided?...Was Paul crucified for you?
Listen to me brothers

Apollos and I are only servants of the *Lord*
Through whom you came to *believe*
God made your faith grow, after Apollos watered
I merely planted the *seed*

The one who plants and the one who waters
Only have *one* goal
Each will be rewarded according to his labor
As we fulfill our role

And you should know that you are God's temple
For His Spirit *lives* in *you*
But if anyone destroys God's temple
God will destroy him too

If someone is sexually immoral or greedy
Yet says he's a brother in the Lord
If he's a slanderer, a drunkard, a swindler or idolater
Association with *him*...you can not afford

While God will judge those outside of the church
Let me tell you this
We *are* to judge those in the church, for it is written,
"Expel the wicked from your midst"

The wicked will not *inherit* the kingdom of God
And though wicked were some of *you*
You were washed and sanctified in the blood of Jesus
And justified in His name too

The sins a man commits are outside of his body
But he who sins *sexually*
Sins against his *own* body...*and* against God
From immorality...you must flee

You are not your own...you were bought with a price
Honor God with your body my brother
And those who are married, your bodies are not your own
Your bodies belong to each other

Do not deprive each other...except for a while
And only by mutual consent
To devote yourself to prayer, then come together again
So that Satan will not tempt

It is good for the unmarried to stay unmarried
But a spouse, they *should* acquire
If they can't control themselves, it is better to marry
Than for them to burn with desire

And in the Lord's Supper...he who drinks of the cup
Or *he* who eats of the bread
In an unworthy manner...sins against the Lord
And sin will be on his head

You'll be guilty if your spirit isn't right with the Lord
So examine yourself inside
This is why many among you are weak and sick
And a number of you have died

Now to each of us, the manifestation of the Spirit
Is given for the common good
One receives from the Spirit, the gift of wisdom
To another, knowledge understood

Another receives faith...another the gift of healing
To another...prophecy He gives
Some speak in different tongues or interpret them
The gift disbursement is His

To some...He gives miraculous powers
And others can discern the spirits
But it is *He alone* who does *all* of these things
He determines the proper fits

If I speak in the languages of men and angels
And yet I don't have love
I am nothing more than a clanging cymbal
No matter my gift from above

If I have the gift of knowledge and understanding
To unravel mystery
Or I have faith enough to move a mountain
Or the gift of prophecy

Yet I have not love...I am still nothing
And even if I give to the poor
Everything I own...but I still have not love
I gain nothing...for sure

Love is patient, love is kind, it does not envy
It does not boast...It is not proud
Love is not rude...It is not self-seeking
Nor easily angered and loud

Love keeps no record of being wronged
In evil, it does not delight
Instead...love rejoices whenever truth wins
On the side of what is right

Love never gives up and never loses faith
It always hopes and will always endure
In every kind of situation, love never fails
Yet a time will come for sure

Prophecies will cease and tongues will be stilled
Knowledge will become obsolete
We know and prophesy in part...but when *perfection* comes
The imperfect disappears...complete

When I was a child, I thought and acted like a child
When I grew older, I put that away
Now we see things...as in a misty mirror
But there will come a day

When we see face to face...and we will fully know
All that comes from above
But for now...faith and hope and love remain
And the greatest of these is love

So let love be your goal...and *desire* the gifts
Especially the ability to prophesy
It is even *more* important than speaking in tongues
And here is the reason why

Speaking in tongues is between a person and God
And it's *good* that the person is edified
But even *more* so, the whole *church* is lifted up
When someone has prophesied

If unbelievers should come into your church
They'll think you've lost your mind
If everyone is speaking in unknown languages
But if prophesying, they find

Then these people will be convinced of sin
And judged by what you say
The secrets of their hearts will be exposed
And they'll fall on their knees and pray

When you assemble, one will sing, another teach
One will have a revelation to share
One will speak in tongues...another will interpret
All done for the good of all there

God is not a God of confusion but of peace
So when you gather to pray
Be eager to prophesy and do not *forbid* tongues
But do *everything*...in an orderly way

Now I want to remind you of the Gospel I taught you
And the *most important thing*
Jesus died for our sins…He was buried and He rose
For our salvation to bring

He appeared to Peter and then to the twelve
And then to five hundred more
So all else aside…hold *firmly* to the Gospel
That is what we *preach* it for

Now I am going to tell you a mystery
That we will not all die
But we will all be changed in a flash
In the twinkling of an eye

For the trumpet will sound…and the dead will rise
To the living….change He'll bring
Prophecy fulfilled…"O death where is your victory?
O death where is your sting?"

2 Corinthians

We do not use deception in our ministry
Nor do we distort God's word
And if our Gospel is hidden to those who are lost
Even though they have heard

It's because the god of this world has blinded them
Blinded the minds of the unbeliever
So the light of the Gospel won't shine in their hearts
They are fooled by the deceiver

Do not become partners with unbelievers
What can this relationship afford?
What do light and darkness have in common?
"Be separate from them," says the Lord

As to giving, whoever plants just a few seeds
Will have a small crop in their field
But whoever is planting *generously*
Much will their harvest yield

So decide in your heart how much you will give
Don't give with reluctance or fear
Don't give in response to pressure on you
God *loves* those who give with cheer

Also in your faith, don't let anything move you
You must stand strong and remain
Give yourself completely in your work for the Lord
Labor in *Him*...is not in vain

Galatians

Grace and peace to you from God our Father
And the Lord Jesus Christ, His Son
Who gave Himself for our sins, to rescue us from evil
According to the will of the One

Live your life by the power of the Spirit
Not by what your nature requires
For what the Holy Spirit wants, is just the opposite
Of what the sinful nature desires

I have told you that if you partake in sinful acts
Such as sexual immorality
Witchcraft, hostility, outbursts of anger
Selfish ambition and idolatry

Quarreling, jealousy, drunkenness or division
What will happen *then*
Is that you will not inherit the kingdom of God
Now I have warned you *again*

The fruit of the Holy Spirit is self control
Peace and joy and love
Patience, kindness, gentleness and goodness
Qualities from above

You mature Christians should *help* someone
If they have fallen into sin
But be careful, for *you* may also be tempted
While *you* are helping *them*

If you help each other with problems and troubles
You will fulfill Christ's law
Be careful not to think too much of yourself
And here is one thing more

Do not be deceived...God cannot be mocked
Each man will reap what he sows
If you are sowing to please your own nature
You'll reap corruption and woes

But if you are sowing to please the Spirit
And the laws of God you *keep*
And you don't become tired of doing good
Eternal rewards you will reap

So whenever you have the opportunity
Do good to *everyone*
Especially to those who are *believers*
In Jesus Christ . . . the Son

Ephesians

Praises be to God, the Father of our Lord
He has blessed us in the heavenly domain
Before creation He loved us...and chose us in Christ
In *His* eyes...we have *no blame*

I have not stopped thanking God for all of you
And I pray for you *constantly*
That He gives you wisdom...that so much deeper
Your knowledge of Him will be

I also pray that your hearts are enlightened
So you *know* what He calls you to do
And the enormity of the glorious way of life
That He has reserved for you

When we followed the ways of the world
We were all dead in our sin
But His great love for us made us alive in *Christ*
And *now* we are seated with *Him*

For you have been saved by grace through faith
Not because of works by *you*
It is a gift from God, so that no one can boast
About anything *they* might do

You must no longer live as the people of the world
For God...they do not know
They no longer care for what is right or wrong
And to sinful pleasures they go

Do not let the sun go down while you're angry
Don't give the devil a foothold
Do not speak evil...for everything you say
Should serve to help others to grow

And do not grieve the Holy Spirit of God
For He has put a *mark* on you
For the day of redemption...so get rid of all anger
Bitterness and malice too

Show kindness and compassion to one another
And forgiveness too
In the same way...that through Jesus Christ
God has forgiven *you*

Therefore...you should be *imitators* God
And live a life of love
As Jesus loved us...and gave Himself up
As a sacrifice to God above

Wives submit to your husbands as to the Lord
For the husband is the head of the wife
The same way that Christ is the head of the Church
For whom He gave His life

In the same way that husbands love their own bodies
They should also love their wives
They should care for them and protect them
Cherishing their lives

And for this very reason, a man will leave
His father and his mother
And be united to his wife and they become one
As they love one another

Children...obey your parents in the Lord
For this is the right thing to do
Honor your father and mother is the first Commandment
That comes with a *promise* for *you*

That if you respect your parents, you will live long
With good things in your life
Fathers...train your children in the ways of the Lord
Instead of angering them with strife

THE ARMOR OF GOD

Finally my brothers, be strong in the Lord
And in the power of His might
Put on the Armor of God to stand against the devil
With it, you'll be ready to fight

For we wrestle not against flesh and blood
But against principalities and powers
Against the rulers of the darkness of this world
The enemy who devours

Against spiritual wickedness in high places
Put on the Armor of God, therefore
When the day of evil comes, you can stand your ground
Now listen... for there is more

Stand firm with the belt of truth 'round your waist
With the breastplate of righteousness on
Shod your feet with the gospel of peace
And the shield of faith on your arm

With it you can quench the fiery darts of the wicked
For we *know* this shield is hard
Take the helmet of salvation and the sword of the Spirit
Which *is*... the Word of God

And on all occasions, with all prayers and requests
Pray as the Spirit leads
Keep this in mind... be alert and keep praying
For all of the saints and their needs

Philippians

I thank God when I think of you and pray with joy
For we have *always* been in accord
God began a good work in you and He will continue
'Til its completion on the day of the Lord

I want you to understand, my brothers and sisters
That what has happened to *me*
Has *spread* the Gospel...and the whole palace guard
Has now become able to see

They know that I'm a prisoner in and for the *Lord*
And most of the believers *here*
Have become more confident and are speaking boldly
The Gospel...without fear

And while some preach Christ with pure motives
Others are using their voice
To preach out of envy...yet still *Jesus* is *preached*
So what?...I *still* rejoice

Your prayers and the Spirit will lead to my deliverance
And I trust and hope as time goes by
That I will have courage and bring honor to Christ
Whether I live or die

For to me to live is Christ...and to die is gain
Yet, which one would I choose?
I'd rather die and be with Christ which is far better
But more necessary...to live and be used

Whatever happens...conduct yourself in a worthy way
And have Jesus' disposition
For though He was *God*, He made himself *nothing*
Becoming a *servant* by definition

In His appearance as a man, He humbled Himself
Even to the ultimate loss
By becoming obedient...to the point of death
Even to death on a cross

Therefore God exalted Him to the highest position
Gave Him the name above all names
That in the name of *Jesus*, every knee shall bow
And *every* tongue proclaim

That Jesus Christ is Lord, to the glory of the Father
In Heaven, on earth and under
Therefore, continue....to work out your salvation
With fear...and trembling...and wonder

For it is *God* who is working to *cause* the desire
And also the *power* in you
For you to be acting according to *His* purposes
And doing what He wants you to do

Do *everything* without arguing and complaining
So you will be innocent and pure
Children of God....who live among the corrupt
Shining as the stars, for sure

I am not perfect....and I haven't reached my goal
But Christ took hold of *me*
So I keep on struggling and working at it
Because of the goal I see

Forgetting what is behind and straining to what is ahead
Toward the goal I run
So I can win the prize of being called to Heaven
Because of what *Jesus* has done

Now I tell you to rejoice in the Lord *always*
And *again* I say rejoice!
Show gentleness and kindness to *everyone*
Your *actions*....are a *choice*

And do not be anxious about anything
In everything by prayer and thanksgiving
Make all of your requests known unto God
These are the guidelines for living

And the peace of God, which transcends understanding
Will guard your hearts and your minds
This is the way...to approach God and pray
In situations of all kinds

There are things that you should *dwell* upon
Think of things that are *true*
Things that are honest, just and pure
Admirable and excellent too

Things that are lovely and of good report
Things of virtue and praise
These are the things you should *think* about
All throughout your days

And the things that you have learned and received
And heard and seen *me* do
If you *do* these things and *follow* my example
The God of peace....shall be with you

Thessalonians

1 Thessalonians

We always thank God for all of you brethren
And we witness before Him too
Of your hope in Jesus and your faithful work
And the loving deeds you do

We knew that God *chose* you for His own people
When we brought to you the Good News
For the Holy Spirit gave you the conviction
And with power....you were infused

And in spite of the severe suffering that it brought
You *welcomed* the message there
You received it with joy in the Holy Spirit
Then you spread it everywhere

THE LORD'S COMING

We want you to understand the promise of Jesus
To those who are in Him
About those who died....so you don't have to grieve
Like the rest of men

We believe that Jesus died and rose again
And according to what He said
He will come back...and those who died *in* Him
He will bring back from the dead

He will come from Heaven with a loud command
When the voice of the archangel cries
And when the trumpet call of God is sounded
The dead in Christ will rise

And after that, those of us who are still alive
Will be caught up with all of them
To gather in the clouds and meet the Lord in the sky
And to forever *be* with Him

But as to the times and dates of His coming
These we do not know
The day of the Lord will come like a thief in the night
For He has *told* us so

When people are saying, "It is peaceful and safe"
Then destruction will come
As suddenly as labor on a pregnant woman
With no escape....for anyone

But we *know* this is coming and won't be *surprised*
We are children of the day and light
We do not belong to the darkness like others
As those who are drunk in the night

So let us be self-controlled and stay sober
And live in faith...and hope...and love
Rather than face wrath....God wants us to be saved
Through our Lord Jesus Christ above

Jesus *died* for us so that when He returns
Whether we're alive or dead
We can be *with* Him forever and ever
For all of time ahead

So encourage the brethren with these words
And always build up each other
Respect your leaders who guide you in the Lord
Live in peace with one another

Warn the unruly, comfort the shy, help the weak
Be patient with *everyone* you find
Make sure nobody pays back evil for evil
And to everyone be kind

Pray continually...and always be joyful
Give thanks in everything
For this is the will of God for the people
Who belong to Christ the King

Do not suppress the fire of the Holy Spirit
Do not stifle *prophecy*
Yet test all things....and keep what is good
And avoid all the evil you see

Now may the God of peace make you holy
Holy through and through
Until the Lord comes....He will keep you blameless
For *He* is faithful and true

2 Thessalonians

We should always thank God for all of you
For your faith grows more and more
And the love that you have for each other increases
We boast of you, therefore

We boast to the churches, of your perseverance
In the trials that you endure
You will be counted worthy of the kingdom of God
Proof that His judgment is sure

To those who trouble you....God will *give* trouble
And He will give *relief* to *you*
When in *blazing fire*....the Lord Jesus returns
Bringing powerful angels too

He will judge and punish those who don't know God
And don't obey the Gospel of the Lord
He'll cast them from His presence, to eternal destruction
But His people...He will reward

On the day the Lord comes, in majesty and power
His holy people will stand in awe
And this includes *you*...for you believed
When we testified to you before

With this thought in mind, we continually pray
That God will always find *you*
Worthy of His calling....and fill you with power
To do what He has you to do

The Lawless One

Now concerning the coming of our Lord Jesus
When *we* will be gathered to *Him*
We don't *want* you to become upset or alarmed
If you hear it has already *been*

So if you should hear of a report or a prophecy
Said to come from us
That says the day of the Lord has already come
This we will *now* discuss

Don't let anyone fool you in any way
For that day *will not come*
Until the rebellion occurs and we have *seen*
The revealing of the *lawless* one

Though doomed to destruction, he will emerge
Everything of God he will oppose
He will set himself up in God's Temple
As his exaltation grows

And now you know what is restraining him
Remember I *told* you this *before*
For he will be revealed….at the appointed time
But rebellion is *already* at the door

For the secret power of his lawlessness
Is already at work in the world
Yet restrained until the restrainer is taken away
And *then*….it will be unfurled

At that time, the lawless one will be revealed
And *him*….the Lord will slay
With the breath of His mouth….and with His appearing
On that glorious day

The lawless one….who is the antichrist
Will come through Satan's works
With all sorts of miracles, signs and wonders
Behind deception he lurks

With all sorts of evil....he will deceive
Those who will be lost
For they *refuse* to love Truth and be *saved*
Never realizing the cost

So God will send a delusion and they will believe
The lies that are put in their heads
They will be condemned for rejecting the truth
And enjoying the evil instead

STAND FIRM

We thank God for choosing you from the beginning
So stand firm in His Word
He *chose* you to share in the glory of the Lord
Hold *fast* to the truth you have heard

May our Lord Jesus Christ....and God our Father
Who gave comfort and hope to you
Encourage and strengthen you in every good thing
The good things you say and do

Pray that the Word of the Lord spreads quickly
And with enthusiasm, is met
And pray we are delivered from evil people
Remember and never forget

That the Lord is faithful and will strengthen you
And protect you from the evil one
May the Lord direct your hearts....into the love of God
And the perseverance of Christ....His Son

Now stay away from the brethren who are idle
Who don't live according to the Word
We said, "If a man doesn't work, he doesn't eat"
So remember what you have heard

For some people are idle and are busybodies
Urge them to change their ways
Take note of anyone among you who is like this
Anyone who disobeys

Do not associate with him so he will be ashamed
Ashamed in front of the others
Yet do not consider him to be an enemy
Warn him as a brother

Now may the Lord of Peace give you peace in all things
And may peace *in* you....always dwell
And may the grace of our Lord Jesus Christ
Be with you all....as well

Timothy

1 Timothy

A letter from Paul, an apostle of Jesus
To Timothy, in faith, my son
Grace and mercy and peace from God the Father
And Jesus the Holy One

I urged you to remain there in Ephesus
So you can command certain men
To refrain from teaching false doctrines
Which cause controversy then

The goal of this command is love from pure hearts
Good conscience and faith sincere
Because some want to teach but they have strayed
And meaningless talk they hear

THE GRACE OF THE LORD

I thank the Lord Jesus, who gave me strength
And appointed me to serve
Though I blasphemed Him and persecuted His people
He gave me grace I did not deserve

I was acting in ignorance and unbelief
When the Lord showed mercy on me
And His grace, along with His faith and love
He poured out abundantly

For Jesus came into the world to *save* sinners
Of which *I* am the very worst *one*
I'm a prime example of the unlimited patience
That the Lord has for *everyone*

So now others can realize that eternal life
They can *also* receive
They need only to come to Jesus Christ
And in *Him*...believe

Instructions to the Church

To God be the honor and the glory forever
He wants all to be saved...and then
They will *know* that the only mediator is Jesus
The *ransom* for all men

I was appointed an apostle and I'm telling the truth
And I want everyone....everywhere
Without anger or quarreling or resentment
To lift holy hands in prayer

If a man wants to become a church leader
He must lead a *respectful* life
And be willing to learn and able to teach
A good leader of his children and wife

For if he cannot be a good leader in his own home
Then a church....how can he lead?
And he must also be respected by those outside
So they can say nothing bad indeed

He must not get drunk or become violent
He must be gentle and kind
He must not love money or be a *new* Christian
And have self-control of his mind

Likewise, deacons must be men of respect
From drunkenness....they must abstain
They must be tested and lead their own homes well
And not pursue dishonest gain

In the same way *wives* of leaders and deacons
Must be women of respect
Not gossips, but temperate, faithful in everything
It is important their behavior is correct

TREATMENT OF OTHERS

Treat older men as though they are your fathers
And older women as mothers
Treat younger women as sisters with absolute purity
And younger men as brothers

Take care of the widow, who *has* no one else
If the widow is *truly* alone
But her care is the first duty of her *descendants*
If she has children of her own

If anyone does not provide for their own relatives
And especially their own house
They deny the faith and are worse than unbelievers
So care for parents, children and spouse

And those who are rich in worldly possessions
Do not put your faith in *there*
For it is *too* unreliable....put your faith in God
And be generous and willing to share

2 Timothy

FALSE TEACHERS AND THE LAST DAYS

The Spirit has said clearly that in the later times
The true faith...some will leave
For by demonic teachings and evil spirits
They...will be deceived

They will be fooled when people come to them
And put false teachings in their heads
These teachers are liars and hypocrites
Whose consciences are dead

In the last days, there will be *terrible* times
For the way that people will be
They will love themselves and be boastful
The truth they will not see

They will love their money and be brutal
And they will also *abuse*
They will be ungrateful, unholy, unforgiving
And people....they will use

They will be disobedient to their parents
The good....they will not love
They will be lovers of fun and pleasure
Instead of God above

These people will have a *form* of godliness
But they will deny His *power*
Ruthlessly they will seek gain for themselves
Hour upon hour

These kinds of people will worm their way
Into the *homes* of needy women
Women who are swayed by evil desires
And loaded down with sin

These women are forever going after new teachings
But the truth....they never learn
Time and again....they become exploited
Yet again and again they return

PAUL'S CHALLENGE

Now I challenge you, in the presence of God and Jesus
Who will judge the living and the dead
Preach the Word of God in good times and bad
For there comes a time ahead

When people will not *want* to hear the truth
And instead, the people will seek
Teachers who tell them what they want to hear
And they'll listen to the lies they speak

But keep your mind clear and do not be afraid
To suffer for what is true
Be an evangelist and preach the gospel
Do the work God has given to you

Now I am already being poured out like an offering
The time of my departure is at hand
I have fought the good fight, I have finished the race
In the faith I have taken a stand

I have kept the faith and now for me
The Lord has laid up a crown
Which the righteous Judge will *award* to me
Heed what I'm writing down

For a crown of righteousness is not just for *me*
Let me make this *clear*
A crown of righteousness will be given to *all*
Who *long* for the Lord to appear

Titus

To Titus, my true son in our common faith
The reason I left you in Crete
Was for you to appoint elders in every town
And arrange things that weren't complete

An elder you choose must be blameless
The husband of one wife
With believing children above accusation
Of excessive living or strife

As God's steward he must not be arrogant
From violence he must refrain
Not given to drunkenness or a quick temper
Or pursuit of dishonest gain

Rather, he must be hospitable to strangers
A lover of what is good
Sober-minded, righteous, kind, self-controlled
Holding to the Word as he should

That he may be able to excel in *sound* teaching
Thereby encouraging the brothers
And also refuting the ones who oppose it
Who are deceiving many others

For there are many insubordinate people
Deceivers who talk in vain
Teaching things that they ought *not* to teach
For the sake of dishonest gain

Therefore, rebuke these people severely
So in the faith they will be sound
And will ignore those who are rejecting truth
And are spreading myths around

To those who are pure...all things are pure
To the corrupted...*nothing* is pure
These people are claiming that they know God
But their actions deny Him for sure

You must teach in accord with sound doctrine
Teach the men who are mature
To be sober, dignified, sound in faith and love
With patience to endure

Likewise, you must teach the older *women*
To live in a *Godly* way
To be teachers of good...not enslaved to much wine
Or slanderers in things they say

Then *they* can train the *younger* women
To love their children and spouses
To live good and pure and sober lives
And be keepers of their houses

To teach them to be subject to their husbands
So no one can malign God's word
In like manner, teach the younger *men*
These things already heard

To be sober-minded and self-controlled
And in everything *you* do
Show them by *example*, a pattern of good works
So no one can speak evil of *you*

Live your life in an incorruptible manner
Be serious in your speech
Show integrity and sound thinking in your living
By example...you will teach

Servants are to be subject to their employers
And be pleasing in everything
Not talking back and not stealing from them
Glory to our Savior this will bring

For God's saving grace was manifested to all men
It teaches us to say, "No"
To ungodliness and worldly desires
And to live with self-control

While we ourselves wait for the blessed hope
And the glorious to appear
Our great God and Savior Jesus Christ
Who sacrificed Himself here

To ransom us from all lawlessness
And for Himself...to purify
A peculiar people...eager to do good
These teachings you should apply

Remind the people to be subject to authorities
And to be ready to do what is good
To slander no one...to be peaceful and kind
And show humility as they should

For we too were foolish, disobedient and deceived
Serving pleasures and lust
Living in malice and hating each other
In envy and distrust

But the kindness and love of our Savior came
Not due to anything we had done
In mercy He saved and renewed us in the Spirit
Which He poured on us through His Son

And now we have the hope of eternal life
As heirs...justified by His grace
I want you to stress these things to believers
So devotion to good works they embrace

Hebrews

God spoke to our forefathers through prophets
In many times and many ways
But now He has spoken to us through His Son
He has spoken in these last days

God named His Son Jesus, as Heir to all things
And it was *through* His Son
That God created the entire *universe*
Jesus *is*...a reflection of the One

And when Jesus had cleansed us from our sins
He sat down at God's right hand
Having a place so much higher than the angels
As was the Father's plan

For God was speaking to His *Son*....*not* the angels
When He made His intentions *concrete*
Saying, "Sit at my right side until I make your enemies
A footstool for your feet"

So we must pay careful attention to remember
What the Lord was the first to tell
If we don't take the way to Heaven that He *gave* us
What makes us think we won't go to hell?

And since we *have* our High Priest...Jesus the Son
Let us hold firm our faith in *Him*
He understands....for He *faced* our temptations
And yet...He did not sin

So let us come with confidence to the throne of God
Where mercy....we will receive
And where we will also find the grace to help us
In our time of need

Jesus came as High Priest of the *good* things to come
And He entered the Most Holy Place
Heaven's Tabernacle...by His own blood sacrifice
For our sins....to erase

The blood of animals is sprinkled on people
This is done to sanctify them
How much *more* is done by the blood of *Christ*
Through the sacrifice of *Him*?

For the Law says that without the shedding of blood
There can be no forgiveness of sin
But *Christ* was sacrificed...once and for all
So we could be cleansed through *Him*

Because of the sacrificed body and blood of Jesus
We can enter the Most Holy Place
So let us come to God with pure sincere hearts
And *confidence* in our faith

Let us see how we can encourage one another
To do deeds in a loving way
And do not give up gathering together
Even more as we approach the Day

But if we should *deliberately* keep on sinning
After the truth....we have learned
There is *no more sacrifice* to cover *those* sins
Only judgment that we have earned

Only terrible expectation of judgment and fire
That consumes God's enemies
And for those who would trample on the *Son* of God
The worst punishment waits for these

For those who don't treat the blood of the covenant
As a most holy thing
And have insulted the Holy Spirit of God
Judgment...God will bring

We know the One who said...."It is mine to revenge"
He who said, "*I* will repay"
He also said, "The Lord will judge His people"
On that great and terrible day

Now remember back in the earlier days
When you had *received* the word
You suffered much....but stood your ground
Standing for what you had heard

At times you were publicly insulted and persecuted
At times with others...you stood
And since you knew you had better things in Heaven
You accepted when they took your goods

So do not abandon your confidence *now*
You will have a rich reward
If you are patient and continue to do God's will
You'll receive the promises of the Lord

For in just a little while, the One will be coming
He will come and not delay
He takes pleasure in those who live by faith
But not in those who turn away

We are not those who turn to their own destruction
We are faithful and saved shall we be
And *faith* is being *confident* in what we hope for
Certain of things we don't see

Pay Attention to God

Make every effort to live in peace with all men
And to live a holy life
Without holiness, no one will see the Lord
So avoid unholiness and strife

Watch out for each other so no one misses
Receiving God's wonderful grace
Be careful that bitterness doesn't come up
Causing trouble for those in your place

See that no one is sexually immoral or godless
Or they may suffer Esau's fate
Who traded his inheritance, for just one meal
Then cried...but it was too late

Now you have not come to a mountain
Where you must tremble with fear
It is Mount Zion, the Heavenly Jerusalem
Where you are drawing near

Where countless angels are joyfully gathered
In the *city*....of the Creator
The place of God....the Judge of all
And *Jesus*....the Mediator

Do not refuse Him who speaks from Heaven
He has shaken the earth in the past
He said He'll shake it again and also the heavens
Then only the *unshakable* will last

Be thankful for a kingdom that *cannot* be shaken
And we should also aspire
To serve God acceptably with reverence and awe
For our "God is a consuming fire"

Concluding Words

Now remember to love each other as brothers
Entertain strangers coming and going
For by doing so, some people have entertained
Angels without knowing

Remember those in prison as though *you* were there
And those who are mistreated too
For you are also subject to suffering
And it can happen to *you*

God will judge the adulterer and sexually immoral
So keep pure the marriage bed
Do not love money, be content with what you have
And remember what God has said

"I will never leave you...I will never forsake you"
So we can have courage, you see
And say, "The Lord is my helper, I will not be afraid
Of what man will do to me"

James

James wrote a letter to the twelve tribes of Israel
Scattered among the nations
In his letter he covered many topics
Starting with trials and temptations

You should all consider it absolute joy
When facing trials of all kinds
For when you are tested, you develop perseverance
And maturity in your minds

You should all ask God for wisdom
For the Lord gives *generously*
But you must *believe* and not doubt when you ask
Or you're like a wave upon the sea

Tossed about and blown around by the wind
A man with a double-mind
Unstable in everything and though he asks
Nothing...will he find

The humble should take pride in their high position
And the rich take pride in their low
For as flowers in the sun....the rich will wither
As about their business they go

God promised those who persevere in trial
That when they have stood the test
That they will receive the crown of life
They will be truly blessed

No one should say, "God is tempting me"
For God will tempt *no one*
Each one is tempted by his own evil desires
And sin leads to death....when it's done

You should *know* that every good and perfect gift
Comes from God above
Who does not change like shifting shadows
He is steadfast in His love

And everyone should be quick to listen
And yet…slow to speak
Slow to anger…you should live God's word
And purity you should seek

Believers should *never* show favoritism
Honoring rich over poor
If you keep the Law and stumble on *one point*
You break *all* of it, for sure

Judgment without mercy will be shown to those
Who were *not* merciful, Jesus said
Also, what good is faith without deeds?
Faith without action is dead

Not many of you should presume to be teachers
For judgment will be stricter on *them*
And tame your tongues…They are full of poison
They praise God…yet they curse men

Who is wise and understanding among you?
His good life should tell
But if his heart has envy and selfish ambition
His wisdom is from the devil in hell

But the wisdom that comes from Heaven
Is sincere…and first of all *pure*
Peace-loving, considerate, submissive
And merciful for sure

Know that the peacemakers, who sow in peace
Raise a harvest of righteousness
But what is it that causes quarrels among *you*?
It's your inward desire to possess

You kill and covet, but can't get what you want
You don't have, because you don't ask the Lord
When you ask you don't receive…for your motives are wrong
It's *pleasures* you want to afford

Friendship with the world, is hatred toward God
You adulterous people should see
That those who choose friendship with the world
Become God's enemy

Scripture tells us that God opposes the proud
But grace the humble will see
So submit yourselves to God and resist the devil
And from you he will *flee*

You should know that if you draw *near* to God
He will draw near to *you*
Wash your hands sinners….and purify your hearts
As the Lord wants you to do

Remember, there is only one Lawgiver and Judge
Who are *you* to judge your brother?
There is only One…who can save or destroy
So do not slander one another

And do not be *boasting* to each other
Of the *things* you plan to do
For you have no way of knowing at all
What will happen to you

Your life is a mist…that appears for a while
And then…you will be gone
Say instead…"If it is the will of the Lord"
That *then* you will carry on

If you don't do the good that you know you should
You're sinning in God's eyes
To the rich among you, who cheat the innocent
The Lord has *heard* their cries

And as a farmer waits patiently for the coming rain
Wait patiently for the coming of the Lord
Meanwhile…do not grumble against each other
For the *Judge*…is standing at the door!

You have all heard about the perseverance of Job
And saw what the Lord finally brought
For the Lord is full of compassion and mercy
And with Job....a lesson was taught

Look at the prophets in the face of suffering
As an example...look to them
And above all else, never swear by anything
Or you...God will condemn

If anyone is in trouble...he should pray
If happy...sing *songs* of praise
The elders should anoint the sick with oil
And the sick....the Lord will raise

So pray for each other, so you may be healed
To each other...confess your sin
For a righteous man's prayer is powerful and effective
And forgiveness and healing will begin

Elijah was a man just like us...and *he prayed*
That it wouldn't rain back then
For three and a half years, it was *dry* on the earth
Until he prayed it would rain *again*

And if one of you should wander from the truth
And someone brings him back one day
They'll save him from death, and cover a multitude of sins
When they turn a sinner from the error of his way

Peter

1 Peter

Rid yourselves of all malice and hypocrisy
Envy, slander and deceit
Instead, you must crave spiritual things
So your growth can be complete

We know that Jesus is the believers' Cornerstone
And though precious to you all
He's the Stone that causes nonbelievers to stumble
He's the *Rock*....that makes them fall

But *you* people are a *chosen* people
Royal priesthood...holy nation
Praise *God* for calling you out of darkness
And giving you salvation

But you must submit yourselves to authority
As Jesus told us then
For it is the will of *God*, that by doing *good*
You silence talk...of foolish men

Christ suffered for us and bore our sins
In His body on the tree
So we could die to sin and live in righteousness
As the Lord wants us to be

And by His wounds, you have been healed
You were like sheep astray
But now you've returned to the Shepherd
The One who showed you the way

Wives...non-believing husbands can be won over
By submissive wives
When they see the behavior and the purity
And the reverence of your lives

Your beauty should not come from adornment
Fine clothes...gold jewelry...braided hair
But instead from the beauty of a quiet gentle spirit
Your *inner* selves...not what you wear

Husbands...you who received the gracious gift of life
Should treat your wives as fellow heirs
Treating them with respect and consideration
So that nothing will hinder your prayers

And all of you should be living in harmony
In harmony with one another
Being humble, sympathetic and compassionate
And loving each other as brother

Though pagans abuse you and think it is strange
That believers no longer live in sin
These people will stand before God, who will judge
And give account of themselves to *Him*

You should offer hospitality and above all else
Treat each other with love
Serving others by using whatever gifts
You received from God above

Do not be surprised when you *suffer* for Christ
Or the painful trial you feel
But rejoice so that you may be overjoyed
When His glory is revealed

If you're insulted because of the name of Jesus
You are truly blessed
For the Spirit of glory...and of God
Upon *you*...rests

You *elders*...be shepherds of God's flock
For the flock is under your care
The elders should be serving as overseers
Of the younger Christians there

Because you are willing…not because you must
Is how God wants you to be
Eager to serve and not greedy for money
For the younger ones will see

So instead of lording it over them
Be examples every day
When Jesus appears…you'll receive a crown of glory
That will never fade away

Young men…be *submissive* to the elders
And clothed in humility
For God resists the proud…and gives peace to the humble
These words….can set men free

So humble yourselves under God's mighty hand
He will lift you when time is due
And cast all of your cares upon *Him*
Because He cares for you

Always be self-controlled and alert
Every day and every hour
For the devil prowls like a roaring lion
Seeking whom he may devour

Resist the devil and stand strong in the faith
For you know that there are others
All over the world…and the same kind of suffering
Is happening to your brothers

2 Peter

It was through the divine power of Jesus our Lord
That we received everything we need
For life and godliness…through our knowledge of Him
For it was through *His* deed

He gave His great and precious promises
Through which you can take part
In *His* divine nature…and escape corruption
Caused by evil desires of the heart

Make every effort to add to your faith
These things that I speak of
Goodness, knowledge, self-control, perseverance
Godliness, kindness and love

For if you have these qualities in increasing measure
Increasing throughout your life
They will keep you from being unproductive
In your knowledge of our Lord, Jesus Christ

But if anyone does *not* possess these qualities
He is nearsighted and blind
And forgot that he has been *cleansed* from sin
It is important to keep this in mind

And *always* remember that we do not follow
A cleverly written *story*
For we *witnessed* the voice that came to Jesus
From the Majestic Glory

Saying, "This is my Son...whom I love"
With our *own ears* we *heard*
"With Him I am well pleased," said the voice
We were *there* when this occurred!

Take heed and pay attention to the prophets
For prophecy wasn't wrong
The *messages* of the prophets came from *God*
As the Holy Spirit carried them along

But there are also *false prophets* and teachers
And they are there with *you*
They preach heresy and deny the sovereign Lord
Bringing destruction on themselves too

In their greed these teachers will exploit you
With stories they have made
But condemnation is hanging over them
For their sins...they will be paid

God did not spare the angels when *they* sinned
But sent them straight to hell
And in the day of Noah...God sent a flood
Condemning *those* sinners as well

Yet at that time, He protected Noah and others
And when Sodom, He condemned
A righteous man, Lot, and his family lived there
And yes...the Lord spared them

For the Lord knows how to rescue the godly
While at the very same time
He can judge and punish the *unrighteous* ones
For their evil lives of crime

Bold and arrogant, these men are not afraid
To slander a celestial being
Yet powerful *angels* wouldn't do such a thing
In the presence of the Lord's seeing

But these men go and blaspheme in matters
They don't even understand
They will be paid for the harm they have done
Punished...by God's hand

These men carouse in broad daylight
Reveling in their pleasures
With eyes full of adultery...they continuously sin
On *them*...He will use strong measures

And for those who have *known* our Lord and Savior
And *then* turned *back* to sin
Better for them to have *not* known righteousness
Than to turn their *backs* on *Him*

THE DAY OF THE LORD

You must understand that in the last days
Scoffers indeed will come
Saying, "Where is the coming He *promised*?"
Mocking the Holy One

They will say that since the beginning of creation
All things are the same as then
But as God used a flood...now *fire* is reserved
To destroy these ungodly men

But with the Lord...a day is like a thousand years
And a thousand years like a day
He is not slow in keeping His promise...but patient
Not wanting *anyone* to perish away

But the day of the Lord will come like a thief
Surprising everyone there
The heavens will disappear...the elements will burn
Everything on earth...laid bare

And since everything will be *destroyed* in this way
What kind of people ought you to be?
You ought to live lives, that are holy and godly
I am trying to make you see

For the heavens will be destroyed by fire
The elements will melt
Yet we look forward to His promise of a *new* Heaven and earth
After His judgment....has been dealt

So try hard to be blameless and at peace with *Him*
Since *this*, you look forward to
Remember...the patience of the Lord means salvation
And Paul *also* wrote that to you

Therefore dear friends, do not be led astray
And drop your guard...*never*
But grow in the grace and knowledge of our Lord
To *Him* be the glory....now and forever

1 John

What we have seen and heard and touched
We now proclaim to you
So that you may also have *fellowship* with us
And the Father and His Son too

And to make our joy complete
Is the reason that we write
For the message we have heard from Him
Is that God is light

In Him, there is no darkness at all
But if fellowship with Him, we imply
Yet walk in darkness, and don't live by truth
Then we are living a lie

But if indeed...we walk in the light
And fellowship with each other and Him
Then the blood of Jesus Christ, His Son
Purifies us...from sin

But if we claim that we do not *have* any sin
It's ourselves that we deceive
If we *confess* our sin, He is faithful and just
And forgiveness we will receive

And if we claim that we have *never* sinned
We make a liar out of *Him*
And His word doesn't have a place in our lives
Only *He* committed no sin

My dear children...I am writing this to you
So that you will *not* sin
But if you *do*, we have an *intercessor*
And our defenses...are in Him

Jesus Christ, who is the Righteous One
The atoning sacrifice
For our sin and all the sins of the world
He already *paid* the price

His love is complete in us if we obey Him
And do not do....what He forbid
And this is how we *know*...that we are in Him
If we *walk*....as *Jesus* did

But if you love the world or anything in it
The Father's love is not in you
For worldly things are cravings and lusts
And boasts of what you have and do

The man who does the will of God lives forever
The world and its desires pass away
Beware of those who deny that Jesus is the Christ
They are trying to lead you astray

My dear children...continue in the Lord
So that when He *does* appear
We can stand confident and unashamed before Him
This is why I write you here

This is how we recognize the children of God
And the children of the other
If they do not do right, they are not God's children
Nor are those who don't love their brother

And if someone has material possessions
And sees his brother in need
And yet does nothing...is the love of God in him?
Not without action...indeed

Jesus Christ laid down His life for us
This is how we *know* what love *is*
So for *our* brothers...we should lay down *our* lives
As Jesus laid down His

If our hearts don't condemn us we can go before God
And receive whatever we ask
He commands us to believe in His Son, Jesus Christ
That is our given task

God also commands us to love one another
And those who obey live in Him
And this is how we *know*...that He lives in *us*
By the Spirit He gave us within

But dear friends, do not believe every spirit
Test the spirits to see
If they *are* from God...for many false prophets
In the world shall be

Every spirit that acknowledges that Jesus is Lord
Is a spirit that comes from God
But every spirit that does *not* acknowledge *Jesus*
Their holiness...is a façade

For they are the spirit of the antichrist
They're already in the world today
But you are from God, and have *overcome* them
You *know*, that Jesus is the way

Remember that greater is He who is in *you*
Than he who is in the world...so *then*
Whoever knows *God*....will listen to *us*
But the *world* will listen to *them*

My dear friends....let us love one another
Love comes from God above
Who sent His only Son, as a sacrifice for us
Because God Himself...*is* love

And since God so loved us, dear friends
We should also love each other
He *lives* in us and His love is made complete
If *we* love one another

So we will be confident on the day of judgment
For there is no fear in love
And perfect love drives out all fear
Of punishment thereof

And *we* love…because He first loved *us*
But if anyone hates his brother
And says he loves God…then he is lying
For He *commands* us to love each other

Remember that God has given us His testimony
Eternal life through Jesus, His Son
And he who has the Son…has life forever
But he who does not…has none

And we have *confidence* in approaching God
If we ask *anything* according to His will
We know that He hears us…and whatever we ask
We *know* our request…He'll fulfill

We also know that anyone born of God
Does *not* continue to sin
For the *One* who was born of God keeps him *safe*
And the enemy…cannot *harm* him

We know that the evil one controls the world
And we children of God know too
That the Son of God gave us understanding
So we can know Him who is true

And we are *in* the One who is true
Even in His Son, Jesus Christ
Avoid all idols…for Jesus is the *true* God
In *Him*…is eternal life

Jude

Jude wanted to write a letter to the Christians
About the salvation they all shared
But instead, he felt the need to *warn* them
So they would be prepared

Beware...for some have slipped in among you
And deception you can ill afford
They use the grace of God....as a license to *sin*
And deny Jesus Christ as Lord

Remember when the Lord delivered His people
Out of Egypt...then *again*
Some disbelieved and worshiped idols
And He *destroyed* those men

Sodom and Gomorrah should be an example
Of the punishment of eternal fire
To those who disobey....the laws of God
For *they* will suffer His ire

Woe to those who pollute their bodies
For God is *always* seeing
And woe to those who reject authority
Or slander a celestial being

The archangel Michael argued with the devil
But he *knew* what he had to do
Michael did not slander and accuse him
He said, "The *Lord* rebuke you!"

Men who are shepherds, feeding only themselves
Fruitless trees...uprooted...twice dead
Blackest darkness forever is reserved for them
And will fall upon each head

Enoch, the descendant of Adam prophesied
Warning about these men
He said the Lord will come to judge everyone
And convict those who sin against Him

In the last days, there will be scoffers
Following ungodly desires
Build yourselves in faith and pray in the spirit
And snatch others....from the fires

And to Him who is able to keep you from falling
Majesty and glory be
And to the one and only...God our Savior
Be power and authority

Revelation

While John was exiled on the island of Patmos
Where he remained for many a year
God gave him visions, which have since filled hearts
With both hope and fear

For John was shown the end of days
In the visions which God sent
He was shown the coming of the Lord
And the day of great judgment

John was told to write down what he saw
For generations to come
The visions were both a promise and a warning
A message for everyone

He wrote that he saw the Lord come in the clouds
And that every eye would see
And because of the Lord, the people would mourn
He wrote, "So shall it be"

ONE LIKE A SON OF MAN

I heard behind me, a loud voice like a trumpet
"Write on a scroll what you see," it said
Then I turned and saw the risen Lord Jesus
And before Him I fell…as though dead

He was wearing a robe that reached to His feet
His hair was white as snow
He wore a sash of gold around His chest
His eyes were as *fire*…aglow

His feet were like bronze…glowing in a furnace
His voice…like a rushing water sound
A double-edged sword, came out of His mouth
His face shone like the sun…all around

He touched me and said…"Do not be afraid
I am the first and the last"
And standing there…was the Son of Man
The Lord of the future and past

The Letters to the Churches

Then the Lord told John to write to the churches
And He told him what to say
So John wrote letters to the seven churches
Showing them the way

He wrote that the Lord sees the good things they do
And He also sees the bad
For they all did things that were pleasing to Him
And things that made Him sad

The letters encouraged them to follow in His ways
And in the faith to stay strong
For though they may suffer for His Name's sake
He'll come for them before very long

But for those who are neither hot nor cold
He wished they were either one
For those lukewarm…He will spit them out
This is a promise from the Son

He rebukes and disciplines those He loves
To be earnest and repent
"I stand at the door and knock," He said
His message clearly sent

"And if anyone hears my voice," He continued,
"And opens up the door
I will come in and eat with him"
And then He told him more

He said those who manage to overcome
Will *sit* with Him on His throne
Those with an ear….should listen to the Spirit
For now His words are known

THE LORD SHOWS THE FUTURE

After this, I looked up and before me
Standing open...was a door
And a voice said, "Come up," and I was transported
And this is what I saw

A throne in Heaven...and looking like jewels
Was the one who on it...sat
Around the throne was a rainbow like an emerald
And twenty-four thrones 'round that

On *those* sat twenty-four elders in white
Each wearing a crown of gold
From the center throne, came flashes of lightning
And peals of thunder bold

And there in front of the center throne
Seven lamps met my gaze
The lamps were the seven spirits of God
Appearing as lamps ablaze

And as I continued to look, I saw
What appeared to be
Shining and sparkling in front of the throne
A crystal clear...glass sea

Around the throne were four winged creatures
Covered with eyes...all around
As the creatures continually praised the Lord God
The elders bowed down to the ground

THE LAMB AND THE SCROLL

The One on the throne, held a scroll which was sealed
As the vision continued to unfold
An angel said, "Who is *worthy* to break the seals
And open up the scroll?"

But no one was able to open the scroll
Or even look inside
And since no one was found who was worthy
I bowed my head and cried

Then one of the elders said, "Do not weep"
And I looked and saw the Lamb
Who approached the One who sat on the throne
And took the scroll from His hand

The Lamb who was slain...The Lion of Judah
Was the only worthy one
Then a hundred...million...angels gathered
Singing praises to God's Son

THE SEALS

Then the Lamb began to open the seals
And when He opened the very first one
One of the four winged creatures called out
And in a voice like thunder...said, "COME!"

As I looked I saw a white horse and rider
The rider carried a bow
He was given a crown, and he rode like a conqueror
And off to conquer he rode

And then the Lamb opened the second seal
And the second creature said, "COME!"
I saw a rider who was given the power to make war
His horse was a fiery *red* one

The Lamb opened the third...the third creature said, "COME!"
Then I saw a horse that was *black*!
And its rider was carrying a pair of scales
As he rode upon its back

I then heard a voice, from among the winged creatures
I listened and heard it say
That a quart of wheat or three quarts of barley
Would cost the wages of a day

"And do not damage the oil and the wine,"
The voice went on to say
The Lamb opened the fourth...the fourth creature said, "COME!"
In the very same way

This final horse was pale...its rider called Death
Hades followed close behind
They had sword...famine...plague and beasts
To kill a quarter of mankind

The Lamb opened the fifth seal and under the altar
I could see the souls of those slain
They were martyred because of the Word of God
And the testimony they maintained

"How long sovereign Lord, holy and true,"
In a loud voice, they cried,
"Until you judge...and avenge our blood?"
Pled the people who had died

Then each was given...a white robe to wear
And told they would have to wait
A little while longer...'til their *fellow* servants
Had also met *their* fate

Then I watched as the Lamb opened the sixth seal
And there came a great *earthquake*
Every mountain and island was moved from its place
As I watched everything shake

The sun turned black...the moon blood red
As the cataclysm took its toll
Then the stars in the sky...fell to the earth
And the sky rolled up like a scroll

Everyone on earth, from the greatest to the least
Tried to hide throughout the land
They cried out to the rocks to fall on them
To hide them...from God and the Lamb

THE 144,000

Then I saw four angels, holding *back* the wind
So it wouldn't blow on the land
And an angel came from the east, carrying the seal
Of the living God in his hand

The angel called to the four other angels
To not harm the trees, land or sea
Until seals were on the foreheads of the servants of God
Then I *heard* who they would be

A hundred and forty-four thousand people
From the Israel tribes would be sealed
And I continued to watch in amazement
As prophecy was revealed

I saw a great multitude, which couldn't be counted
Standing with palms in hand
Wearing white robes…crying out in loud voices
Praising God and the Lamb

The angels were also in praise and worship
An elder spoke as he turned his head,
"Who are these in white robes….and where did they come from?"
"Sir…you *know*"…I said

"These have come out of the great tribulation"
The elder, responding, began,
"They have washed their robes and made them white
In the blood of the Lamb"

He said they serve God…day and night
And there will be no more cries
For the Lamb will be their shepherd
And God will wipe every tear from their eyes

THE SEVENTH SEAL

There was silence in Heaven for about half an hour
When the seventh seal was opened by the Lamb
And I saw the seven angels who stand before God
Each given a trumpet in his hand

Then another angel came and stood before the altar
Burning incense in a censer of gold
Prayers of saints and the incense went up before God
Then much more did I behold

For the angel filled the censer with fire from the altar
Hurled to earth...across the land
There were voices and thunder and flashes of lightning
And a mighty earthquake began

THE TRUMPETS

The seven angels with trumpets, prepared to sound them
And when the first one of the seven
Blew on his trumpet...fire, hail and blood
Rained down on earth from Heaven

I watched as the scene continued to unfold
And the wrath of God I learned
As a third of the earth and a third of the trees
And all of the grass was burned

When the second angel sounded his trumpet
A blazing mountain was thrown to the sea
Which became one-third blood...and a third of the creatures
And the ships would no longer be

At the third trumpet sound...a star named Wormwood
Fell blazing to earth from the sky
And a third of the rivers and streams were made bitter
And the water made many people die

The fourth trumpet sounded...a third of the sun was struck
And a third of the day had no light
And likewise, a third of the moon and the stars
Were dark...a third of the night

Then an eagle called, "Woe to the inhabitants of earth
Because of the trumpet blasts
About to be sounded by the *other* three angels!"
Now *these* would come to pass

When the fifth trumpet sounded...a star fell to earth
And the star was given a key
To open the Abyss...and when he did
Great smoke was what I did see

Then out of the smoke, locusts came on the earth
And the locusts were given power
To sting those who had *not*...the seal of *God*
Like scorpions...hour after hour

The locusts looked like horses prepared for battle
They had teeth as those of a lion
They had faces as a man and hair as a women
Their breastplates appeared as iron

On their heads was something like crowns of gold
The sound of their wings filled the sky
Sent not to kill...but to torture for five months
Causing men to desire to die

Their power to hurt was in their scorpion tails
Over *them* they had a king
The angel of the abyss...Now the first woe has passed
Two woes come after these things

When the sixth angel sounded his trumpet
From the altar came a voice...well-defined,
"Release the four angels who are bound at the Euphrates"
They would kill a third of mankind

To accomplish this deed they would use an army
I looked and saw it then
And I heard the number of mounted troops
Two hundred million men

Their breastplates were dark blue and yellow
And also a fiery red
And looking more like a lion, than a horse
Was each horse's head

Their power was in their mouths and in their tails
Each tail like a snake with a head
From their mouths came fire, smoke and sulfur
Then a third of mankind...was dead

Yet after this happened, the rest of the people
Who were *not* killed by these plagues
Still did not repent of their evil works
And turn to God to be saved

They continued to worship gold and demons
And idols that can't walk or see
They continued their murders, their thefts, their magic
And sexual immorality

THE ANGEL AND THE LITTLE SCROLL

A *mighty* angel came from Heaven...his face as the sun
With a little scroll, opened in his hand
With legs like fire...he put his right foot on the sea
And his left foot on the land

He shouted like a lion...and seven thunders spoke
And as I looked around
A voice said, "Seal what the thunder said
And do not write it down"

The angel raised his right hand to Heaven and swore
By the One who forever lives
The Creator of the heavens, earth and sea
And all that in them...is

The mighty angel raised his voice and said,
"There will be no more delays!
When the seventh angel is about to sound his trumpet
The mystery of God will be completed in those days!"

The Two Witnesses

I was told that the Gentiles will trample the holy city
For many months...forty-two
But that God would give power to two witnesses
And I was told what they would do

For twelve hundred sixty days they will prophesy
And in sackcloth they will be clothed
They are the lampstands and olive trees of the Lord
And by many, they will be loathed

But if anyone tries to harm these two
Fire from their mouths will come
And devour their enemies...and they will die
One...by one

These men will have power to turn waters to blood
And cause it not to rain
Power to strike the earth with plagues
And cause the people pain

But when they have finished their testimony
The beast from the Abyss
Will attack the witnesses and kill them
And the people will gloat over this

Their bodies will lie in the streets of the city
Where the Lord was crucified
The people will celebrate and give each other gifts
When they hear that the prophets have died

But at three and a half days...a breath of life from God
Will enter them and they will stand
And terror will fall upon those who see them
Then the prophets will *leave* the land

For a voice from Heaven will say, "Come up!"
And they will go to Heaven in a cloud
And at that very hour...an earthquake will strike
Devastating and loud

A tenth of the city...will be destroyed
Seven thousand people will have died
Then those who survive will give glory to God
Because *they* will be *terrified*

THE SEVENTH TRUMPET

At the seventh trumpet blast...voices rose in Heaven
"The kingdom of the world," they said together,
"Has become the kingdom of our Lord and His Christ
And He shall reign forever and ever"

Then the twenty-four elders who sat on the thrones
Upon their faces fell
They worshiped God and called for judgment
Rewards in Heaven and hell

The temple of Heaven was opened and inside
Was the Ark of the Covenant
There was lightning, thunder, earthquake and hail
All from Heaven sent

THE WOMAN AND THE DRAGON

Then a wondrous sign appeared in Heaven
A pregnant woman clothed with the sun
Moon under her feet...a crown of twelve stars
And her labor...had begun

Crying out in pain, she was ready to give birth
But she faced a giant dragon of red
The dragon had seven heads and he had ten horns
And a crown upon on each head

The dragon would devour the child when it was born
Defenseless and alone
But when the woman gave birth...the child was snatched
Up to God and His throne

Then the woman fled to a place in the desert
Which God had prepared before
Then Michael and his angels, fought the dragon and *his*
In a mighty Heavenly war

But the dragon and his angels weren't strong enough
So their victory could never be
And the great deceiver of the world and all his angels
Were hurled to the earth and the sea

Then I heard a great voice saying in the Heavens,
"Now salvation has come
And the power and the kingdom of our God
And the authority of Christ, His Son

"For cast down was the accuser of the brethren
He accused before God constantly
But they overcame him by the blood of the Lamb
And the word of their testimony

"They did not love their lives so much
As from death to shrink away
Because of this...be glad you Heavens
And those who in Heaven stay

"But because the devil has gone down to you
Woe to the earth and the sea
For the devil knows that his time is short
And he is filled with fury"

When hurled to the earth, he pursued the woman
But God protected her again
So the dragon was furious and went to make war
On the rest of her offspring then

THE BEAST OUT OF THE SEA

Then I looked and saw a beast...coming from the sea
Like a leopard with feet like a bear
The beast had seven heads...and it had ten horns
On each horn, a crown it did wear

The mouth of the beast was like that of a lion
A blasphemous name on each head
And one of the heads had a wound that was healed
A wound that had rendered it dead

From the dragon the beast received power
Authority and a throne
The world was *amazed* and *followed* the beast
Worshiping him and the dragon alone

"Who is like the beast?" the people asked
"Who can war against him?" they said
He blasphemed God and slandered His name
Many hearts were filled with dread

He was given a mouth to blaspheme and boast
He was given authority too
Which he would possess for forty-two months
To do what he would do

He slandered Heaven and those living there
He had authority over all men
He was given power to make war against the saints
And to *conquer* them

Everyone on earth would worship the beast
Except for those whose names
Were written in the Lamb's book of life
The Lamb who had been slain

The saints will need patience, endurance and faithfulness
Of these, their hearts should be filled
For there will be those...who *will* be arrested
Those who will be *killed*

The Beast Out of the Earth

Then I looked and I saw *another* beast
Out of the earth he came
With two horns like a lamb...he spoke like a dragon
And acted in the first beast's name

He made all of the people worship the first beast
Performing miraculous signs
Causing fire to come down from Heaven
Deceiving everyone's minds

He ordered the people to set up an image
In honor of the first beast
Then he ordered that everyone *worship* the image
From the greatest to the least

He was given power to give breath to the image
And also to give it speech
So that the image could kill...all who refused
To *worship* the image of the beast

He forced the people to receive a mark of the beast
Upon their forehead or right hand
And without it....no one could buy or sell
Anywhere in the land

The mark is the name or the number of his name
On each hand or head affixed
Let anyone who has insight...calculate
The number is 6-6-6

The Lamb and the 144,000

Then I looked up again and I saw the Lamb
Who stood on the Zion Mount
And with Him were tens of thousands of faithful
A hundred forty-four thousand....the count

They had the name of the Lamb on their foreheads
And also His Father's name
They kept themselves pure...no lies in their mouths
Redeemed from the earth, they came

THE THREE ANGELS

Then I looked and I saw *another* angel
Flying in midair
He had the eternal Gospel to proclaim
For those on earth everywhere

"Fear God and give Him glory," he shouted,
"For the hour of His judgment has come"
Then he told all to worship the One who created
Everything and everyone

"Fallen! Fallen is Babylon the Great,"
Was a *second* angel's cry,
"Which *made* the nations drink...the mad wine of her adulteries!"
He said as he flew by

Then a *third* angel followed and shouted a warning
To the greatest and the least
To *not* receive the mark on their forehead or hand
Or worship the image and the beast

For they *too* would drink the wine of God's fury
Poured *full strength*....in the cup of His wrath
And be tormented forever....with burning sulfur
If they *chose* to follow that path

"No rest day or night, for those who worship
The beast and his image," he proclaimed
It was clear they would suffer, forever and ever
If they *received* the mark of his name

Then a voice from Heaven told me to write
"Blessed are the dead
Who die in the Lord from now on," said the voice
And *then* the Spirit said:

"Yes…they will *rest* from their labors
For their deeds will follow them"
It was *clear* that God will bless the faithful
And *those* He will *not* condemn

The Harvest of the Earth

Then I saw a white cloud…and seated upon it
Was One….like a Son of Man
He had a crown of gold upon His head
And a sharp sickle…in His hand

Then an angel came out of the temple and called
To Him who sat on the cloud,
"Take your sickle and reap…for the time has come"
He said in a voice clear and loud

"For the harvest of the earth is ripe," he said
And then the *Holy One*
Swung His sickle…over the earth
The harvest…had begun

Then *another* angel came out of the temple
He carried a sharp sickle *too*
Then the angel in charge of the *fire*
Told *that one* what to do

"Take your sickle and gather the clusters
Of the vine of the earth," he said,
"For its grapes are ripe"…And the angel raised
The sickle…over his head

Then he swung his sickle over the earth
And when it made its pass
The grapes that it gathered…all were thrown
Into the winepress of God's wrath

Then the grapes were trampled in the winepress
Blood flowed…for quite a while
It rose as high as the horses' bridles
For a hundred and eighty mile

SEVEN ANGELS WITH SEVEN PLAGUES

Then seven other angels came out of the temple
Wearing shining linen to their feet
They were given the *final* bowls of God's wrath
Which would make God's wrath complete

Then I looked and I saw a sea of glass and fire
And standing next to the sea
Were those who were victorious over the beast
Now these souls were free

They were holding harps, given them by God
And they raised their voices in praise
And sang the songs of Moses and the Lamb
Praising the Lord and His ways

THE SEVEN BOWLS OF GOD'S WRATH

Then a voice from the temple told the seven angels
To pour out the bowls from each hand
So the *first* angel tilted his bowl of God's wrath
And poured it...on the land

All of the people with the mark of the beast
Who worshiped his image too
Were afflicted with ugly and painful sores
And there was *nothing* they could do

Then the *second* angel poured his bowl on the *sea*
Which turned to blood *so* red
And though the sea was full of life *before*
Now everything in it...was dead

Then the *third* angel poured his bowl of wrath
On the rivers and the springs
And those waters *also* turned to blood
Killing all of the living things

The fourth angel poured *his* bowl on the sun
It scorched the people with fire
But instead of repenting...they cursed God's name
Choosing to receive His ire

The fifth bowl was poured on the throne of the beast
Into darkness, his kingdom was sent
Men were in agony...yet *still* they cursed God
And *still*....they refused to repent

The sixth bowl was poured on the River Euphrates
To prepare for the kings from the East
The water dried up...evil spirits like frogs
Came out of the mouth of the beast

And out of the mouths of the dragon and the prophet
And on the earth they trod
Doing miracles and gathering kings to Armageddon
For the battle on the great day of God

Then the seventh angel poured his bowl in the air
And a loud voice came from the throne
"It is done," said the voice....and thunder was heard
And flashes of lightning shone

Then a *great* earthquake started...like no other
That had ever been before
It split the great city...into three parts
The cities of the nations...no more

God remembered *Babylon*...and He sent His fury
The fury of His wrath to its ground
And the islands of the world....all disappeared
And the mountains couldn't be found

Then hailstones weighing a *hundred pounds*
Fell from the sky on men
But *still* the people would not repent
And cursed God...yet again

THE WOMAN ON THE BEAST

One of the seven angels then said to me, "Come
I will show you the punishment
Of the great prostitute...who sits on many waters"
And in the spirit we went

Then I saw a woman dressed in purple and scarlet
Glittering with precious gems and gold
On a scarlet beast, covered with blasphemous names
Which she sat upon...proud and bold

The kings of the earth had committed adultery
With the woman on the beast
The people were *intoxicated* with the *wine* of her adulteries
From the greatest to the least

The beast had seven heads...and it had ten horns
And the woman held a golden cup
Abominable things and the filth of her adulteries
All had filled it up

The woman was drunk...but not from the cup
Which she was holding in her hand
She was drunk with the blood of the saints who had died
Faithful...to the Lamb

Then the angel explained the mystery of the woman
And also the beast she rode
"The beast that you saw...once was...now is not,"
To me the angel told

"It will come from the Abyss and go to its destruction,"
The angel went on to say
"And the people whose names aren't in the book of life
Will be astonished on that day

"Astonished when they see...the beast who once was
Now is not and yet will be," he said
"This calls for a mind with wisdom," he continued
And then some light, he shed

He told me the seven heads are seven hills
Which the woman sits upon
They are also seven kings and five have fallen
And then the angel went on

"One king is….and the other has not yet come
Yes, but when he does
He must remain….for a little while
And then the beast who was

"And now is not…will be the *eighth* king
And he belongs to the seven
And he is going to his destruction,"
Continued the angel from Heaven

"Ten kings who had not yet received a kingdom
Are the ten horns you did see
And aligned with the beast…for one hour
They receive authority

"And though these kings have authority
Only for an hour
They have one *purpose*…to give to the *beast*
Their authority and their power

"They will make war…against the Lamb
But the Lamb will overcome
For he is King of kings and Lord of lords"
And *He*….is the *only* One

"And with Him will be His faithful followers
And the *waters* that you saw
Where the prostitute sits, are the people and nations"
Then the angel told me more

"The beast and the ten horns will hate the prostitute
And she will feel their ire
They will bring her to ruin and leave her naked
Eat her flesh…and burn her with fire

"To accomplish His purpose...God has put it
Into their hearts to agree
To give to the beast, their ruling power
Until God's words come to be"

THE FALL OF BABYLON

Now the woman that I saw is that great city
Ruling over earth's kings
Then *another* angel came down from Heaven
And showed me *other* things

This angel had great authority and the earth was *lit up*
Illuminated by his splendor
And with a mighty voice, the angel shouted
The message he came to render

"Fallen, fallen is Babylon the Great!"
And then he went on to tell
That the city was home to all kinds of demons
And unclean spirits from hell

He said that all of the nations of the world
All had drunk of her wine
All the kings had committed adultery with her
For that was their design

The merchants of the earth grew rich with her
From her luxuries in excess
Then *another* voice came out of Heaven
God's people...to address

"Come out of her my people," said the voice,
"So you will not share in her sin"
The voice was calling His people from the city
Before His wrath would begin

"Her sins are piled up to Heaven," said the voice
"God has remembered her crimes"
Babylon will be paid for what she had done
Multiplied by two times

Babylon will suffer torture and grief
Famine, death and mourning
And Babylon will be consumed by fire
The voice called out the warning

The kings of the earth will be terrified
They will stand far off and cry
Saying, "In one hour your doom has come"
As they watch the city die

The merchants of the earth will weep and mourn
Now who will buy their freight?
"Your riches and splendor have vanished," they'll cry
On that fateful date

And every person on every ship
Upon the oceans deep
Will see the smoke of her burning
They will mourn and they will weep

Then I saw a mighty angel pick up a boulder
And throw it into the sea
Saying, "Thus with violence will Babylon be cast
Never again found will it be"

Then I heard the roar of a great multitude
Coming from Heaven with a shout
Praising the Lord God for His judgments
And for avenging...the devout

The twenty-four elders and the four living creatures
Worshiped before the throne
Then the great multitude, rejoiced and shouted
Sounding like a rushing water tone

"Hallelujah! For the Lord God Almighty reigns!"
Like thunder, their voices, as one
"Let us rejoice and be glad and give Him glory
For the wedding of the Lamb has come!

"His bride has made herself ready," they shouted
"Fine linen, bright and clean
Was given her to wear"... Then an angel spoke
As I stared in awe at the scene

He said, "Write down, 'Blessed are those invited
To the wedding supper of the Lamb'"
The angel said those... were the true words of God
God the Great I Am

Then I fell at his feet to worship the angel
But the angel made me see
I should worship only God for the testimony of Jesus
Is the spirit of prophecy

THE RIDER ON THE WHITE HORSE

Then Heaven stood open and I saw a white horse
Its Rider called Faithful and True
His eyes blazed like fire... He wore many crowns
And as He came into view

A name unknown to all but the Rider
I was able to see
It was written on the Rider... and that *name*
Added to the *mystery*

Dressed in a robe that was dipped in blood
The Word of God is His name
And the armies of Heaven, riding white horses
Behind the Rider came

And from His mouth, to strike down the nations
There appeared a sword
On His robe and His thigh was written the name
King of kings and Lord of lords

Then an angel who was standing in the sun
To the birds of the air did call
To gather together... to eat the flesh
Of the people great and small

Then I saw the beast and the kings of the earth
And their armies gathered together
To make war against the Rider and His army
For the greatest battle ever

But the beast was captured....and with him the prophet
Who performed the miraculous signs
That deluded the people who received the mark
People of all kinds

Then thrown alive...into the lake of fire
Were the false prophet and the beast
Then the sword of the Rider killed their followers
And on their flesh...the birds did feast

The Thousand Years

Then I saw an angel, coming out of Heaven
And down from Heaven he came
The angel was carrying the keys to the abyss
He also carried a great chain

He *seized* the dragon who is *really Satan*
Who inflicted generations with fears
Then the angel bound him and threw him in the Abyss
Where he'll stay for a thousand years

Then I looked and saw judges, sitting on thrones
And I also saw many a soul
Of those beheaded for taking a stand for Jesus
While the beast was in control

They refused to worship or take his mark
And now they came to life
And during the thousand years to come
They will reign with Christ

But the rest of the dead did not come to life
Until the thousand years end
Blessed are those in the *first* resurrection
Second death has no power over *them*

THE DOOM OF SATAN

And when the thousand years are over
Satan will be released
And he will go out to deceive the nations
From the greatest to the least

They will gather for battle, in great numbers
Like the sands upon the shore
Surrounding God's people in the city He loves
But then...they will be no more

For fire will rain down from Heaven above
Devouring them where they stand
Then the devil will be thrown into the lake of fire
Defeated by God's hand

The devil will *join* the beast and false prophet
Where they will pay for their crime
Tormented day and night forever
Until the end of time

THE GREAT WHITE THRONE JUDGMENT

Then I looked and saw a great white throne
And on the throne sat the One
The earth and the sky fled from His presence
The Judgment....had begun

The books were opened and the great and small
Stood before the throne
Their deeds were recorded...and they would be judged
On what the books had shown

Then I saw that another book was opened
The book of life...its name
And anyone not found written in it
Was thrown into the lake of flame

The New Jerusalem

Then I looked and saw….a *new* Heaven and earth
For the first had passed away
And I heard a loud voice, coming from the throne
I listened and heard it say

That the dwelling of God would now be with men
He will wipe each tear from their eye
And there will be no more pain or death
And no one will mourn or cry

Then He who was seated upon the throne said,
"I am making everything new!"
Then He turned to me and said, "Write this down
For these words are trustworthy and true"

He said that He is the Alpha and the Omega
And He said that it is done
He said that he who overcomes will inherit all of this
And they will be His son

But the cowards, the unbelievers, the vile, the murderers
The whoremongers and the liars
The idolaters and those who practice magic arts
Will be thrown in the lake of fires

Then one of the seven angels who had seven bowls
Came to me to say,
"Come…I will show you the bride of the Lamb"
And he carried me away

The angel carried me in the spirit
To a mountain great and high
Where I saw the Holy City…Jerusalem
Coming down from Heaven in the sky

Its brilliance like that of a precious jewel
It shone with the glory of God
Like a jasper, clear as crystal
Twelve gates on its facade

Around the city stood a great, high wall
At each gate, an angel did stand
The twelve tribe names were written on the gates
There was never a city so grand

Three gates on the north and three on the south
Three on the east and west too
There were twelve foundations, under the walls
With names that I well knew

The names of the apostles of the Lamb
Were written on the foundations
Then with a golden rod the angel measured
The length....and elevations

The city was laid out like a square
As deep as it was wide
It measured fourteen hundred miles
Top to bottom...side to side

The walls, made of jasper, were very thick
Two hundred feet thick, the measure
The foundations covered in precious stones
Like a magnificent treasure

The first foundation was made of jasper
Then sapphire, clear and blue
The third was quartz, the fourth was emerald
Each stone, a brilliant hue

The fifth, sardonyx, the deepest of black
With streaks of orange and red
The sixth was carnelian, the seventh, chrysolite
In the sparkling foundation bed

The eighth was beryl, a refracting prism
As I had never seen
The ninth, topaz...the tenth, chrysoprase
A glittering, transparent green

The eleventh foundation was covered in jacinth
Clear red flashing stones
The twelfth was amethyst, the color of royalty
Brilliant purple tones

Now the city itself…was made of pure gold
Gold as pure as glass
Each gate was formed…from a single pearl
Through which everyone would pass

As I looked….I saw no *temple* in the city
For God Almighty and the Lamb
Are the temple and the lamp….and the city is lit
From the glory of the Great I Am

The kings of the earth will bring it their splendor
The nations will walk by its light
And the gates will always stand open
For there will be no night

Only those whose names are in the Lamb's book of life
Shall be permitted in
Those who are deceitful and things impure
Shall *never* enter therein

The River of Life

Then the angel showed me the river
The river of the water of life
It was clear as crystal and flowed from the throne
The throne of God and Christ

It flowed down the middle of the great wide street
The street was made of pure gold
Which glittered like transparent glass
Almost too much to behold

And on each side of the river
Stood the tree of life
To give fruit every month and to heal the nations
No longer, curse or strife

The throne of God and the Lamb will be in the city
He will be in His servants' sight
His name will be on their foreheads
And there will be no night

Then the angel spoke and said to me,
"These words are trustworthy and true
The Lord, the God of the spirits of the prophets
Sent His angel to you

"To show His servants the things," he continued,
"That must soon take place"
Then I bowed down to worship the angel
Down to the ground with my face

But again the angel would not allow it
For he is a servant too
Then he said to worship only *God*
For *that* is the right thing to do

JESUS IS COMING

"Behold...I am coming soon," said Jesus
And then He said, "Blessed is he
Who is keeping the words of this book
The words of the prophecy"

Then the angel said, "Do not seal up the words
Of the prophecy of this book
For the time is near," he said to me
As I continued to look

Then Jesus said, "Behold...I come quickly
My reward I bring with me
And according to the work that each has done
So his reward will be

"I am the Alpha and the Omega
The First...and the Last
The Beginning and the End," He said for *He*
Is God of the future and past

He said, "Happy are those doing His commands
That they may have the right
To the tree of life and to enter the city"
The city that has no night

"But the dogs will be left outside," He said,
"Those who practice magic arts
The murderers, the idolaters, the whoremongers"
Those with evil in their hearts

He said that those who love and practice lies
Will not be allowed inside
He sent His angel with this testimony for the church
The church...which is His bride

He said, "I am the Root and the Offspring of David
The Bright and Morning Star"
And the Spirit and the Bride say, "Come"
Come...whoever they are

He who is hearing...let him say, "Come"
And whoever the thirsting may be
And he who is willing, let him take the gift
Of the water of life which is free

I testify to everyone who hears the words
Of the prophecy of this scroll
If anyone adds to them, God will add to *him*
The plagues herein foretold

And if anyone may take away from these words
God will take away his share
In the book of life and in the holy city
Which are both described in here

Then Jesus who testified to all of these things
Promised us again
"Yes...I am coming quickly," He said
Come Lord Jesus....Amen

¤

The grace of Our Lord Jesus Christ is with you all
Amen

Appendix A

Modern Day Names and/or Locations of Cities, Nations and Bodies of Water Spoken of in the Bible

Note: Many no longer exist

Adullam—Was possibly twenty miles west of Bethlehem

Alexandria—Is a seaport city in northern Egypt

Amman—Is in northern Jordan

Antioch—Is now known as Antakya, Turkey

Arabah—Is on the border between Israel and Jordan

Aram—Was south of Damascus in present-day Syria

Ashdod—Is on the southern coast of Israel

Ashkelon—Is now known as Ashqelon on the southern coast of Israel

Assyria—Was the Tigris River area in nothern present-day Iraq

Aswan—Is on the Nile River in southern Egypt

Baal Meon—Is now known as M'ain in Israel

Babel—Is now known as Babylon in present-day Iraq

Babylon—Is fifty-five miles south of present-day Baghdad in Iraq

Babylonia—Area now known as eastern Iraq and western Iran

Beersheba—Is in present-day Negev Desert in southern Israel

Berea—Is now known as Veria in Greece

Besor Ravine—Is now known as Nahal Besor, south Negev

Bethany—Is one and one-half miles east of Jerusalem

Bethel—Was twelve miles north of Jerusalem

Bethlehem—Is in the central present-day West Bank

Bethsaida—Is in the central present-day Golan Heights

Beth Shemesh—Is now known as Beit Shemesh, Israel

Beth Togarmah—Believed to be in present-day Armenia

Bozrah—Is now known as Bouseira in south present-day Jordan

Caesarea—Ruins on the coast of northern Israel

Caesarea Philippi—Is now known as Marjeyoun, Lebanon

Cana—Believed to have been north of Nazareth

Canaan—Was the region encompassing: present-day Israel, Lebanon, Palestinian Territories, adjoining coastal lands and parts of Jordan, Syria and northeastern Egypt

Capernaum—Is on the Sea of Galilee in nothern Israel

Cappadocia—Was a region in present-day Turkey

Chaldea—Was in central present-day Iraq

Cilicia—Is now known as Çukurova in southern present-day Turkey

Corinth—Is in southern Greece

Crete—Is a southern island of Greece

Cush—Area that is now known as Egypt and Sudan

Cyprus—Is an island in the Mediterranean Sea

Cyrene—Is on the northern coast of present-day Libya

Damascus—Is the capital of present-day Syria

Dedan—Is now known as Al-'Ula in present-day Arabia

Derbe—Is in southern present-day Turkey

Desert of Ziph—Was in Judea, south of Hebron

Eden—Was possibly in present-day Iraq

Edom—Was in central present-day Jordan

Ekron—Was located in southwestern Canaan

Elam—Was in southwest present-day Iran

Emmaus—Was about seven miles northwest of Jerusalem

Endor—Was a Canaanite village

Ephah—Was on the east shore of the Dead Sea

Ephesus—Is in eastern present-day Turkey

Ephraim—Was about twenty-five miles north of Jerusalem

Euphrates River—Is in present-day Syria and Iraq

Fair Havens—Was on the southern coast of present-day Crete

Ford of Jabbok—Is now known as Zerka, east of Jordan

Galatia—Was an area in central present-day Turkey

Galilee—Is a large region in northern Israel

Gath—Was on the southern coast of Canaan

Gaza—Is in the present-day Gaza Strip

Geba—Was about five and one-half miles north of Jerusalem

Gennesaret—Was south of Capernaum in northern Israel

Gerasa—Is now known as Jerash in northern present-day Jordan

Gihon River—Was one of four rivers in Eden

Gilead—Mountainous region in present-day Jordan

Gilgal—Is in Israel

Gomorrah—Was possibly in present-day Jordan

Hadrach—Was in Aram in present-day Syria

Hamath—Northern present-day Syria

Hamonah—Is now known as Hama in central present-day Syria

Haran—Is now known as Harran in southern present-day Turkey

Hebron—Is in present-day West Bank

Horeb—May be Sinai in present-day Sinai Peninnsula

Iconium—Is now known as Konya in present-day Turkey

Jericho—Is in the present-day West Bank

Jerusalem—Is in Israel

Jeshimoth—Was east of Jordan in the Moab Desert

Joppa—Is now known as Tel Aviv, coast of Israel

Jordan River—Between the West Bank and Jordan

Judah—Was southern present-day Israel

Kebar River—Is in present-day Babylon, Iraq

Keilah—Was in Judah, present-day Israel

Kiriathaim—Was east of Jordan

Koa—Was in the Babylonian empire

Lystra—Was in southern present-day Turkey

Macedonia—Is north of Greece

Malta—Is an island south of Sicily, Italy

Mede—Was in northwest present-day Iran

Mesopotamia—Area now known as northern Iraq and eastern Syria

Midian—Area is now known as Saudi Arabia

Migdal—Is in northern Israel

Migdol—Was in present-day Egypt

Moab—Was east of Dead Sea in present-day Jordan

Moreh Plain—Was in present-day West Bank

Mount Ararat—Is in present-day Turkey

Mount Carmel—Is in northern Israel

Mount of Olives—Is in Jerusalem

Mount Sinai—Is in the present-day Sinai Peninsula

Mysia—Was in area in eastern present-day Turkey

Nain—Was in northern Israel

Naphtali—Was on the eastern side of the Galilee

Nazareth—Is in northern Israel

Nineveh—Was in northern present-day Iraq

Nob—Was on north side of present-day Jerusalem

Pamphylia—Was a region in south present-day Turkey

Parthia—Is a region in northeastern present-day Iran

Perga—Ruins on southern coast of present-day Turkey

Pergamum—Ruins in eastern present-day Turkey

Persia—Area in southern present-day Iran

Philippi—Is in northern Greece

Philistia—Was the southern coast of Canaan

Phoenix—Was on the coast of present-day Crete

Pishon River—Was one of four rivers in Eden

Pisidia—Was a region in southern present-day Turkey

Pontus—Was a region in northern present-day Turkey

Put—May be a region in present-day Libya

Rameses—Was in Egypt

Samaria—Was in the area of present-day West Bank

Sea of Galilee—Is in northern Israel

Sea of Tiberias—Is now known as the Sea of Galilee, Israel

Seir—Region from the southern Dead Sea to the Red Sea

Sheba—Was area in present-day Yemen

Shechem—Was in present-day West Bank

Sidon—Is on the coasts of present-day Lebanon

Sodom—Was possibly in Jordan

Succoth—Was in northern Egypt

Susa—Is now known as Shush in western present-day Iran

Tarsus—Is on the southern coast of present-day Turkey

Teman—Is probably now known as Yemen

Thessalonica—Is now known as Thessaloniki in Greece

Tigris River—Is in Iraq

Troas—Is on the east coast of present-day Turkey

Tyre—Is on the coast of present-day Lebanon

Ulai Canal—Was in Elam in present-day Iran

Ur—Was in southeast present-day Iraq

Valley of Jehoshaphat—Between Jerusalem and the Mount of Olives

Zarephath—Is now known as Surafend in present-day Lebanon

Zebulun—Was in Galilee

Ziklag—Was in Judah, present-day Israel

Zoar—Was southeast of the Dead Sea

Zorah—Was in Judah, present-day Israel

Appendix B

Bibliography

BIBLES

Young's Literal Translation. Robert Young, ed. Grand Rapids, MI: Baker Book House, 2003.

The Darby Translation.

The American Standard Bible. La Habra, CA: The Lockman Foundation, 1975.

The King James Version.

The Holy Bible, New Living Translation. Wheaton, IL: Tyndale House Publishers, Inc., 2007.

The Holy Bible, New Century Version. Dallas, TX: Word Publishing, 1991.

The Holy Bible, New International Version of the Bible. Grand Rapids, MI: Zondervan, 2008.

The Daily Bible Devotional: A One-Year Journey Through God's Word in Chronological Order. F. LaGard Smith, ed. Eugene, OR: Harvest House, 2009.

OTHER RESOURCES

Then and Now Bible Maps. Torrance, CA: Rose Publishing, 2007.

www.BibleGateway.com

www.ChristianAnswers.net

www.Wikipedia.com

To Contact the Author

www.TheAmazingWordofGod.com

Penny Zee

P.O. Box 23366

Ft. Lauderdale, FL 33307